The New Economics of Fast Food

Robert L. Emerson
President, Stonehill Capital Management

VNR Van Nostrand Reinhold
New York

Library of Congress Catalog Number
ISBN 0-442-23431-7

Printed in the United States of America

Van Nostrand Reinhold
115 Fifth Avenue
New York, New York 10003

Van Nostrand Reinhold International Company Limited
11 New Fetter Lane
London EC4P 4EE, England

Van Nostrand Reinhold
480 La Trobe Street
Melbourne, Victoria 3000, Australia

Nelson Canada
1120 Birchmount Road
Scarborough, Ontario M1K 5G4, Canada

16   15   14   13   12   11   10   9   8   7   6   5   4   3   2   1

Library of Congress Cataloging-in-Publication Data
Emerson, Robert L., 1946-
    The new economics of fast food / by Robert L. Emerson.
        p.   cm.
    ISBN 0-442-23431-7
    1. Fast food restaurants—United States.   2. Fast food
restaurants—Economic aspects—United States.   I. Title.
TX945.E65   1990
338.4'76479573—dc20   89-78146
                                             CIP

To all the Putnam Emersons

Contents

List of Tables

Preface

The $60 billion quick-service restaurant industry is important in many respects: it is among the nation's largest employers, it accounts for 40 percent of restaurant sales and more than 10 percent of total American food expenditures, and has probably made more millionaires than any other business except for real estate and natural resources. The industry's growth and profitability have recently entered a new phase, one where pressures of labor cost, oversaturation of outlets, and soaring real estate costs have squeezed profitability.

Fast food has always been an industry in flux, where new chains spring up to replace more mature, stagnating systems. The industry has experienced periods of dramatic shakeout, such as the early 1970s, when a large number of chains closed their stores. Even in the face of such adverse conditions, however, different entrants came along to offer new concepts, for example, drive-through windows or breakfast, to expand the market.

The late 1980s have seen a more permanent and widespread dislocation, however. The third quarter of 1989 marked the first time in history that fast-food sales showed a decline from the prior year. McDonald's now opens more than half of its company-operated units in foreign markets. Numerous erstwhile industry leaders, including Church's Fried Chicken, Wendy's, Friendly Ice Cream, and Winchell's Donut Houses, are seeing many of their stores being converted to newer, more profitable fast-food concepts. The second-largest pizza chain is for sale; the largest fast-food fish chain has recently been acquired at distressed prices, and the nation's best coffee shop operator, Shoney's, has undergone a recapitalization that will slow its expansion for the foreseeable future.

The argument of this book is that a labor shortage has forced chain restaurants to raise prices, thereby depriving consumers of the price-value relationship that prevailed in the 1960s, 1970s, and early 1980s. As a result, the growth of fast food has slowed sharply, exacerbating the problem of overstoring or saturation.

The best hope for profitable growth in the future lies in three areas: foreign markets, recycling real estate, or offering new dining experiences that either give consumers superior value (buffet concepts with very high food costs and huge capital turnover) or that offer consumers at least the illusion of great quantity at low prices (pizza or Mexican chains).

Even in this difficult environment, however, new ideas are being tested: whether the double drive-throughs developed by Rally's will survive McDonald's backlash remains to be seen, but a few heroic entrepreneurs have always emerged to confound the skeptics.

Acknowledgments

Countless people in the restaurant industry helped in the research and preparation of this book. I am particularly indebted to Michael R. Quinlan, chairman and chief executive officer of McDonald's Corporation.

Paul Schrage, McDonald's senior executive vice president and chief marketing officer, and Jack M. Greenberg, McDonald's chief financial officer, contributed valuable insights in their respective fields. Sharon L. Vuinovich, director of investor relations, has organized meetings for financial analysts that are probably the most informative of those offered by any consumer products company and has also provided the answers to countless questions about financial minutiae on the company.

Franchisees often provide the most valuable insights into the workings of their industry. Jamie Coulter, a leading Pizza Hut franchisee, remains, in my opinion, the nation's shrewdest and most knowledgeable observer of the fast-food industry, while at the same time operating some of the industry's most profitable restaurants.

John Weiss, partner at Montgomery Securities, and his colleague, Michael Mueller, continue to do some of the most provocative and thorough work on both financial and operating trends within the industry.

Steven A. Rockwell of Alex Brown & Sons organizes an annual conference of restaurant operators that provides a splendid forum for meeting senior managements of a vast number of restaurant companies.

William Tilley, chairman of the Jacmar Companies, provided key insights into real estate issues and the whole economics of PepsiCo's restaurant operations.

Finally, I wish to thank Bert Fingerhut and Robert S. Salomon, Jr., for their help in the creation of Stonehill Capital Management and their support in investing in a venture dedicated to in-depth research.

Introduction

The New Economics of Fast Food

In recent years the quick-service restaurant industry has begun to be adversely affected by two factors that will become far more damaging in the future. First, overstoring and saturation have begun to crop up in earnest. This problem has always been part of the financial community's concern about the industry. The issue has not been *whether* the industry would become saturated, the question has been *when*. The answer, as we shall see, is that the problem is now at hand in a way that has never occurred before.

This development is not entirely negative, however. The recycling of real estate locations to newer, more effective kinds of foodservice operators will provide opportunities for the alert investor and operator. The shrewd investor who can identify underutilized real estate sites controlled by a failing fast-food chain has probably earned greater returns in recent years than all but a handful of operators of profitable chains. This movement toward acquiring chains for their real estate will continue.

Deteriorating Demographic Outlook

The second negative influence is demographic. The fact that young people (the principal consumers of fast food) are declining as a proportion of the total populace is well known. Individuals who are 18 to 24 years old consume 4.8 meals away from home weekly, compared with 3.7 meals for all consumers. The number of Americans in this age group nearly doubled between 1960 and 1980, but will drop 20 percent by the year 2000.

People over 65, in contrast, eat out only 1.8 times per week, on average, and will be among the most rapidly growing age groups for the rest of the century. The negative implications on demand for fast food of this shift in the age of the population have received considerable attention. What has received less attention, however, is the negative implications of this demographic shift for labor costs.

Labor Costs Pressures and Forced Menu Price Increases

The past decade has seen labor costs rise as a percent of sales for virtually every major fast-food chain. Interestingly, this has occurred in a period when minimum wage legislation has generally been absent, except at the state level. It is the free market, not government interference, that has supplied the labor cost pressure. Ironically, the restaurant industry had coped very well with legislated minimum wage hikes for the prior 25 years.

In order to combat rising labor costs, most of the major fast-food chains have raised prices to a degree that has far outrun the rise in food costs. This has caused the relative value of eating out versus eating at home to deteriorate.

Less Value for Consumers

The decline in food costs as a percent of sales in recent years shows up clearly in both industry aggregate data and in the income statements of the individual companies. Consumers no longer feel that quick-service restaurants provide them with good value for their money. As a result, the growth in the overall market for food consumed away from home has stagnated, hastening the onset of saturation noted above.

In this context, it is noteworthy that the most dramatic improvement in profitability of any major restaurant chain in recent years has been the explosion in sales and earnings at PepsiCo's Taco Bell following the chain's adoption of a new low-priced strategy beginning in late 1988.

The twin problems of deteriorating demographics and impending saturation have grave implications for most established restaurant operators and their franchisees. Yet even in the midst of this economic crisis, there is hope for new concepts that can take advantage of the new economics.

Most Promising New Concepts

The concepts that can offer low labor costs and high capital turnover, particularly if they feature a relatively inexpensive food line, may be able to take advantage of the pricing umbrella being constructed by the major chains. To this end, buffet concepts, which absorb very high food costs in order to offer the consumer great value, may come increasingly into vogue.

New Menu Items Not the Answer

The inevitable response of chains when sales and profits soften is to offer new menu items. In an environment of critical labor shortages and deteriorating service standards, however, such an approach may be futile.

One of the hallmarks of successful chains throughout the history of the industry has been reliance on an extremely limited range of menu offerings. Indeed, a chain's attempts to introduce new products, while they may be greeted with a strong initial trial, almost inevitably signal impending deterioration in its basic business.

Chapter 1

Evolution of the Fast-Food Industry

Changes in the Industry in the 1980s

The history of the restaurant industry has been one of a limited number of ventures growing very rapidly and profitably while many new entrants fail and many erstwhile industry leaders decay and shrink in size. This phenomenon, which I have dubbed "the endless shakeout" in an earlier work, continues in the current environment. The process has become more complex in recent years, however.

Turnarounds a Decade Ago

A decade ago, few fast-food firms had successfully recovered from unsatisfactory profitability. Those companies that had encountered problems in the industry's first major shakeout in the early 1970s for the most part languished in permanent obscurity and eventually closed stores and underwent gradual liquidation. In the 1980s, however, a series of impressive recoveries have been engineered, often by private investors who have taken over either distressed public companies or divisions of large public companies.

   The turnaround at Kentucky Fried Chicken engineeered by Michael Miles and Richard Mayer is probably the most noteworthy, but there have been others. Hardee's, since its acquisition by Imasco, has quietly become the second most profitable hamburger chain. The leveraged buyout firm of Gibbons, Green van Amerongen achieved dramatic success in improving the results of Jack-in-the-Box after acquiring the firm from Ralston Purina.

Different Solutions for Turnarounds

Each of these three situations has been solved by different approaches: Kentucky Fried Chicken began with a new emphasis on quality of operations at the store level; Hardee's benefited from the massive success of a new breakfast program; and Jack-in-the-Box's recovery was at least partly achieved by closing unprofitable stores in areas far removed geographically from the chain's core markets.

Real Estate Opportunities in the 1980s

A new development is just beginning as the decade draws to a close: cannibalizing unsuccessful chains for their locations. The idea is to acquire a chain, no matter how badly it may be failing as an ongoing operating entity, in order to gain control of the company's underlying real estate. This is the motivation behind Tennessee Restaurant's acquisition of Friendly Ice Cream Corporation from Hershey Foods; it is the motivation behind the purchase of Winchell's Donut Houses from TW Services by the Canadian investment group, Shato Holdings; and it explains the purchase of Church's Fried Chicken by A. Copeland Enterprises, Inc. It may well be the fate of numerous other chains that are earning an inadequate return on investment.

Former Profit Leaders

The most profitable companies of a decade ago are, with the exception of McDonald's, Pizza Hut, and Taco Bell, no longer among the industry leaders. Church's Fried Chicken, Denny's, and Wendy's registered far better financial results in the late 1970s than virtually all of their competitors, yet Church's has been acquired by the parent company of Popeye's, a privately owned firm that was an obscure new entrant in the late 1970s, while Wendy's suffers from deteriorating volume, inadequate profitability, and store closings by its franchisees. Denny's, which was taken private by its management, has since deteriorated in profitability and has been passed from one buyer, TW Services, to GTO, the acquirer of TW Services.

The Old Economics of Fast Food

A decade ago, the pattern of growth and profitability for successful restaurant chains was straightforward. Chains would achieve between $1.00 at the low end to $1.45 at the high end of sales for every dollar invested in land, building, and equipment required to construct a restaurant. The restaurant would achieve profits at the store level in the range of 17.0 to 21.0 percent of sales. At the individual restaurant level overall unleveraged profitability in terms of return on investment, then, would fall in a range of 22.0 to 24.0 percent before taxes.

Heavy Financial Leverage

Most publicly held successful chains maintained a ratio of total debt to stockholders' equity of 2:1. On the face of it, this appears to be a very high degree of leverage. However, the stability of the companies' business justified the reliance on heavy borrowing: during the severe recession of 1973-74, most of the publicly held fast-food firms actually managed to *improve* their fixed-charge coverage.

Table 1.1

Fixed-Charge Coverage in Recession

Chain	1973	1974	1975
Chart House	2.3	2.3	2.3
Church's Fried Chicken	4.0	5.9	6.5
Denny's	1.6	1.9	2.1
Friendly Ice Cream	5.9	6.6	6.6
Hardee's	2.1	1.3	1.6
Jerrico	4.3	5.0	6.5
McDonald's	3.6	3.6	3.6
Pillsbury*	2.4	2.2	2.3
Pizza Hut	2.3	2.3	2.3
Ponderosa	3.7	1.3	1.3
Sambo's	2.6	2.9	2.6
Victoria Station	2.6	2.2	3.0
Wendy's	3.1	4.1	4.8

*Restaurant operations only.

Source: Company reports on SEC Form 10-K, annual reports and author's calculations.

The Recession of 1974

Table 1.1 illustrates the improvement in fixed-charge coverage experienced by thirteen major chain restaurant operators in the mid-1970s. "Fixed-charge coverage" is defined as pretax income before rental and interest costs divided by rental and interest costs. Note that ten of the thirteen chains shown either maintained or improved their fixed-charge coverage ratios during the recession of 1974–75. Restaurant companies are not put out of business by economic downturns alone.

Of the thirteen companies examined in the preceding table, two have since filed for bankruptcy, one (Pizza Hut) was bought out by PepsiCo and has prospered after an initial collapse and a lengthy turnaround effort, seven have since been bought out under adverse conditions at depressed prices, Wendy's is looking for a buyer, Hardee's was acquired by Imasco and has done well, and McDonald's has created an empire. But the failures were not brought on by economic conditions, nor were they caused by saturation in the companies' respective market segments.

High Return on Equity

These unhappy endings were all in the future in the mid-1970s. With a pretax interest cost in the range of 8.0 to 10 percent, total pretax return on equity approaching 50 percent could be achieved. (An unleveraged return on total investment of 23 percent translates into a 46.0 percent pretax return on equity, assuming a 2:1 debt-equity ratio and a 10 percent cost of debt.) With federal, state, and local taxes typically taking 48 percent of pretax income, after-tax return on equity averaged around 23.9 percent.

Since most of the companies involved paid little if any dividend, the retention rate approached the after-tax return on beginning equity. As a result, the companies could finance growth at rates in the low 20 percent area while maintaining their capital structures at constant levels.

Saturation Fear

In the seventies, the only issue of concern appeared merely to be one of saturation: How many restaurants could be cloned at identical rates of return to that of the existing ones? Saturation is a condition easier to identify in retrospect than·on a real-time basis, and the current state of saturation is analyzed at great length later in this book. The conclusion suggested in the analysis of the industry in late 1989 is that overstoring is now definitely a major problem for the industry.

However, saturation by itself was not what effectively drove Burger Chef out of business nearly two decades ago; it is not what destroyed Kentucky Fried Chicken in 1971, and it is not the explanation for the collapse of Sambo's or Victoria Station.

Other Chains Prosper

In each of the aforementioned cases many other chains prospered for years in the segment in which these victims crashed. McDonald's has prospered mightily in the segment from which Burger Chef (and Borden Burger and Wetson's and, more recently, perhaps, Wendy's) have been driven. Church's Fried Chicken was one of America's fastest-growing companies in the decade after Kentucky Fried Chicken floundered. Numerous dinner houses have succeeded in the market where Victoria Station failed. Shoney's continued to thrive by operating coffee shops more than a decade after Sambo's filed for bankruptcy.

Saturation may well prove to be the downfall of the chain restaurant industry in the 1990s, but it cannot be the explanation for the disasters of ten or twenty years ago. Too many vital new entrants have sprung up to suggest that overstoring of the industry alone was the problem.

Growing Chains Keep Managers

One critical flaw in the economics of the restaurant industry, and particularly the fast-food segment, is the need for growth in order to attract ambitious, effective management. The economics of restaurants, particularly comparatively small units with less than $1 million in annual sales, are not well-suited toward paying management a competitive wage. The growing chain, however, can offer the prospects of advancement: the diligent store manager can believe that he or she won't have to be merely a unit manager for long.

As a result, restaurant companies that have been profitable eventually tend to falter in one of two ways. Some chains overexpand, thereby exceeding either geographical limitations or the size of the niche market that they have secured. Examples include Friendly Ice Cream, Jack-in-the-Box, Gino's, Victoria Station, Chi-Chi's, and Wendy's.

Alternatively, companies may accurately gauge the size of their market and halt expansion before overstoring becomes a problem for them. However, slow decay of the organization inevitably sets in, leading to deterioration of operations as store managers leave. Customer counts eventually fall as a result of poor quality, and profitability suffers.

Chain restaurants are not good cash cows. Very few, if any, chain restaurants have ever made the successful transition from growth companies to annuities. The lone exception may prove to be Shoney's, which offered a unique stock option program to all levels of management, including store managers and area supervisors, after its recapitalization. As a result, management was provided with powerful economic inducements to perform well even with a reduced rate of store openings.

Stages of Development of the Fast-Food Industry

Some perspective on the history of the fast-food industry is useful in understanding the current economics of the business. While it is customary to date the beginning of the fast-food era to the early 1950s, when the corporate entities we now know as McDonald's, Burger King, and Kentucky Fried Chicken were founded, the origins of the industry actually go back to the late 1920s and early 1930s. The first White Castle was opened by E. W. Ingram in Wichita, Kansas, in 1921. The A&W Root Beer chain was founded in 1922 by Roy Allen and Fred Wright.

Origination in California

The concept of serving people in their cars, like most American restaurant trends, got its start in California, with a drive-in restaurant with carhop service called the Pig Stand, which opened in Hollywood in 1932. Another California chain, Bob Wian's Bob's, Home of the Big Boy, began franchising of a drive-in featuring a double-decker hamburger in the early 1940s. Foodmaker, which became the owner of the Jack-in-the-Box chain, was founded in California in 1941.

Meanwhile, several early east coast entries were created during the same period. The first Howard Johnson's opened in Quincy, Massachusetts, in 1925, while the Blake brothers opened the initial Friendly Ice Cream store in Wilbraham, Massachusetts, in 1935. Two transplanted New Englanders moved to California and laid the foundation for what was to become the greatest success in the restaurant industry. Two brothers from New Hampshire, Richard and Maurice McDonald, opened a modest hot dog stand near Pasadena, California, in 1937.

The First McDonald's

The first McDonald's restaurant included a dozen stools and also offered carhop service. Three years later, a larger store was opened by the McDonald brothers in San Bernardino. This unit, which was 600 square feet in size, featured the stainless steel fixtures and open kitchen to which a later generation of McDonald's executives attributed so much of the chain's success. The menu, however, initially did not emphasize hamburgers, but rather featured pork sandwiches and ribs.

With $200,000 in annual sales and a 25 percent profit margin, the restaurant was staggeringly profitable in terms of return on capital. Although the cost of the initial unit is unknown, even a decade later a McDonald's unit of 600 square feet cost less than $70,000 to buy and equip. Hence, the annual return on investment, unleveraged, on the initial McDonald's must surely have approached 100 percent before taxes.

A Change in Format

Eventually, however, competitive pressure caused sales to decline, and in 1948 the McDonald's brothers elected to close their drive-in, remodel it, and reopen as a fast-service, limited-menu hamburger stand. After slow initial response, the low-priced ($0.15 apiece) hamburgers caught on, and by 1951 the store achieved annual sales of $277,000, rising to $350,000 by the mid-1950s. The prices, which included a $0.12 bag of french fries and a shake for $0.20, were not raised for nearly twenty years. The first increase in the price of the small hamburger (to $0.18) was put in place in 1967. Interestingly, McDonald's Corporation's average sales per store did not achieve the level of the original unit in San Bernardino in 1951 until 1966.

It was this store that Mr. Ray A. Kroc, a milkshake machine salesman for Chicago's Multimixer, first visited in July of 1954. It may have been Kroc's obsession with cleanliness and his intuitive understanding of Americans' preoccupation with the subject, more than speed of delivery or low prices that allowed him to build the world's largest food-service empire.

The Secret of McDonald's Early Success

In explaining Kroc's contribution to the industry, McDonald's president Edward Schmitt observed twenty-five years later:

> What McDonald's did—I think what was really a stroke of genius on Ray's part—was the fish-bowl type of atmosphere at McDonald's. You not only see the people scurrying around inside of it—which itself, by the way, is entertaining. It really is: watching those kids work back there. How they work and get 26 people on the floor and trying to figure out why they don't bump into each other. But the other thing is, if a fellow dropped a patty on the floor you could see him doing it, and maybe you wouldn't eat there. You can also see the cleanliness of the stainless steel. Ray really could have gone cheaper and got the black iron or galvanized iron finishes on the equipment. But he chose stainless steel, and he did it because it shows blemishes and it shows dirt and you can see from outside how clean the place is that they are cooking the food in. This was something revolutionary. How many kitchens do you know in the United States of established restaurants where you look into their food facilities and preparation area? Man, very few. Because people could see what was happening, they not only got a sense of value for what they were getting for fifteen cents (that probably could have even been a little negative: how could you possibly sell it for fifteen cents?) but they saw the food being prepared. They knew that some greasy guy wasn't drunk in the backroom, like there always was in any other kitchen. They could see the cleanliness of the atmosphere and how it was prepared from the point of the grill, right to them. They could watch that product and know the safety of taking their children to eat at McDonald's. Where else can you do that? (*Endless Shakeout*, p. 279)

This theme of obsessive cleanliness recurs in conversations with fast-food pioneers. In response to the author's question about the single most important contribution that Pizza Hut had made, founder Frank Carney replied simply: "Hygiene."

Other Chains Spring Up

On March 1, 1954, Mr. James McLamore opened his first Burger King in Miami. In the same year Harland Sanders began his efforts to franchise his unique method of frying chicken to restaurant operators in the southeast. (Kentucky Fried Chicken was not the first of the fried chicken chains, though it did become the largest. The first Church's Fried Chicken unit was opened in San Antonio, Texas, in 1952.) Colonel Sanders (the honorary title was bestowed upon him by Kentucky governor Ruby Laffoon as a tribute to Sanders's contribution to Kentucky's culinary arts) had developed his own method of slow pan-frying chicken in the 1930s. His method of franchising was simple: he charged 4 cents (later increased to a nickel) for each chicken sold using his cooking formula, and his franchisees paid him on the honor system.

Chain Growth in the 1960s

In the following decade the three aforementioned chains grew quickly, with Burger King opening 100 units by the end of 1965, McDonald's, 738, and Kentucky Fried Chicken, 1000. Another newcomer, Burger Chef, had 325 units in operation by 1965.

Even with the prodigious growth of the hamburger chains during the decade, however, they were still dwarfed by long-established purveyors of ice cream and soft drinks. By the end of 1965, for example, the A&W Root Beer, Tastee-Freeze, and International Dairy Queen systems operated a combined total of 7500 stores! In dollar volume, the largest restaurant chain in 1965 was Howard Johnson, with sales of $300 million, equal to the systemwide sales of McDonald's, Burger King, and Kentucky Fried Chicken combined.

Stock Offerings

Following the initial public stock offerings of Kentucky Fried Chicken in 1964 and McDonald's in 1965, the new chains proliferated rapidly. Kentucky Fried Chicken grew from 1000 stores in 1965 to 4000 by 1971. Burger King's systemwide stores rose from 100 to 800 during the same period.

McDonald's store growth, while very impressive by most standards, actually lagged that of its competitors in percentage terms. The number of units in the McDonald's system rose from 738 units in 1965 to 2272 by 1972. Burger Chef nearly quadrupled, from 325 stores in 1965 to almost 1200 in 1972.

Acquisitions of Leading Chains

Although some of the fast-food operators of the period financed their growth through public stock offerings, others were purchased by giant packaged foods operators. In 1967 the Pillsbury Company acquired Burger King for $19 million. In 1968 General Foods bought Burger Chef for $20 million. During the same period, Ralston-Purina acquired Jack-in-the-Box, United Brands bought A&W, and Great Western acquired Shakey's Pizza.

In the late 1960s it was by no means clear who the ultimate survivors in the fast-food business would be. When Burger Chef was acquired by General Foods, for example, the chain had 850 stores in operation, compared with McDonald's 970, and was opening stores at an annual rate of 300 units in contrast to the more deliberate pace of McDonald's 100 new store openings.

With the financial resources of a stable, highly profitable food processor providing financial wherewithal for opening new restaurants at a rapid clip, a model for aggressive expansion appeared to be in place. Yet the failure of Burger Chef would prove to be only one of the first among many disappointments when packaged food marketers tried to apply their financing and marketing techniques to the promising growth area of fast food.

Richard Mayer, who was one of the architects of the resurrection of Kentucky Fried Chicken by Heublein in the late 1970s, summarized some of the difficulties that packaged foods companies have with restaurant operations.

> "There is a great difference between food service and packaged foods. Food service is a very sensitive operating business. Unless the operations are really humming, marketing isn't going to work. . . . In packaged foods, you never have to worry about Jell-O or Tide not delivering to consumer: that's all controlled by machines at the plant. QSC [quality, service and cleanliness] is typically controlled at the plant level in packaged foods, but not so in the restaurant business." (*Endless Shakeout*, rev. ed., p. 325)

McDonald's Altered Strategy

Some of the seeds of McDonald's ultimate success were sown in the very beginning of Kroc's involvement, particularly the insistence on quality and cleanliness. But some of the key decisions were made in the late 1960s. These changed the chain's operations and distinguished it from all of its predecessors and imitators.

The year 1968 was a particularly eventful one for McDonald's, as the chain put into place several innovations that mark the company's operations to this day. First, the Big Mac sandwich was introduced systemwide in October, having been tested since January 1967. The first McDonald's store to depart from the traditional red and white tiles was opened in Matteson, Illinois: the unit featured the mansard roof decor that is still common in the system. More importantly, it marked the first use of indoor seating, as McDonald's, not content to be merely a drive-in eatery, strove to enter the sit-down restaurant business.

The First Shakeout

The early 1970s saw the first shakeout in the fast-food industry, as well as the first major examples of fast-food chains selling out to a packaged foods company shortly before their operations went sour. Burger Chef's operations deteriorated to the point where its parent company, General Foods, set up a $75.5 million loss reserve (before an estimated tax benefit of $36.5 million) in 1972.

Similarly, Gino's, which had enjoyed great success in the Washington and Philadelphia markets, suffered losses in its initial foray into the California market that nearly forced the chain into bankruptcy. Kentucky Fried Chicken, which had compiled an unbroken string of earnings gains in the late 1960s, was sold to Heublein, a marketer of alcoholic beverages and specialty foods, in July of 1971 in exchange for 5.5 million shares of Heublein stock worth nearly $275 million. In a few short months, Kentucky Fried Chicken was forced to establish reserves for losses totaling $45.5 million.

McDonald's, however, took advantage of the recessions of both 1970–71 and 1974–75 by accelerating its rate of new store openings. The company used its financial muscle by buying sites at depressed prices, raising its expansion rate, and thereby opening up an insurmountable lead over its competitors.

Most of the chains that experienced operating difficulties in the early 1970s never recovered. Examples include Burger Chef, Gino's, Borden Burgers, Wetson's, and A&W. The lone exceptions were chains like Kentucky Fried Chicken and Jack-in-the-Box that, after several corporate reorganizations and sales at distressed prices were, with infusions of new capital, able to resume operations on a scaled-down basis.

Founding of Wendy's

Even during this difficult period, however, new chains were emerging that were to prosper for the rest of the 1970s and, in several cases, beyond. Wendy's first store was opened in Columbus, Ohio, in 1969 by a former Kentucky Fried Chicken franchisee, R. David Thomas. While Wendy's was a latecomer to the hamburger segment, a business that was already seeing a severe initial shakeout, it was a chain with a difference. Thomas hit on the idea of a larger, more expensive sandwich than that offered by McDonald's. His quarter-pound sandwich sold for $0.55 in 1969, more than three times the price of McDonald's small $0.18 sandwich.

The emphasis on the larger sandwich was important because it enabled Wendy's to prepare its product in the early days with much lower labor costs than its better-established competitors: no more cooks were required to prepare a quarter-pound sandwich for $0.55 than the small sandwich at McDonald's for $0.18. As a result, Wendy's labor cost as a percent of sales in the mid-1970s averaged only 17.0 percent of sales, compared with 22.5 percent for McDonald's, 25.4 percent for Hardee's, and 25.0 percent for Burger King. Wendy's profit margins at the store level (21.0 percent) were more than double those of Burger King (10.5 percent) and Hardee's (8.5 percent) and far exceeded those of McDonald's (16.9 percent).

Drive-Through Windows

Thomas's second innovation was to offer sales via a drive-through window, which served to increase sales per square foot for his restaurants, providing him with lower financing costs than the typical hamburger operator. Table 1.2 illustrates the superior sales productivity achieved by Wendy's compared with its larger competitors in 1974.

The competitive advantage of the drive-through for Wendy's proved to be short-lived: McDonald's began adopting the innovation for its own units, as did Burger King. As a

Table 1.2

Sales and Capital Cost per Store, 1974

Chain	Sales per Store ($)	Capital Cost per Store ($)	Sales per $ of Capital
Burger King	460,000	347,000	1.32
McDonald's	671,000	438,000	1.53
Wendy's	490,000	280,000	1.75

Source: Company reports to SEC on Form 10-K, annual reports, and author's calculations.

Table 1.3

Unit Economics of Hamburger Chains, 1980

Chain	Capital Cost per Store ($)	Area per Store (ft^2)	Sales per Store ($)	Sales per ft^2 ($)	Sales per $ Capital
Burger King	790,000	2750	748,000	272	0.95
Hardee's	480,000	2250	410,000	182	0.85
McDonald's	650,000	3700	942,000	255	1.45
Wendy's	529,000	2400	627,100	261	1.19

result, the sales per dollar of capital cost advantage that Wendy's enjoyed in the early 1970s had largely slipped away by 1980. Table 1.3 shows the sales per store, sales per dollar of capital, and sales per square foot of the four leading hamburger chains in 1980.

Note that Burger King, Wendy's, and McDonald's were all quite similar in terms of sales per square foot, though Hardee's lagged far behind. One should keep in mind, too, that by this time McDonald's had introduced breakfast in its stores, thereby creating higher sales than those enjoyed by the other chains, none of which had successfully created sales in the morning hours.

The first of many medium-sized dinner house chains emerged in the late 1960s and early 1970s, too. Victoria Station opened its first store in San Francisco in 1969, while Steak & Ale opened its first unit in Dallas in 1966.

Market Share Determined

During the recession of 1973–74, the leadership of the fast-food hamburger industry was established. McDonald's, under the leadership of new chairman Fred Turner, actually accelerated its rate of store openings during the economic downturn, thereby permanently ensuring its dominance in the hamburger segment. At the same time, however, numerous smaller operations were forced to curtail their operations.

A cataloging of expansion and contraction in the hamburger industry during the mid-1970s is helpful here, because it was generally those chains that expanded in this

Table 1.4

Fast-Food Hamburger Units and 1974 Recession

Chain	1973	1974	1975	Percent Change, 1973–75
McDonald's	2,717	3,232	3,706	36.4
Burger King	1,190	1,395	1,603	34.7
Hardee's	889	929	913	2.7
Jack-in-the-Box	750	865	859	14.5
Burger Chef	1,050	960	950	−9.5
A&W	2,450	1,964	1,842	−24.8
Gino's	316	329	338	7.0
Sonic Drive-In	201	274	406	102.0
White Castle	129	133	135	4.7
Krystal	155	155	160	3.2
Wendy's	32	93	252	687.5
Whataburger	145	166	200	37.9
Steak&Shake	78	89	106	35.9
Carroll's	129	149	134	3.9
Borden Burgers	89	86	88	−1.1
Pioneer Take-Out	75	95	105	40.0
Burger Queen	53	54	70	32.1
White Tower	178	173	118	−33.7
Jack's	63	74	81	28.6
Eat 'N Park	36	38	40	11.1
Spudnut	318	120	130	−59.1
Mister Quick	69	67	69	0.0
Wetson's	54	36	29	−46.3
Winky's	35	46	42	20.0
Total	11,201	11,522	12,376	10.5

period that were the most successful for the next decade. Table 1.4 shows the number of units open at year-end 1973, 1974, and 1975 for the twenty-four identifiable fast-food hamburger chains (in this instance, those with thirty or more units and $10 million or more in sales for 1973).

Note that six of the twenty-four chains actually reduced the number of stores in their systems during this two-year period, while another showed no growth. Eight of the chains, *including four of the six largest,* closed more stores than they opened during 1975 alone. Of the chains that shrank during the 1974–75 recession, none is a significant factor in the industry today. A&W has one-quarter the number of units it operated 15 years ago, while Burger Chef has virtually disappeared and Gino's no longer exists, having been acquired and cannibalized for their sites by Hardee's and Marriott, respectively. (A small number of Burger Chef stores are still in operation, with the most profitable probably being one located on North Gilbert Street in Danville, Illinois.)

On the other hand, of the eight chains that expanded at a 30 percent rate or faster during the 1973–75 period, six are among the nine largest chains today.

Market Segment Established by 1973

For each major segment of the fast-food industry, the concept that had achieved dominance by 1973 remains the largest factor in its segment today. McDonald's, Pizza Hut, Kentucky Fried Chicken, Long John Silver, and Taco Bell were all the largest entrants in their respective sectors and remain so today. In other respects, however, the situation has been more fluid in other segments than in the hamburger business.

Table 1.5 shows expansion in the pizza segment in the mid-1970s. In this segment the ultimate shape of the competitive battle was not yet evident. While Pizza Hut's expansion clearly enabled the chain to outpace its peers, the growth of the smaller factors bore little relationship to the ultimate survival of the other chains. Domino's and Little Caesar currently dwarf Pizza Inn in sales, number of units, and profitability. Moreover, three of the eight largest pizza chains in 1989 were not even in existence in the mid-1970s.

Table 1.5

Pizza Chain Units and 1974 Recession

Chain	1973	1974	1975	Percent Change, 1973–75
Pizza Hut	1487	1875	2321	56.1
Shakey's	490	494	516	5.3
Pizza Inn	261	350	435	66.7
Pasquale	230	240	225	−2.2
Village Inn	132	132	145	9.8
Roundtable	81	94	118	45.7
Domino's	91	104	116	27.5
Little Caesar	125	130	135	8.0
Cassano	102	108	93	−8.8
Dino's	85	100	100	17.6
Total	3084	3627	4204	36.3

Table 1.6

Fried Chicken Chain Units and 1974 Recession

Chain	1973	1974	1975	Percent Change, 1973–75
Kentucky Fried Chicken	3799	3935	4060	6.9
Church's	525	565	634	20.8
Lum's	357	318	312	−12.6
Golden Skillet	180	200	219	21.7
Famous Recipe	134	140	135	0.7
Chicken Unlimited	226	239	185	−18.1
Brown's Chicken	0	0	94	NM
Total	5221	5397	5639	8.0

In the fried chicken segment, too, the clear leader was already established by the early 1970s. As indicated in Table 1.6, however, Kentucky Fried Chicken was no longer growing rapidly. The second-largest entry, Church's, was expanding far more aggressively. The chain that is now second-largest, Popeye's, which is the owner of Church's since September 1989, had barely started its operations and does not appear on the list of significant participants in 1973. The first Popeye's was opened in New Orleans in 1972.

Seafood Shakeout

In the fast-food seafood industry, the ultimate winner was by no means certain in the mid-1970s. In 1974, Arthur Treacher had 356 units in operation with sales of $73 million, not far short of the $82 million in sales on 373 stores achieved by segment leader Long John Silver.

Mexican Niche

In the Mexican segment, Table 1.7 indicates that Taco Bell's total dominance was well-established by the early 1970s. No other chain has made a dent in the fast-food Mexican segment, though there have been several entries into the Mexican dinner house business.

By the fourth quarter of 1989, Taco Bell had maintained a staggering 70 percent of the quick-service Mexican food industry, according to PepsiCo's market research. No restaurant chain enjoys a share of its segment even approaching this level. Indeed, very few brands in *any* consumer products category have been able to achieve such a high market share.

Coffee Shops Lose Market Share

One final note on the competitive shape of the chain restaurant industry in the mid-1970s must be mentioned. Howard Johnson's, it has already been noted, was by far the largest restaurant company in 1965. The coffee-shop segment, which was dominated by three operators: Howard Johnson's, Denny's, and Sambo's, had more than 5700 chain units in operation at the end of 1975, or nearly half the number of stores operated by the hamburger

Table 1.7

Mexican Fast-Food Chain Units and 1974 Recession

Chain	1973	1974	1975	Percent Change, 1973–75
Taco Bell	562	628	673	19.8
El Chico	71	77	78	9.9
Taco Charlie (Calny)	59	62	66	11.9
El Taco	77	84	84	9.1
Taco Time	85	95	124	45.9
Taco Tico	0	0	100	NM
Pup 'n Taco	76	83	87	14.5
Total	930	1029	1212	30.3

chains. It was equal in size to the fried chicken segment in terms of number of units and was 50 percent larger in sales volumes. The coffee-shop chains had 40 percent more units in operation than did the pizza chains, and enjoyed volume nearly triple that of the pizza segment. Today the pizza chains enjoy triple the number of units operated by the coffee-shop chains, while the hamburger chains outnumber the coffee shops by a factor of 5 to 1.

Analysts of the fast-food industry often speak of the fast-food chains capturing share of market from the independent "mom 'n' pop" operators. This has surely been true, but with less fanfare the fast-food giants have also ground down the more labor-intensive coffee shops that dominated the scene as recently as the mid-1960s.

The Recession of 1974–75

The chains that emerged successfully from the recession of 1970–71 held up remarkably well during the next economic downturn. Particularly striking was their success at the individual store level during the recession of 1974–75, especially considering the impact of the first OPEC oil embargo beginning in November 1973. Virtually every publicly held restaurant chain managed to register increases in customer counts during the recession, which was the most severe since the 1930s. Table 1.8 shows the growth in comparable store sales in real, that is, inflation-adjusted, terms for nine major food-service chains in 1974 and 1975. Note the general pattern of consistent increases. The decline in McDonald's sales per store in 1974 probably reflects some natural slowdown from an inflated base created by the successful introduction of the Quarter-Pounder sandwich in 1973. (The chain's sales per store had risen 22.3 percent in 1973, by far the largest increase in McDonald's history.)

The more benign economic climate of the late 1970s, however, saw the emergence of operating difficulties for most of the large chains. This, in turn, led to a large number of acquisitions by food and beverage operators, with generally the same unhappy results. Between 1976 and 1978, Friendly Ice Cream, Gilbert Robinson, Lum's, Pizza Hut, Taco Bell, and Steak & Ale were all acquired by major food and beverage companies. Sambo's

Table 1.8

Percentage Gains in Real Sales per Store

Chain	1974	1975
Denny's	3.1	2.7
Friendly Ice Cream	5.9	2.4
Long John Silver	6.4	15.1
McDonald's	(4.8)	3.9
Pizza Hut	3.0	6.2
Sambo's	3.9	0.2
Victoria Station	0.0	8.0
Wendy's	12.0	9.8
Winchell's Donut Houses	0.2	1.9

Source: Company reports and author's calculations.

was nearly acquired by conglomerate W. R. Grace, although the talks were suspended and Sambo's eventually plunged into bankruptcy. Hardee's was acquired by Imasco, a Canadian conglomerate, in 1980. Victoria Station, unable to find a buyer, filed for bankruptcy in 1986.

The crisis of the late 1970s was a result of several factors. In the case of Friendly Ice Cream, the chain proved unable to adapt to new geographical markets. Unfamiliar with advertising techniques, the chain entered midwestern markets hoping to rely on the word-of-mouth reputation that had worked in its heavily saturated New England market.

Hobbled by a name that belied its restaurant offerings, the chain floundered and was acquired by Hershey Foods Corporation in 1979. Hershey, in turn, found itself unable to turn the chain's operations around, and sold the chain to a group headed by Richard Rainwater and former Burger King president Donald Smith in early 1989. The intent of the acquiring group is to sell part of the chain for its underlying real estate value.

For Sambo's, the problem was one of alleged fraud in its scheme for compensating store managers. The plan, known as the "fraction of the action," was in some sense a pyramiding scheme that rewarded managers with percentage interests in the profits of newly opened stores throughout the system. When the Securities and Exchange Commission made inquiries into the chain's accounting method, store managers deserted in droves and the chain filed for bankruptcy. Some of the stores are operated today under different names by a chain called Vicorp.

For Victoria Station, which relied heavily on sales of a particular item, prime rib, that was difficult to make at home, the problem became one of boredom with the limited menu coupled with the chain's railway motif. Attempts to broaden the menu met with price resistance, and the chain lost its identity with even its loyal customer base.

Few Chains Remain Unscathed

Of the fifteen largest publicly held restaurant companies in 1976, all but four have either gone bankrupt or been sold. Of the remaining four, Dunkin' Donuts is the subject of a takeover battle at this writing, while Wendy's, crippled by losses and franchising woes, sells at a lower stock price than it did a decade earlier and is down nearly 75 percent from its high price of 1986. The chain has reportedly tried to sell its company-operated stores to franchisees of other chains.

Shoney's, citing lack of expansion opportunities, went through a recapitalization in July 1988 that paid its shareholders a large cash dividend and permanently curtailed expansion plans.

McDonald's Strongest

Only McDonald's has emerged unscathed. Its stock price is up sixfold in a decade; it is a component of the Dow-Jones Industrial Average; it is the most heavily advertised brand name in the world; and it is the creator of perhaps more millionaires among its franchisees, stockholders, and suppliers than any business enterprise in history.

New Chains Emerging

Yet for all of the fallout of the older chains, newer ones have sprung up, evincing the never-ending vitality of this protean industry. Some have been buffet chains, like Ryan's Family Steak Houses and Buffets, Inc., offering all-you-can-eat food bars to value-conscious patrons. Some have been upscale concepts, a step above fast food in price and quality, such as Chili's (run by Steak & Ale founder Norman Brinker). Still others, like Sbarro's, compete with the giant pizza chains by offering a more varied Italian menu in mall locations. Most recently, a concept called Rally's, developed by Long John Silver's creator James Patterson, has achieved astonishingly high sales per store with its double drive-through hamburger concept.

The New Wendy's?

Rally's may have some of the advantages that Wendy's brought to the industry when it attacked McDonald's and Burger King in the early 1970s. With low prices (one-third less than those of the larger chains), high turnover in a small facility, and the ability to serve very quickly, Rally's produces a ratio of sales to invested capital nearly half again as high as McDonald's and nearly double that of Wendy's.

Chapter 2

Size and Growth of the Fast-Food Industry

Refining the Concept of Fast Food

The very term "fast food" is ambiguous and has, in some instances, come to be synonymous with food served at chain restaurants of every description. Even the adjective "fast" may be a misnomer: the consumer waits for his pizza as long at Pizza Hut as he does at a traditional Italian restaurant. The issue of coffee shops in this context is difficult: if one includes the traditional breakfast at Denny's or Howard Johnson's as fast food, then any chain restaurant would seem to qualify.

Defining "Fast Food"

As used in this book, "fast food" generally means food served to a patron at a self-service counter or through a drive-through window. It may be prepared in advance, as at McDonald's, or it may be cooked to order, as is generally true of the pizza chains. The term is not necessarily confined to large corporate foodservice entities, although virtually all of the analysis in this monograph is directed at large chains.

The very term "fast food" is anathema to managements in the industry: McDonald's management prefers "QSR" (quick-service restaurant). Wendy's founder and chairman R. David Thomas once remarked, "When you say 'fast food,' that's a New York analyst talking. Our investment bankers gave us that handle, which I think is really terrible." (*Endless Shakeout*, p. 53)

Relative Size and Composition of the Restaurant Industry

Discussions of the size of the restaurant industry must begin with some definitions and distinctions. The National Restaurant Association (NRA) estimates that sales at "eating places," including restaurants and lunchrooms ($70.6 billion), limited-menu restaurants and refreshment places ($60.4 billion), commercial cafeterias, social caterers, and ice cream or frozen custard stands, totaled $138.2 billion in 1988. Bars and taverns provided another $9.6 billion, bringing total sales at eating and drinking establishments to $147.8 billion.

Hotels and motels provided food sales of $13.3 billion in 1988, while foodservice facilities operated at retail outlets other than restaurants, including drug stores and variety and convenience stores, totaled $16.6 billion.

"Food contractors," which provide foodservice at plants, schools, hospitals, and other facilities owned by others, accounted for estimated revenues in 1988 of $11.5 billion. "Institutional foodservice," which the NRA defines as "business, educational, government or institutional organizations which operate their own foodservice," achieved sales of $23.1 billion. Finally, military foodservice amounted to $1.0 billion.

The grand total of total food prepared away from home, then, was $213.5 billion, of which eating and drinking places accounted for 69.2 percent, while limited-menu restaurants ("fast food") accounted for 28.2 percent.

Sales at eating and drinking places of $147.8 billion accounted for 9.0 percent of total U.S. retail trade in 1988 of $1629 billion. The largest components of retail trade were auto dealers (total sales of $369 billion) and food stores ($332 billion).

Restaurant Sales and Food Expenditures

Restaurant sales have risen slowly as a percentage of total food expenditures. By 1988, slightly over 28 percent of the American food dollar was spent at eating and drinking places, in contrast to 20 percent two decades earlier and 25 percent in the late 1970s. These data are shown in Table 2.1. Note that the percentage of food expenditures spent at restaurants peaked in 1986 and declined slightly in 1987, showing only partial recovery in 1988.

Differences in Data Series

These data on sales of restaurants, or more strictly "eating and drinking places," maintained by the Department of Commerce, are not all-inclusive in that they do not include food eaten away from home at convenience stores, ballparks, and in company cafeterias. A more complete picture of the size and growth of the market for all food consumed away from home, developed by the National Restaurant Association, is shown in Table 2.2. Note that the growth in sales of food prepared away from home showed its lowest growth ever in 1988.

The series in Table 2.2 includes as its largest component "commercial foodservice sales," a category which in turn comprises sales of restaurants, snack bars, fast-food restaurants, hotels, caterers, and bars. The category also encompasses food contractors, defined as commercial ventures that prepare food for clients in the customers' own facilities, including colleges, hospitals, manufacturing plants, and offices. This segment is not to be confused

Table 2.1

Restaurant Sales and Food Expenditures

Year	Restaurant Sales ($ million)	% Change	Total Food Expenditures ($ billion)	% Change	Restaurant Sales as % of Food Expenditures
1967	22,518		112.3		20.05
1968	25,279	12.3	121.6	8.3	20.79
1969	27,173	7.5	130.5	7.3	20.82
1970	30,476	12.2	142.1	8.9	21.45
1971	32,321	6.1	147.5	3.8	21.91
1972	35,738	10.6	158.5	7.5	22.55
1973	40,290	12.7	176.1	11.1	22.88
1974	44,606	10.7	198.2	12.5	22.51
1975	51,067	14.5	218.7	10.3	23.35
1976	57,331	12.3	236.2	8.0	24.27
1977	63,370	10.5	255.9	8.3	24.76
1978	71,828	13.3	282.2	10.3	25.45
1979	82,110	14.3	317.3	12.4	25.88
1980	90,058	9.7	349.1	10.0	25.80
1981	98,118	8.9	376.5	7.8	26.06
1982	104,593	6.6	398.8	5.9	26.23
1983	114,869	9.8	421.9	5.8	27.23
1984	124,741	8.6	448.5	6.3	27.81
1985	133,457	7.0	471.6	5.2	28.30
1986	144,966	8.6	500.0	6.0	28.99
1987	147,717	1.9	529.2	5.8	27.91
1988	157,504	6.6	559.7	5.8	28.14

Compound Annual Growth Rate (%)

1983–88		6.5		5.8	
1978–83		9.8		8.4	
1967–78		11.1		8.7	
1967–88		9.7		7.9	

with institutional food prepared for their own account by such organizations, which are listed separately.

The segment of commercial foodservice also includes sales made by retail outlets that are not primarily engaged in foodservice, including drug stores, department stores, convenience stores, and gas stations. Finally, the category includes drive-in movies, bowling alleys, vending machines, and recreational facilities.

The growth in commercial foodservice is illustrated in Table 2.3. Note that commercial foodservice comprises nearly 90 percent of all foodservice and has consistently grown about half a percent faster than other foodservice business annually. Again, note that 1988 marked the slowest rate of growth in commercial foodservice since the NRA has been tracking the data.

Table 2.2

Total U.S. Foodservice Sales

Year	Grand Total Foodservice Sales ($ million)	% Change
1970	42,780	
1971	46,070	7.7
1972	49,930	8.4
1973	56,322	12.8
1974	62,867	11.6
1975	70,313	11.8
1976	78,380	11.5
1977	86,834	10.8
1978	97,615	12.4
1979	109,576	12.3
1980	119,617	9.2
1981	131,399	9.8
1982	140,437	6.9
1983	152,121	8.3
1984	164,953	8.4
1985	174,767	5.9
1986	188,909	8.1
1987	203,063	7.5
1988	213,526	5.2

Compound Annual Growth Rate (%)

1970–88	9.3
1970–80	10.8
1980–88	7.5
1983–88	7.0

Source: National Restaurant Association.

Table 2.3

Commercial Foodservice Sales (Including Restaurants and Hotels)

Year	Total Commercial Foodservice Sales ($ million)	% Change	As % of Total Foodservice
1970	34,829		81.4
1971	37,686	8.2	81.8
1972	41,062	9.0	82.2
1973	46,450	13.1	82.5
1974	51,884	11.7	82.5
1975	58,392	12.5	83.0
1976	65,635	12.4	83.7
1977	73,140	11.4	84.2
1978	82,673	13.0	84.7
1979	93,105	12.6	85.0
1980	101,529	9.0	84.9
1981	112,058	10.4	85.3
1982	119,992	7.1	85.4
1983	131,266	9.4	86.3
1984	143,265	9.1	86.9
1985	152,864	6.7	87.5
1986	166,322	8.8	88.0
1987	179,669	8.0	88.5
1988	189,331	5.4	88.7

Compound Annual Growth Rate (%)

1970–88	9.9
1970–80	11.3
1980–88	8.1
1983–88	7.6

Source: National Restaurant Association.

Growth of Individual Segments

Before examining the growth rates of the individual segments within the commercial foodservice segment, a brief exploration of the other noncommercial forms of foodservice is worthwhile. Table 2.4 illustrates the comparatively small and slow-growing category of employee foodservice, that is, industrial and commercial organizations that operate their own foodservice programs. The NRA estimated that in 1967 approximately 3465 facilities were operated in this way.

Table 2.5 recounts the size of the educational foodservice market, again confining the data to organizations that operate their own facilities rather than employing a food contractor to do so. Here, too, the growth has been modest. The totals include locations at 91,000 public and parochial elementary and secondary schools and nearly 1100 public colleges and 1700 private colleges and universities.

Table 2.4

Institutional Foodservice Sales

Year	Sales ($ million)	% Change
1970	688	
1971	692	0.6
1972	736	6.4
1973	903	22.7
1974	1034	14.5
1975	1072	3.7
1976	1133	5.7
1977	1245	9.9
1978	1373	10.3
1979	1535	11.8
1980	1635	6.5
1981	1762	07.8
1982	1733	−1.6
1983	1767	2.0
1984	1904	7.8
1985	1971	3.5
1986	1976	0.3
1987	2021	2.3
1988	2113	4.6

Compound Annual Growth Rate (%)

1970–88	6.4
1970–80	9.0
1980–88	3.3
1983–88	3.6

Source: National Restaurant Association.

Table 2.5

Educational Foodservice Sales

Year	Sales ($ million)	% Change
1970	2102	
1971	2374	12.9
1972	2410	1.5
1973	2605	8.1
1974	2923	12.2
1975	3184	8.9
1976	3318	4.2
1977	3502	5.5
1978	3791	8.3
1979	4176	10.2
1980	4610	10.4
1981	4900	6.3
1982	5248	7.1
1983	5509	5.0
1984	5749	4.4
1985	5979	4.0
1986	6253	4.6
1987	6485	3.7
1988	6716	3.6

Compound Annual Growth Rate (%)

1970–88	6.7
1970–80	8.2
1980–88	4.8
1983–88	4.0

Source: National Restaurant Association.

Table 2.6

Hospital Foodservice Sales

Year	Sales ($ million)	% Change
1970	2991	
1971	3019	0.9
1972	3227	6.9
1973	3553	10.1
1974	4033	13.5
1975	4346	7.8
1976	4654	7.1
1977	5012	7.7
1978	5437	8.5
1979	6055	11.4
1980	6668	10.1
1981	7183	7.7
1982	7641	6.4
1983	7375	−3.5
1984	7391	0.2
1985	7104	−3.9
1986	7170	0.9
1987	7196	0.4
1988	7368	2.4

Compound Annual Growth Rate (%)

1970–88	5.1
1970–80	8.3
1980–88	1.3
1983–88	0.0

Source: National Restaurant Association.

Table 2.7

**All Other Foodservice Sales
(Prisons, Nursing Homes, and Military)**

Year	Sales ($ million)	% Change
1970	2170	
1971	2299	5.9
1972	2495	8.5
1973	2811	12.7
1974	2993	6.5
1975	3319	10.9
1976	3640	9.7
1977	3935	8.1
1978	4341	10.3
1979	4705	8.4
1980	5175	10.0
1981	5496	6.2
1982	5823	5.9
1983	6204	6.5
1984	6644	7.1
1985	6849	3.1
1986	7188	4.9
1987	7692	7.0
1988	7998	4.0

Compound Annual Growth Rate (%)

1970–88	7.5
1970–80	9.1
1980–88	5.6
1983–88	5.2

Source: National Restaurant Association.

Table 2.6 recaps the growth of hospital feeding, the lone category in all foodservice that has shown no growth at all in the past five years. A total of nearly 6800 hospitals are included in the listing.

Other noncommercial foodservice sales are summarized in Table 2.7. The data include a wide array of outlets, including prisons, the military, nursing homes, clubs, seminaries, and transportation companies.

The most important point in observing growth of the various foodservice categories is that commercial foodservice grows faster than any noncommercial segment. Within commercial foodservice, in turn, the fast-food segment achieves above-average growth. However, *fast food is no longer the most rapidly growing segment of commercial foodservice.* That distinction is now held by retailers whose primary purpose is offering some product other than foodservice.

Within commercial foodservice, the largest category is restaurants other than fast-food units. This broad category includes everything from diners to coffee shops to expensive gourmet restaurants. The historical size and growth of this market is illustrated in Table 2.8. Note that the category's share of total commercial foodservice remained almost precisely constant from 1970 through 1985, but has declined slightly in the most recent three years. The NRA estimated in 1987 that there were 128,000 restaurants of this type in the United States.

Fast-Food Sales Growth

Sales at fast-food restaurants, the subject of this book, are tabulated in Table 2.9. Note the consistent gains in share of market until the last two years. Observe, too, that the annual growth rate of the fast-food segment was nearly twice as fast in the 1970s as it has averaged over the past five years. The NRA estimates that 131,000 fast-food restaurants were in operation in 1987.

Table 2.8

Sales at Restaurants and Lunchrooms (Excluding Fast Food)

Year	Sales ($ million)	% Change	% of Total
1970	13,347		38.3
1971	14,300	7.1	37.9
1972	15,514	8.5	37.8
1973	17,616	13.5	37.9
1974	19,895	12.9	38.3
1975	22,677	14.0	38.8
1976	25,421	12.1	38.7
1977	28,045	10.3	38.3
1978	32,174	14.7	38.9
1979	36,228	12.6	38.9
1980	39,307	8.5	38.7
1981	43,527	10.7	38.8
1982	46,443	6.7	38.7
1983	50,530	8.8	38.5
1984	55,112	9.1	38.5
1985	58,444	6.0	38.2
1986	62,391	6.8	37.5
1987	66,634	6.8	37.1
1988	70,574	5.9	37.3

Compound Annual Growth Rate (%)

1970–88	9.7
1970–80	11.4
1980–88	7.6
1983–88	6.9

Source: National Restaurant Association.

Table 2.9

Sales at Fast-Food Restaurants

Year	Sales ($ million)	% Change	% of Total
1970	6,190		17.8
1971	7,011	13.3	18.6
1972	8,037	14.6	19.6
1973	9,684	20.5	20.8
1974	11,365	17.4	21.9
1975	13,597	19.6	23.3
1976	16,346	20.2	24.9
1977	19,358	18.4	26.5
1978	22,285	15.1	27.0
1979	25,902	16.2	27.8
1980	28,699	10.8	28.3
1981	32,202	12.2	28.7
1982	35,357	9.8	29.5
1983	39,494	11.7	30.1
1984	43,719	10.7	30.5
1985	47,191	7.9	30.9
1986	52,509	11.3	31.6
1987	57,234	9.0	31.9
1988	60,425	5.6	31.9

Compound Annual Growth Rate (%)

1970–88	13.5
1970–80	16.6
1980–88	9.8
1983–88	8.9

Source: National Restaurant Association.

Table 2.10

Sales at Bars and Taverns

Year	Sales ($ million)	% Change	% of Total
1970	5008		14.4
1971	5199	3.8	13.8
1972	5333	2.6	13.0
1973	5535	3.8	11.9
1974	5729	3.5	11.0
1975	5988	4.5	10.3
1976	6233	4.1	9.5
1977	6444	3.4	8.8
1978	6701	4.0	8.1
1979	7184	7.2	7.7
1980	7785	8.4	7.7
1981	8026	3.1	7.2
1982	7912	−1.4	6.6
1983	8157	3.1	6.2
1984	8255	1.2	5.8
1985	8428	2.1	5.5
1986	8976	6.5	5.4
1987	9434	5.1	5.3
1988	9626	2.0	5.1

Compound Annual Growth Rate (%)

1970–88	3.7
1970–80	4.5
1980–88	2.7
1983–88	3.4

Source: National Restaurant Association.

Table 2.11

Sales of Contract Feeders

Year	Sales ($ million)	% Change	% of Total
1970	2,442		7.0
1971	2,790	14.3	7.4
1972	3,003	7.6	7.3
1973	3,475	15.7	7.5
1974	3,934	13.2	7.6
1975	4,169	6.0	7.1
1976	4,504	8.0	6.9
1977	4,989	10.8	6.8
1978	5,549	11.2	6.7
1979	6,242	12.5	6.7
1980	6,818	9.2	6.7
1981	7,344	7.7	6.6
1982	7,708	5.0	6.4
1983	8,242	6.9	6.3
1984	8,907	8.1	6.2
1985	9,460	6.2	6.2
1986	10,095	6.7	6.1
1987	11,075	9.7	6.2
1988	11,550	4.3	6.1

Compound Annual Growth Rate (%)

1970–88	9.0
1970–80	10.8
1980–88	6.8
1983–88	7.0

Source: National Restaurant Association.

Tavern Sales Slowest

Sales at bars and taverns have grown at a very modest rate, as indicated in Table 2.10. Note the persistent drop in share of the total commercial foodservice market, as well as the actual decline in the recession year 1982. The NRA estimates that 32,000 bars and taverns in the United States serve food. They further estimate that 87.5 percent of the sales of bars and taverns consist of alcoholic beverages, so their importance to the foodservice market addressed by fast-food operators is minimal.

Contract feeders' revenues are shown in Table 2.11. The gradual decline in the percentage of total commercial foodservice accounted for by contractors is a source of opportunity for other foodservice establishments. Note, however, that the contract feeders do continue to capture a share of the total in-plant market from institutions that prepare their own food. The NRA estimates that 9000 feeding contractors operate in the United States.

Foodservice sales of hotels and motels are shown in Table 2.12. An estimated 27,000 lodging places maintain their own foodservice operations. Growth of this segment has kept pace with that of total commercial foodservice.

Other Retailers Add Fast Food

The category of other retailers engaged in foodservice has shown rapid growth, and *growth has accelerated in recent years*. This phenomenon is analyzed more fully in the discussion of convenience stores below, and it is a major drag on the growth rate of the fast-food industry. The NRA estimates a total of 108,000 retail outlets are engaged in some form of foodservice. The historical growth of this form of foodservice is recounted in Table 2.13.

Table 2.12

Food Sales at Lodging Places

Year	Sales ($ million)	% Change	% of Total
1970	2,585		7.4
1971	2,716	5.1	7.2
1972	2,999	10.4	7.3
1973	3,358	12.0	7.2
1974	3,662	9.1	7.1
1975	4,093	11.8	7.0
1976	4,595	12.3	7.0
1977	5,030	9.5	6.9
1978	5,677	12.9	6.9
1979	6,244	10.0	6.7
1980	6,768	8.4	6.7
1981	7,630	12.7	6.8
1982	8,286	8.6	6.9
1983	9,165	10.6	7.0
1984	10,026	9.4	7.0
1985	10,699	6.7	7.0
1986	11,383	6.4	6.8
1987	12,328	8.3	6.9
1988	13,303	7.9	7.0

Compound Annual Growth Rate (%)

1970–88	9.5
1970–80	10.1
1980–88	8.8
1983–88	7.7

Source: National Restaurant Association.

Table 2.13

Foodservice Sales of Other Retailers

Year	Other Retail Sales ($ million)	% Change	% of Total
1970	1652		4.7
1971	1788	8.2	4.7
1972	1942	8.6	4.7
1973	2117	9.0	4.6
1974	2192	3.5	4.2
1975	2259	3.1	3.9
1976	2403	6.4	3.7
1977	2495	3.8	3.4
1978	2724	9.2	3.3
1979	2998	10.1	3.2
1980	3264	8.9	3.2
1981	3697	13.3	3.3
1982	4108	11.1	3.4
1983	4690	14.2	3.6
1984	5395	15.0	3.8
1985	6195	14.8	4.1
1986	7052	13.8	4.2
1987	7827	11.0	4.4
1988	8907	13.8	4.7

Compound Annual Growth Rate (%)

1970–88	9.8
1970–80	7.0
1980–88	13.4
1983–88	13.7

Source: National Restaurant Association.

Table 2.14

Miscellaneous Foodservice Sales

Year	Miscellaneous Sales ($ million)	% Change	% of Total
1970	3,605		10.4
1971	3,882	7.7	10.3
1972	4,234	9.1	10.3
1973	4,665	10.2	10.0
1974	5,107	9.5	9.8
1975	5,609	9.8	9.6
1976	6,133	9.3	9.3
1977	6,779	10.5	9.3
1978	7,563	11.6	9.1
1979	8,307	9.8	8.9
1980	8,888	7.0	8.8
1981	9,632	8.4	8.6
1982	10,178	5.7	8.5
1983	10,988	8.0	8.4
1984	11,851	7.9	8.3
1985	12,447	5.0	8.1
1986	13,916	11.8	8.4
1987	15,137	8.8	8.4
1988	14,946	−1.3	7.9

Compound Annual Growth Rate (%)

1970–88	8.2
1970–80	9.4
1980–88	6.7
1983–88	6.3

Source: National Restaurant Association.

Miscellaneous foodservice includes nonstore retailers (e.g., the coffee wagon), vending machines, bowling alleys, and recreation centers. The category is slowly declining as a percent of total foodservice. The data for this segment are shown in Table 2.14.

Food Consumed Away from Home and Disposable Personal Income

Restaurant sales rose very slightly as a percent of disposable personal income (DPI) throughout the 1970s. Table 2.15 shows the relationship between the two series since 1967. Particularly noteworthy is the fact that in the two severe recessions of 1974–75 and 1982 the restaurant industry not only continued to grow but actually managed to increase its share of DPI. Clearly, the total amount of dollars spent at restaurants is not sensitive to the overall economy.

On the other hand, signs of imminent maturity in the growth of restaurant sales have appeared. Although it may be premature to declare that a trend is in place, restaurant sales have dropped as a percent of DPI in each of the last two years. Such a development is not unprecedented: the same pattern was evident in 1979–81, yet reversed itself in subsequent years. However, at that time the nation suffered its second oil shock, which did serve to dampen highway travel considerably. The slowdown in 1987 and 1988 has no such obvious explanation and may, at long last, signal a peaking of demand relative to overall income.

Table 2.15

Restaurant Sales and DPI

Year	Restaurant Sales ($ million)	% Change	DPI ($ billion)	% Change	Restaurant Sales as % of DPI
1967	22,518		562.1		4.01
1968	25,279	12.3	609.6	8.5	4.15
1969	27,173	7.5	656.7	7.7	4.14
1970	30,476	12.2	715.6	9.0	4.26
1971	32,321	6.1	776.8	8.6	4.16
1972	35,738	10.6	839.6	8.1	4.26
1973	40,290	12.7	949.8	13.1	4.24
1974	44,606	10.7	1038.4	9.3	4.30
1975	51,067	14.5	1142.8	10.1	4.47
1976	57,331	12.3	1252.6	9.6	4.58
1977	63,370	10.5	1379.3	10.1	4.59
1978	71,828	13.3	1551.2	12.5	4.63
1979	82,110	14.3	1729.3	11.5	4.75
1980	90,058	9.7	1918.0	10.9	4.70
1981	98,118	8.9	2127.6	10.9	4.61
1982	104,593	6.6	2261.4	6.3	4.63
1983	114,869	9.8	2428.1	7.4	4.73
1984	124,741	8.6	2670.6	10.0	4.67
1985	133,457	7.0	2841.1	6.4	4.70
1986	144,966	8.6	3022.1	6.4	4.80
1987	147,717	1.9	3205.9	6.1	4.61
1988	157,504	6.6	3477.8	8.5	4.53
Compound Annual Growth Rate (%)					
1983–88		6.5		7.5	
1978–83		9.8		9.4	
1967–78		11.1		9.7	
1967–88		9.7		9.1	

Source: U.S. Department of Commerce.

The restaurant industry's growth is tracked most closely by an industry trade group called CREST, which is an acronym for Chain Restaurant Emerging Share Trend. The study's survey found that, for the first time since it began gathering data in the mid-1970s, the fast-food segment of the restaurant industry experienced negative customer counts in the third quarter of 1989.

Expenditures for food consumed away from home vary widely by state and region. As might be expected, restaurant sales are positively correlated with DPI. However, the income elasticity of expenditures at restaurants is very low; that is, the percentage of income spent at restaurants by high-income individuals is not significantly different from that of lower-income people. The explanation for this is that restaurant spending is not primarily recreational or discretionary: most dining-out occasions are an adjunct either to working or to shopping.

Table 2.16 shows year-end 1987 population, DPI, and sales at eating and drinking places for each of the fifty states and the District of Columbia. Table 2.17 shows per capita expenditures at eating and drinking places, as well as eating and drinking expenditures as a percentage of DPI and per capita DPI.

Table 2.18 sorts states by their per capita spending at eating and drinking places. Several of the states at the top of the list, including Hawaii, the District of Columbia, Alaska, California, Wyoming, Vermont, New Hampshire, and Nevada enjoy unusually high levels of spending on tourism (for a fuller discussion, see Chapter 5). Even adjusting for this factor, however, it is clear that residents of states in the Northeast and Middle Atlantic states spend considerably more per capita at restaurants than do residents of states in the Southeast and rural western states.

Table 2.19 ranks the states according to per capita DPI. A similar pattern is evident, with the highest levels of DPI per capita again being found in the Northeast. Table 2.20 shows the states ranked by the percentage of DPI spent at restaurants. Note that in the case of the Middle Atlantic states, a comparatively low percentage of DPI is spent at restaurants, though as we have seen the absolute dollars are quite high. It may be inferred, then, that the income elasticity of total spending at restaurants is comparatively low. Expenditures rise with income, which is to be expected, but do not necessarily rise as a percentage of income.

According to a study by the National Restaurant Association, (*Meal Consumption Behavior,* p. 4) members of households with annual incomes in 1985 of over $50,000 ate 4.7 meals per week away from home; those earning $35,000 to $50,000 ate 4.5 meals away from home weekly; those with incomes of $10,000 to $15,000 ate 3.1 meals out per week and those from households with incomes below $10,000 consumed only 2.8 meals out weekly.

Table 2.16

Sales at Eating and Drinking Establishments by State

State	Population 12/31/87 (000)	DPI ($000)	Sales ($000)
Alabama	4,137.1	40,984,198	1,562,801
Alaska	545.7	7,876,698	539,218
Arizona	3,441.1	41,699,594	2,072,473
Arkansas	2,420.0	24,543,098	886,842
California	27,939.0	426,008,347	21,054,569
Colorado	3,346.3	44,085,675	2,441,362
Connecticut	3,242.5	57,378,965	2,606,333
Delaware	642.5	8,645,997	386,973
D.C.	623.3	10,538,992	740,111
Florida	12,163.9	157,045,634	8,441,975
Georgia	6,295.2	72,490,751	3,754,827
Hawaii	1,088.8	14,683,991	1,351,540
Idaho	1,033.9	10,269,197	456,269
Illinois	11,657.6	164,545,300	6,831,008
Indiana	5,570.8	65,622,147	3,186,125
Iowa	2,860.7	34,680,083	1,502,467
Kansas	2,495.0	33,350,083	1,277,002
Kentucky	3,771.5	39,226,173	1,877,207
Louisiana	4,517.8	45,171,584	2,283,753
Maine	1,191.8	13,998,698	786,336
Maryland	4,562.6	67,037,678	2,903,958
Massachusetts	5,884.1	92,327,918	5,438,655
Michigan	9,262.9	118,111,734	5,370,774
Minnesota	4,292.3	58,403,780	2,701,359
Mississippi	2,676.2	23,011,966	841,893
Missouri	5,173.6	63,129,786	3,011,580
Montana	832.1	8,959,694	463,942
Nebraska	1,616.8	20,330,263	977,280
Nevada	1,026.7	13,584,697	759,731
New Hampshire	1,060.1	15,372,986	788,361
New Jersey	7,728.6	128,510,480	4,517,623
New Mexico	1,525.0	15,141,196	856,906
New York	17,964.0	269,717,767	10,994,956
North Carolina	6,463.6	71,496,746	3,334,259
North Dakota	694.3	8,394,203	347,264
Ohio	10,834.9	135,446,212	6,483,849
Oklahoma	3,344.4	35,503,942	1,818,513
Oregon	2,738.4	30,535,274	1,728,314
Pennsylvania	11,973.4	154,931,090	6,263,727
Rhode Island	990.0	13,354,993	720,468
South Carolina	3,458.4	34,730,221	1,751,158
South Dakota	721.9	8,073,294	385,425
Tennessee	4,899.5	53,370,919	2,370,808
Texas	16,888.0	198,762,908	10,071,669
Utah	1,712.4	16,676,933	634,112
Vermont	550.3	6,460,990	408,910
Virginia	5,943.2	80,729,925	3,434,823
Washington	4,548.9	62,090,277	3,091,423
West Virginia	1,934.6	18,888,190	721,433
Wisconsin	4,836.6	60,917,768	2,950,551
Wyoming	500.4	5,998,096	375,460
Total U.S.	245,622.7	3,202,847,131	150,558,375

Source: U.S. Department of Commerce, Survey of Buying Power.

Table 2.17

Food and Drink Sales per Capita and as Percent of DPI, by State

State	Food & Drink Sales per Capita ($)	% DPI	DPI per Capita ($)
Alabama	378	3.81	9,907
Alaska	988	6.85	14,434
Arizona	602	4.97	12,118
Arkansas	366	3.61	10,142
California	754	4.94	15,248
Colorado	730	5.54	13,174
Connecticut	804	4.54	17,696
Delaware	602	4.48	13,457
D.C.	1187	7.02	16,908
Florida	694	5.38	12,911
Georgia	596	5.18	11,515
Hawaii	1241	9.20	13,486
Idaho	441	4.44	9,932
Illinois	586	4.15	14,115
Indiana	572	4.86	11,780
Iowa	525	4.33	12,123
Kansas	512	3.83	13,367
Kentucky	498	4.79	10,401
Louisiana	506	5.06	9,999
Maine	660	5.62	11,746
Maryland	636	4.33	14,693
Massachusetts	924	5.89	15,691
Michigan	580	4.55	12,751
Minnesota	629	4.63	13,607
Mississippi	315	3.66	8,599
Missouri	582	4.77	12,202
Montana	558	5.18	10,768
Nebraska	604	4.81	12,574
Nevada	740	5.59	13,231
New Hampshire	744	5.13	14,501
New Jersey	585	3.52	16,628
New Mexico	562	5.66	9,929
New York	612	4.08	15,014
North Carolina	516	4.66	11,061
North Dakota	500	4.14	12,090
Ohio	598	4.79	12,501
Oklahoma	544	5.12	10,616
Oregon	631	5.66	11,151
Pennsylvania	523	4.04	12,940
Rhode Island	728	5.39	13,490
South Carolina	506	5.04	10,042
South Dakota	534	4.77	11,183
Tennessee	484	4.44	10,893
Texas	596	5.07	11,769
Utah	370	3.80	9,739
Vermont	743	6.33	11,741
Virginia	578	4.25	13,584
Washington	680	4.98	13,650
West Virginia	373	3.82	9,763
Wisconsin	610	4.84	12,595
Wyoming	750	6.26	11,987
Total U.S.	613	4.70	13,040

Source: U.S. Department of Commerce, Survey of Buying Power.

Table 2.18

Food and Drink Sales per Capita, by State

State	Food & Drink Sales per Capita ($)
Hawaii	1241
D.C.	1187
Alaska	988
Massachusetts	924
Connecticut	804
California	754
Wyoming	750
New Hampshire	744
Vermont	743
Nevada	740
Colorado	730
Rhode Island	728
Florida	694
Washington	680
Maine	660
Maryland	636
Oregon	631
Minnesota	629
New York	612
Wisconsin	610
Nebraska	604
Delaware	602
Arizona	602
Ohio	598
Georgia	596
Texas	596
Illinois	586
New Jersey	585
Missouri	582
Michigan	580
Virginia	578
Indiana	572
New Mexico	562
Montana	558
Oklahoma	544
South Dakota	534
Iowa	525
Pennsylvania	523
North Carolina	516
Kansas	512
South Carolina	506
Louisiana	506
North Dakota	500
Kentucky	498
Tennessee	484
Idaho	441
Alabama	378
West Virginia	373
Utah	370
Arkansas	366
Mississippi	315
Total U.S.	613

Source: U.S. Department of Commerce, Survey of Buying Power.

Table 2.19

DPI per Capita, by State

State	DPI ($)
Connecticut	17,696
D.C.	16,908
New Jersey	16,628
Massachusetts	15,691
California	15,248
New York	15,014
Maryland	14,693
New Hampshire	14,501
Alaska	14,434
Illinois	14,115
Washington	13,650
Minnesota	13,607
Virginia	13,584
Rhode Island	13,490
Hawaii	13,486
Delaware	13,457
Kansas	13,367
Nevada	13,231
Colorado	13,174
Pennsylvania	12,940
Florida	12,911
Michigan	12,751
Wisconsin	12,595
Nebraska	12,574
Ohio	12,501
Missouri	12,202
Iowa	12,123
Arizona	12,118
North Dakota	12,090
Wyoming	11,987
Indiana	11,780
Texas	11,769
Maine	11,746
Vermont	11,741
Georgia	11,515
South Dakota	11,183
Oregon	11,151
North Carolina	11,061
Tennessee	10,893
Montana	10,768
Oklahoma	10,616
Kentucky	10,401
Arkansas	10,142
South Carolina	10,042
Louisiana	9,999
Idaho	9,932
New Mexico	9,929
Alabama	9,907
West Virginia	9,763
Utah	9,739
Mississippi	8,599
Total U.S.	13,040

Source: U.S. Department of Commerce, Survey of Buying Power.

Table 2.20

Fraction of DPI Spent on Eating and Drinking

State	DPI Spent on Eating and Drinking (%)
Hawaii	9.20
D.C.	7.02
Alaska	6.85
Vermont	6.33
Wyoming	6.26
Massachusetts	5.89
Oregon	5.66
New Mexico	5.66
Maine	5.62
Nevada	5.59
Colorado	5.54
Rhode Island	5.39
Florida	5.38
Georgia	5.18
Montana	5.18
New Hampshire	5.13
Oklahoma	5.12
Texas	5.07
Louisiana	5.06
South Carolina	5.04
Washington	4.98
Arizona	4.97
California	4.94
Indiana	4.86
Wisconsin	4.84
Nebraska	4.81
Ohio	4.79
Kentucky	4.79
South Dakota	4.77
Missouri	4.77
North Carolina	4.66
Minnesota	4.63
Michigan	4.55
Connecticut	4.54
Delaware	4.48
Idaho	4.44
Tennessee	4.44
Iowa	4.33
Maryland	4.33
Virginia	4.25
Illinois	4.15
North Dakota	4.14
New York	4.08
Pennsylvania	4.04
Kansas	3.83
West Virginia	3.82
Alabama	3.81
Utah	3.80
Mississippi	3.66
Arkansas	3.61
New Jersey	3.52
Total U.S.	4.70

From Table 2.19.

Price Elasticity Higher than Income Elasticity

Although income elasticity does not appear to be an important determinant of fast-food sales, *price elasticity* is a factor. Interesting work done by the team of restaurant analysts at Montgomery Securities in San Francisco (Michael G. Mueller, John W. Weiss, and Lisa Allen Meier) suggests that large price increases at fast-food restaurants lead to declines in traffic. The Montgomery analysts found that between 1974 and 1988, McDonald's raised menu prices more than 5.0 percent in six years. In five of those six years, McDonald's real sales per store fell, with the declines averaging 3.7 percent in each year.

In the nine years in the period under inspection when menu price increases totaled less than 5.0 percent, real sales per store declined only once, experiencing a 0.5 percent decrease in 1988. Real sales per store rose an average of 2.9 percent annually during the nine years of modest price hikes. The lone year of no price increases at McDonald's (1984) showed a gain in real sales per store of 7.2 percent, by far the largest gain since 1973.

The point here is not that McDonald's management makes a mistake every time it raises prices. In order to protect its profitability, the chain naturally must respond to cost pressures by taking some action to protect its margins. It does so at a price, however. What McDonald's experience does represent is a test case of customers' response to price changes, and the message is that perceived value is critical.

Labor Costs Reduce Value of Restaurant Meals

During the inflationary 1970s, chains were often able to raise prices without poor sales results when the cost pressures were provided by higher food costs. In theory, such an environment should be helpful to the restaurant chains, since food is only 25 to 40 percent of the sales dollar. As a result, cost increases in commodities can be passed along with lower percentage increases than grocery store prices, thereby improving the relative value of eating out versus eating at home. In the 1980s, however, the cost pressure from labor factors is more pervasive, and this forces restaurants to raise prices more rapidly than food cost inflation.

The conclusion is that consumers are highly sensitive to price changes at fast-food restaurants, but their consumption patterns are not particularly determined by income. Recessions by themselves need not be the determinant of problems in the restaurant industry. That is the bright side. The dark side is that growth in consumers' incomes will not save a restaurant concept that is priced inappropriately.

Number of Restaurants in the United States

To the casual observer, it may appear that the proliferation of chain restaurant units has resulted in an enormous increase in the total number of restaurants over the past three decades. In fact, for every chain unit that opens, an independent operator's store (or a less successful chain restaurant unit) is closed. The new chain unit is typically larger than the one it replaces, since the industry has shown more rapid growth in sales than in stores, that is, sales per store have increased, but the number of total stores has risen less rapidly than growth in total population.

Table 2.21

Total Number of Restaurants in the United States

Year	Eating Places	Drinking Places	Eating & Drinking Places
1958	229,815	114,925	344,740
1963	223,876	110,605	334,481
1967	236,563	111,327	347,890
1972	253,136	106,388	359,524
1977	275,200	93,729	368,929
1982	301,700	80,000	381,700

Compound Annual Growth Rate (%)

1977–82	1.9	−3.1	0.7
1958–82	1.1	−1.5	0.4
1958–67	0.3	−0.4	0.1
1967–77	1.5	−1.7	0.6

Source: U.S. Bureau of the Census, 1982 Census of Retail Trade.

Total Growth Minimal

The number of restaurants in the United States has increased very slowly in the past three decades. Table 2.21 shows the total number of eating and drinking places established since 1958. These data, taken from the census of manufacturing, are reported only every five years or so, but show a persistent pattern of small gains in the number of eating places and an equally consistent pattern of small declines in the number of drinking places.

Chains Capture Market Share

The story of the growth of the chain restaurant industry, then, is one of well-financed, professionally managed chains capturing share of market from independent operators. Until the early 1980s, the growth of the chains appeared inevitable. More recently, however, a pattern of retrenchment and store closings among some of the largest chains has again become apparent, much as happened once before in the early 1970s. A shakeout of this kind is by no means a new phenomenon, but the magnitude and breadth of problems confronting many of the chains is unique and marks a new stage in the expansion of restaurant chains.

Failure Rates

Precise data on failure rates in the restaurant industry as a whole are difficult to derive. Dun & Bradstreet tracks failure rates for all industries and compiles failure rates, or more specifically bankruptcies per 10,000 firms, in individual industries. Findings from the

Table 2.22

Failure Rate per 10,000 Firms		
Type of Firm	1987	1988
Eating & drinking places	90	89
Drug stores	31	35
Food stores	58	55
Apparel stores	139	144
Sporting goods	91	89
Liquor stores	45	38
Auto dealerships	56	51
Dry cleaners	38	43
Barber shops	24	16
Funeral services	14	15
Advertising agencies	103	117
All retail trade	81	79
All service firms	128	126
All businesses	102	98

Source: The Dun & Bradstreet Corporation, *Business Failures Record,* 1987 final, 1988 preliminary.

most recent such study are summarized in Table 2.22. These data suggest that the incidence of failure in the restaurant industry, while slightly higher than that of retail trade, is considerably below that of most service industries and, indeed, is somewhat below that of all businesses.

Data Weakness

The drawbacks with this approach to determining failure rates are two: the restaurant industry is increasingly dominated by chains with remarkably low failure rates, and when restaurants fail, they seldom actually file for bankruptcy. The Dun & Bradstreet data are specifically oriented toward identifying firms that liquidate or recapitalize and leave unpaid amounts outstanding. Since restaurants seldom have large payables outstanding and usually operate on short-term leases, a restaurateur whose operations are not meeting his or her financial needs can simply break the lease and close down his restaurant without leaving outstanding obligations.

"Discontinuance" versus "Failure"

The term "discontinuance" may be more useful than outright "failure" in terms of defining the difficulty of opening a successful restaurant. Unhappily, data on discontinuances of new restaurant ventures are not available. What *are* available, however, are data for discontinuance of franchised restaurants going back to the early 1970s. These rates of discontinuance are tabulated in Table 2.23.

Table 2.23

Discontinuance of Franchised Restaurants

Year	Company-Owned			Franchisee-Owned		
	Discontinued	Total	As Percent of Prior Year Total	Discontinued	Total	As Percent of Prior Year Total
1972		6,319			26,219	
1973	210	8,316	3.32	619	28,024	2.36
1974	288	10,115	3.46	842	29,681	3.00
1975	281	11,685	2.78	883	31,298	2.97
1976	221	12,562	1.89	981	34,336	3.13
1977	219	14,527	1.74	789	37,445	2.30
1978	334	15,510	2.30	1061	39,802	2.83
1979	376	16,884	2.42	1072	42,052	2.69
1980	392	17,826	2.32	1408	42,133	3.35
1981	401	19,355	2.25	1454	42,491	3.45
1982	354	19,857	1.83	1084	43,700	2.55
1983	445	21,785	2.24	1085	45,743	2.48
1984	306	22,951	1.40	1024	47,544	2.24
1985	537	23,574	2.34	1622	50,318	3.41
1986	601	24,364	2.55	1435	53,839	2.85

Source: "Franchise Restaurants, A Statistical Appendix to Foodservice Trends," Washington, D.C., National Restaurant Association, March 1988.

Note that the data indicate rates of discontinuance for both company-operated and franchised units only of chains that franchise. A certain natural selection process is at work here: a new restaurant concept that opens with no success whatsoever is unlikely ever to reach the stage of being able to find franchisees. Hence, the experience of franchised chains as shown in the accompanying table already presupposes at least a minimal level of success.

Again, bear in mind that the sample includes chains with only minimal levels of discontinuance: McDonald's, for example, has probably closed fewer than ten stores in its entire corporate existence because of losing operations, though it often closes units in order to open new, larger units in the same market area.

With all of the caveats already mentioned, note that the level of discontinuance is far higher than the level of failure found in the Dun & Bradstreet survey. The suggestion, then, is that even within a sample that already eliminates the most unlikely fledgling ventures, the rate of discontinuance is comparatively high. The level of 2.85 percent discontinuance among franchisees in 1986 would correspond to a failure rate of 285 per 10,000 firms, more than twice the level for all service firms and nearly triple the rate for all businesses.

Second Concepts Fail

If the rate of failure for new entrants is high, it is probably no higher than that of successful restaurant chains that try to develop their own new concepts as an adjunct to their existing businesses. The list of failures in the industry by even the best operators is an imposing one:

1. McDonald's failed with Ramon's steak houses and Jane Dobbins Pie Shops.
2. Pizza Hut failed with Flaming Steer, Taco Kid, and Applegate's Landing.
3. Chart House failed with Sea Shack, a fast-food seafood entry.
4. Friendly Ice Cream unsuccessfully developed Jim Dandy.
5. Wendy's failed with Sister's fried chicken concept.
6. Church's had no success with G.W. Jr.'s hamburger units.

Growth of Largest Chains

The nine largest restaurant chains have achieved systemwide sales growth of 14.6 percent annually since the mid-1970s, and currently account for $32.5 billion in annual sales. (See Table 2.24.) This total equals 23.6 percent of the sales of all eating places in 1988. If one excludes the results of Denny's, a broad-menu coffee shop, from the totals, the other eight chains comprise sales of $31.550 billion, or 51.9 percent of the sales of all limited-menu, that is, fast-food, chain restaurants.

Table 2.24

Growth of Nine Largest Chains

Chain	Systemwide Domestic Sales ($ million)		Compound Annual Growth, 1977–88 (%)
	1975	1988	
McDonald's	2478	11,380	12.4
Burger King	751	4,840	15.4
Pizza Hut	375	2,800	16.7
Hardee's	286	2,810	19.2
Kentucky Fried Chicken	1150	2,900	7.4
Wendy's	74	2,720	32.0
Domino's	23	2,300	42.5
Taco Bell	122	1,600	21.9
Denny's	311	1,227	11.1
Total	5570	32,577	14.6

Players Unchanged

In the mid-1970s, the nine largest restaurant chains were the same in Table 2.24, except that Howard Johnson's, Jack-in-the-Box, and Burger Chef were on the list and Wendy's, Domino's, and Taco Bell were not. The sales of the nine restaurants totaled $6.285 billion, which represented 16.0 percent of sales of all eating places in 1975, using NRA data. Taking the eight largest fast-food chains (adding A&W while eliminating Denny's and Howard Johnson's) produced total fast-food sales of $5.904 billion, or 43.4 percent of limited-menu restaurants in 1975.

Hence, the concentration within the industry among the largest chains has gradually increased, with some of the faster-growing chains, such as Taco Bell and Domino's, replacing the more sluggish coffee shops and the burger chains that have not succeeded.

Chain Dominance

A broader picture of chain dominance in the restaurant industry is presented in Table 2.25. The data include sales of chains with 1000 or more units, those chains with 500 to 1000 units, and those chains with 150 to 500 stores.

Note that chains with 1000 or more units accounted for 22.36 percent of all sales at eating and drinking places as tracked by the Commerce Department. Medium and smaller chains have not increased their market share significantly, although this calculation is distorted by

Table 2.25

Growth of Largest Chains

Year	Restaurant Sales ($ million)	% Change	Sales of 1,000+ Unit Chains ($ million)	% Change	1,000+ Chains' Share (%)	500–1,000 Unit Chains ($ million)	% Change	500–1,000 Unit Chains' Share (%)	151–500 Unit Chains ($ million)	% Change	151–500 Unit Chains' Share (%)	Total Chains' Share (%)
1974	44,606		4,808		10.78	1,894		4.25	2026		4.54	19.57
1975	51,067	14.5	5,614	16.8	10.99	2,682	41.6	5.25	2050	1.2	4.01	20.26
1976	57,331	12.3	6,671	18.8	11.64	3,675	37.0	6.41	1990	−2.9	3.47	21.52
1977	63,370	10.5	8,447	26.6	13.33	4,259	15.9	6.72	2750	38.2	4.34	24.39
1978	71,828	13.3	11,400	35.0	15.87	3,514	−17.5	4.89	2929	6.5	4.08	24.84
1979	82,110	14.3	14,408	26.4	17.55	3,010	−14.3	3.67	3905	33.3	4.76	25.97
1980	90,058	9.7	16,579	15.1	18.41	2,863	−4.9	3.18	4343	11.2	4.82	26.41
1981	98,118	8.9	16,720	0.9	17.04	4,176	45.9	4.26	4905	12.9	5.00	26.30
1982	104,593	6.6	19,401	16.0	18.55	4,669	11.8	4.46	4706	−4.1	4.50	27.51
1983	114,869	9.8	22,261	14.7	19.38	5,078	8.8	4.42	5932	26.1	5.16	28.96
1984	124,741	8.6	26,178	17.6	20.99	5,024	−1.1	4.03	6351	7.1	5.09	30.10
1985	133,457	7.0	28,646	9.4	21.46	6,011	19.6	4.50	6930	9.1	5.19	31.16
1986	144,966	8.6	32,420	13.2	22.36	6,778	12.8	4.68	6610	−4.6	4.56	31.60

Table 2.26

Chains' Share of Total Market

Year	Total Restaurant Sales ($ million)	Year-to-Year Change (%)	Sales of 100 Largest Chains ($ million)	Year-to-Year Change (%)	100 Largest Chains' Share of Total (%)
1985	133,457		60,700		45.48
1986	144,966	8.6	67,439	11.1	46.52
1987	147,717	1.9	74,838	11.0	50.66
1988	157,504	6.6	82,401	10.1	52.32

Source: Nation's Restaurant News, U.S. Department of Commerce.

the fact that eventually a growing chain of 800 stores becomes one of the larger chains and leaves the medium-sized category. The real point is that chains with more than 150 units accounted for nearly 32 percent of total restaurant sales in 1986. The dominance is slowly increasing at the rate of roughly one percentage point each year.

Another perspective on the dominance by chains is provided in Table 2.26, which shows the total sales of the 100 largest foodservice chains. These organizations account for more than 52 percent of total restaurant sales and are increasing their share more rapidly than are the larger chains tabulated in Table 2.25.

Still another way of examining chain dominance is to look at the share of the total market held by the largest player. McDonald's has only about 2 percent of the 380,000 eating and drinking places in the United States, yet accounts for 7 percent of sales of food consumed away from home.

Contrast with Other Industries

By the standards of many consumer-oriented industries, this would constitute a very low level of dominance by the largest factor. In the soft-drink industry, for example, Coca-Cola holds over a 44 percent market share of the worldwide industry, Anheuser-Busch commands 42 percent of the U.S. beer industry, and Philip Morris controls 40 percent of the American cigarette market.

The difference is that the fast-food market does not command the same degree of loyalty that the other products mentioned do. Cigarette smokers seldom select anything but their favorite brand, while the typical heavy fast-food consumer may frequent four or five different concepts. Moreover, convenience is a major factor in restaurant selection, which can further serve to dampen consumer loyalty to a given concept.

Consumer Preferences

According to McDonald's senior vice president Winston B. Christiansen, the company's market research has found that convenience is the number one determinant of the consumer's choice of a quick-service restaurant. This view is not universally accepted within the industry, however. Wayne Calloway, chairman of PepsiCo, the largest foodservice operator in terms of number of outlets, insists that "What consumers want most is value. Value and volume go hand in hand, just like Harry and Sally." (Address to security analysts, New York, Oct. 24, 1989)

Each of these views has some merit, yet both presuppose that certain minimum standards have been met. Customers will not patronize a restaurant that they suspect has hygiene problems. A private study on consumer preferences conducted for Burger King in 1975 found that five of the ten leading concerns of fast-food patrons were related to cleanliness. These were *potential* concerns, not actual problems.

Both Burger King and McDonald's (the lone subjects of the study) measured up well in terms of cleanliness, but consumers' concerns were clear. One is reminded of Edward Schmitt's explanation of McDonald's success in the early days being more attributable to sparkling clean facilities than to price.

PepsiCo's Findings

PepsiCo's research divides the quick-service restaurant user base into three categories, each of which accounts for about one-third of the total population. Light users patronize fast-food restaurants once a month; medium users frequent fast-food units three to six times monthly, and heavy users patronize fast-food units an astonishing seventeen times each month! While accounting for only one-third of all customers, the heavy users produce 71 percent of all visits to fast-food restaurants. The importance of the heavy consumer is evident. What are his or her characteristics? Overwhelmingly, the heavy users are young people. Table 2.27 presents a breakdown of the frequency of fast-food consumption related to age of the consumer. Note the consistently low consumption among older people. Any discussion of the demographics of demand inevitably must begin with data on the age of the population. Table 2.28 shows a breakdown of U.S. population by age group, including projections to the year 2000.

Table 2.27

Frequency of Fast-Food Consumption by Age Group
(% of Respondents)

Age	Number of Times Eaten in Fast-Food Place in Two-Week Period						
	0	1	2	3	4	5	6+
18–24	17.5	14.8	13.9	13.0	8.6	6.5	12.8
25–34	17.6	10.9	23.7	12.4	10.0	7.1	18.4
35–44	18.4	12.3	15.6	16.7	12.1	3.4	21.1
45–54	44.5	13.6	12.8	7.6	2.8	5.2	13.0
55–64	46.7	12.4	23.5	4.6	2.3	5.0	5.3
65+	65.3	0.0	8.0	4.8	4.9	4.1	4.9

Source: "Consumer Nutrition Concerns and Restaurant Choices,"
Washington, D.C., National Restaurant Association, September 1986
(survey conducted March 1986).

Table 2.28

Demographic Shifts of U.S. Population (000)

Year	Age Group (yr)							
	18–24	25–34	35–39	40–44	45–49	50–54	55–59	60–64
1960	16,128	22,919	12,984	12,017	11,267	10,234	8,582	7,523
1970	24,711	25,323	11,771	12,498	12,658	11,453	10,372	9,030
1980	30,350	37,626	14,746	12,198	11,469	11,965	11,963	10,465
1985	28,741	42,227	18,685	14,666	12,059	11,193	11,539	11,275
1990*	25,794	43,529	20,654	18,589	14,509	11,818	10,816	10,908
1995*	23,702	40,520	22,536	20,561	18,402	14,237	11,454	10,268
2000*	24,601	36,415	21,914	22,440	20,363	18,063	13,813	10,900
Compound Annual Growth Rate (%)								
1960–70	4.4	1.0	−1.0	0.4	1.2	1.1	1.9	1.8
1970–80	2.1	4.0	2.3	−0.2	−1.0	0.4	1.4	1.5
1980–85	−1.1	2.3	4.8	3.8	1.0	−1.3	−0.7	1.5
1985–90	−2.1	0.6	2.0	4.9	3.8	1.1	−1.3	−0.7
1990–95*	−1.7	−1.4	1.8	2.0	4.9	3.8	1.2	−1.2
1995–2000*	0.7	−2.1	−0.6	1.8	2.0	4.9	3.8	1.2
1980–90	−1.6	1.5	3.4	4.3	2.4	−0.1	−1.0	0.4
1990–2000*	−0.5	−1.8	0.6	1.9	3.4	4.3	2.5	0.0

*Estimated values.

The New Demographics of Demand

The two decades ending in 1980 were nearly ideal from the demographic perspective of the fast-food industry. The outlook for the rest of the century, however, is far less promising. The reason is that in the twenty years leading up to 1980, the number of people in the age groups that are the heaviest consumers of fast food nearly doubled. For the last twenty years of the century, though, these same age groups will actually decline in number. Only those restaurant chains that can position themselves to maintain the loyalty of an aging customer base will be able to prosper in the 1990s.

Profile of the Heavy User

The demand for fast food is highest among young, single males. According to a study conducted by the National Restaurant Association in March 1987, 44 percent of 18- to 24-year-olds eat at fast-food restaurants more than once a week. Of 25- to 34-year-olds, 35.6 percent frequent fast-food units more than once a week. By contrast, only 12.2 percent of those aged 50 to 64 eat at such restaurants more than once weekly. An identical percentage of those 65 and over eat at fast-food restaurants more than once a week. (National Restaurant Association, "Consumer Behavior and Attitudes Towards Fast Food and Moderately Priced Family Restaurants," Washington, D.C. p. 4)

Not surprisingly, a similar age pattern exists among infrequent visitors to fast-food restaurants. Only 1.4 percent of 18- to 24-year-olds and 1.9 percent of 25- to 34-year-olds never eat fast food. A mere 4.6 percent and 5.9 percent of these respective age groups eat fast food less than once a month.

Older People Shun Fast Food

Among older people, infrequent patrons are far more common: 15.3 percent of those 65 and over never eat fast food, and 27.9 percent eat fast food less than once a month. Among those aged 50 to 64, 8.8 percent never eat fast food, and 15.9 percent eat it less than once a month.

Among single people, 31.8 percent are heavy users of fast food (i.e., eat such food more than once a week), while only 22.5 percent of married people can be so characterized. Of men surveyed, 30.6 percent ate at fast-food restaurants more than one time per week, in contrast to the 21.1 percent of women who are heavy users.

Patterns of infrequent usage are not clearly delineated by gender: 6.6 percent of males never eat fast food, not much different from the 6.4 percent of women who never do. An identical 13.1 percent of both men and women frequent fast-food restaurants less than one time per month. Marital status is not a clear determinant of infrequent usage either: 20.2 percent of married people either never eat fast food or consume it less than once a month, compared with 18.5 percent of single people.

Family Size

Family size appears to be an important determinant of the willingness to consume fast food, with 32.0 percent of those from families of three or four people qualifying as heavy users and 27.4 percent of those from families of five or more being heavy users. By contrast, only 20.3 percent of those from single person households or 20.6 percent of those from two-person households qualify as heavy users. Interestingly, only 1.3 percent of those with five or more family members *never* eat fast food.

Income Elasticity

Fast-food consumption bears remarkably little relationship to income levels. Among consumers with household income of $30,000 or more, 28.7 percent are heavy users and an additional 25.3 percent patronize fast-food restaurants once a week. Among those with household income under $15,000, 24.1 percent are heavy users and another 23.3 percent eat fast food once per week. At the opposite end of the spectrum of usage, 4.6 percent of those with household income over $30,000 never eat fast food, substantially identical with the 4.7 percent of those with income below $15,000 who never consume fast food.

Geographical Consumption Patterns

A strong geographical pattern is evident among heavy users: 30 percent of those in the South and the Midwest eat fast food more than once a week, while only 16.5 percent of those in the East are heavy users. Among West Coast residents, 23.0 percent qualified as heavy users.

At the opposite end of the spectrum, 26.4 percent of easterners eat fast food less than once a month (or never) while only 14.1 percent of midwesterners and 19.6 percent of southerners are such infrequent patrons. Among residents of the western part of the country, 18.6 percent may be described as infrequent customers.

When weighted by their frequency of visits, the heavy-using age groups of 18- to 24-year-olds produce nearly twice the level of per capita food consumption as their elders. This has negative implications for the growth rate of fast-food consumption in the 1990s compared with the growth enjoyed during the 1960s, 1970s, and early 1980s.

Aging Population

From 1960 to 1980, the population of Americans aged 18 to 24 rose 85 percent. Between 1980 and 1985 the number of people in that age group was virtually unchanged. From 1985 to 1990, however, the number of consumers in the 18 to 24 age category dropped 13 percent.

A similar, slightly less pronounced pattern is evident among those in the 25 to 34 age group. From 1960 to 1985, the number of Americans in this age group rose 80 percent, but between 1985 and the year 2000 the population of 25- to 34-year-olds will drop 10 percent. The most rapid growth for the rest of the century (22.2 percent) will come from those in the 65-and-over category, which, as we have already seen, has the lowest per capita usage of fast food.

Motivation for Eating Out

The primary motivation for eating at fast-food restaurants rather than some other type of dining establishment relates to lack of time. In a study conducted in 1983, consumers were asked their reasons for eating at different types of restaurants. Fast-food restaurants were chosen 39.7 percent of the time because of lack of time and 40.8 percent of the time for convenience. In contrast, family restaurants were chosen for lack of time only 7.8 percent of the time, and atmosphere restaurants, not surprisingly, a mere 1.4 percent of the time.

Consistency

Consistency of product is particularly important to fast-food patrons: 92.2 percent of the the respondents strongly agreed or agreed that they expect consistency from one visit to the next when they patronize fast-food restaurants. (National Restaurant Association, "Consumer Expectations with Regard to Dining at Fast Food Restaurants," Washington, D.C., p. 26)

Criteria for Restaurant Selection

Having chosen to eat at a fast-food restaurant, how do consumers choose among the various competing alternatives? Their preferences and priorities are not too different from those they hold for moderately priced family restaurants or for upscale atmosphere restaurants. In all three cases, the two most important criteria were quality of food and friendly service.

At this point, however, priorities diverge. For fast-food patrons, the three next-most-important attributes affecting individual restaurant selection are convenient location, fast service, and convenient parking, while atmosphere, variety of menu items, and nutritious food (in slightly different orders) are the most important attributes within the other two categories. Interestingly, the cost of the meal has a relatively low priority in all three types of restaurants, ranking sixth out of thirteen criteria in fast-food restaurant selection, sixth among family restaurants, and tenth among atmosphere restaurants.

Importance of Promotions

Perhaps more significant is the relative lack of importance ascribed to special discounts and promotions, which ranked dead last as a criterion for selection of family and atmosphere restaurants (perhaps simply reflecting the relative infrequency with which they are offered at such dining establishments) and twelfth out of thirteen criteria for selection of fast-food restaurants. (National Restaurant Association, "How Consumers Make the Decision to Eat Out," Washington, D.C., 1982, p. 36)

This is a particularly noteworthy finding because it suggests that the high level of couponing and similar promotions is not responsive to the real desires of the fast-food customer. Indeed, a study by the NRA in 1982 found that 70.1 percent of the respondents to a survey of 1,788 adults and children above the age of 8 agreed with the statement, "I go to restaurants because of the food not because of incentives." Moreover, consumers perceive that promotions, while in themselves representing good value, raise the cost of other items on the menu. In the NRA study, 50.2 percent agreed with the statement, "Incentives increase costs of other products." (National Restaurant Association, "Consumer Reactions to and Use of Restaurant Promotions," Washington, D.C., 1982, p. 114)

Effectiveness of Fast-Food Industry

How good a job does the fast-food industry do of satisfying the wants and needs of its customers? The answer varies according to the different preferences that customers hold. The NRA found that 71.3 percent declared themselves "satisfied" or "very satisfied" with the convenience of the restaurants because the patron did not have to prepare the food himself (sic), and 70.8 percent declared themselves satisfied or very satisfied with the convenience of the location of the fast-food restaurants that they frequent. Speed of service was another related area where the fast-food vendors seem to please their customers: 61.6 percent of the respondents described themselves as satisfied or very satisfied in this regard.

On the other hand, only 32.4 percent of respondents were satisfied or very satisfied with the atmosphere at fast-food restaurants, while a mere 37.3 percent registered high satisfaction levels with the variety of food and beverages offered. ("Consumer Attitudes Toward Fast Food," op. cit., p. 10) So far, so good. Remember that consumers do not *expect* much in the way of atmosphere or menu variety in their fast-food restaurants, nor do they base their choices upon these attributes.

Food Quality Unsatisfactory

The fast-food industry unfortunately falls down in those areas where consumers *do* express their willingness to make competitive choices. Only 37.5 percent of those surveyed expressed satisfaction with food quality, the single criterion that consumers rank highest in importance. Perhaps the notion of high quality, delicious fast food is oxymoronic: maybe the need for speed and uniformity necessarily precludes great taste. But only 51.8 percent of respondents professed satisfaction with the attitude of the server. As we have seen, friendly service is the second most important criterion for selection among patrons of fast-food restaurants (and all other restaurants as well). It is not clear that a sunny disposition and quick service are incompatible, but the demographics of today's labor force make it difficult for the fast-food operator to exercise much leeway in the selection of employees. The fast-food labor market is a seller's market and will continue to be so well into the next century.

Price-Value Discrepancy

Again, the industry does not seem to do well in delivering value for money: a comparatively low 46.1 percent of respondents pronounced themselves satisfied with the price paid for value received. In summary, the fast-food industry is responsive in terms of meeting the need for speed and convenience, but falls short in product quality, friendliness of service, and value for price. Cleanliness, a prime criterion for restaurant selection, was found to be satisfactory or very satisfactory by 51.8 percent of the respondents.

Young People Dissatisfied

One of the more surprising findings of the NRA's research is that young people are less satisfied with food quality in fast-food restaurants than are their elders. The notion that fast food is nourishment fit only for teen-agers with primitive palettes is not supported by the data. Only 33.8 percent of 18- to 24-year-olds found the food at fast-food restaurants satisfying or very satisfying, along with 29.0 percent of those in the 25- to 34-year-old age group.

Among those aged 35 to 49, 35.6 percent found the food satisfying or very satisfying, while 43.2 percent of those 50 to 64 years old found it satisfying or better and 47.3 percent of those 65 and over so described their fast food. Older people may not frequent fast-food restaurants as often as their juniors, but apparently it is not objections to the food that keep them away. (Ibid., p. 21)

Family Restaurants Preferred

The same NRA study presents an interesting contrast between the levels of satisfaction at moderately priced family restaurants in contrast to the fast-food restaurants: both attitude and speed of service produced far higher satisfaction levels at the moderately priced family restaurants than at the fast-food units. Moreover, the disparity in terms of price and value was astonishingly high: 66.7 percent of the respondents professed satisfaction with the price paid for value received at family restaurants, in contrast to the already cited 46.1 percent of fast-food patrons. Whether family restaurants can continue to offer a superior dining experience in the future is open to question. Such restaurants are even more labor-intensive than fast-food units, suggesting they will experience the same labor squeeze in the future (or even a worse one) than will the fast-food operators.

However, the message is clear in terms of fast food not delivering a product at a price that people can accept. The fast-food industry is not doing a good job of convincing its customers that it makes good economic sense: it only succeeds in delivering convenience.

Working Women and Fast Food

The lone source of optimism for the future growth of fast-food consumption lies in the continuing gradual increase in the percent of women in the labor force. The percentage of women who work has increased steadily over the past two decades, as indicated in Table 2.29. Note that the Bureau of Labor projects that this trend will continue through the end of

Table 2.29

Women in the Labor Force

Year	% of All Women
1970	43.4
1971	43.4
1972	43.9
1973	44.8
1974	45.7
1975	46.4
1976	47.4
1977	48.5
1978	50.0
1979	51.0
1980	51.1
1981	52.2
1982	52.7
1983	53.0
1984	53.7
1985	54.5
1986	55.0
1987	55.4
1988	55.9
2000*	62.0

*Estimated value.

the century. Inasmuch as families with two incomes tend to eat out more frequently than single-income households, this trend bodes well for the restaurant industry.

According to the research department of the National Restaurant Association, females who are employed either full time or part time eat out 4.3 times per week, compared with only 2.9 times for women who do not work. ("Meal Consumption Behavior," p. 4) The increasing number of women in the labor force is the impetus behind the increased incidence of eating lunch away from home: in 1981 only 46 percent of women ate at least one commercially prepared lunch per week, while that proportion rose to 51 percent by 1985. (Ibid., p. 4)

Nearly 80 percent of U.S. adults eat at McDonald's at least once a year, while 64 percent eat at McDonald's at least once a month. One-quarter of all breakfasts eaten outside the home are consumed at McDonald's.

According to PepsiCo's research, 60 percent of the quick-service restaurant industry is represented by off-premise, i.e., take-out, sales. Of the 60 percent, 12 percent, or more than 7 percent of the total market, is accounted for by delivery sales. Pizza Hut alone has found that 90 percent of its growth in the three years 1986–89 was accounted for by off-premise sales.

Recycling Issue

As of late 1989, 400 towns across the United States have considered bans on polystyrene packaging. A total of less than 100 bans have been passed, with two actually going into effect. Only one (in Glen Cove, New York) has caused McDonald's to alter its packaging practices. Ironically, waxed paper is not recyclable under existing technology, whereas foam and polystyrene are.

According to Shelby Yastrow, senior vice president and director, environmental affairs, for McDonald's, "for every 100 pounds of trash going into landfills, less than 4 ounces comes from all plastic food packaging."

Convenience Stores

The restaurant industry has begun to suffer increasing loss of market share to convenience stores, prepared food offerings at grocery stores, microwave preparation at home, and even the renaissance of old-fashioned sandwich shops. Although not large in an absolute sense, these competitors are capturing a large portion of the growth experienced in food service.

According to the National Restaurant Association, restaurants in drugstores, convenience stores, gas stations, and variety stores accounted for $8.9 billion in sales in 1988, or 4.2 percent of total food consumption outside the home. This represented an increase of 44 percent from the $6.2 billion or 3.5 percent of the total registered in 1985. The 12.0 percent growth achieved by this segment in 1988 alone was more rapid than any other form of food consumed away from home. Although still small, sales of this form of foodservice accounted for 7.0 percent of the growth in the total industry between 1985 and 1988.

McDonald's market research estimates that convenience stores account for $10 billion in annual sales of carry-out prepared food. This figure is considerably higher than the data compiled by the National Restaurant Association, which are tabulated in Table 2.30.

According to the National Association of Convenience Stores, at year-end 1988 there were 69,200 convenience stores in the United States, with total sales in 1988 (including gasoline) of $61.2 billion. The convenience store industry has suffered an erosion of profitability because of new store openings by the oil companies as adjuncts to existing gasoline stations. Between 1983 and 1988, convenience stores attached to gas stations rose from 16,000 to 30,000. During the same period, profit per store for the convenience operators fell from $23,000 per store to $18,000.

As a result of the competitive incursions from the oil companies (who already have a well-chosen site when they open a convenience outlet), the traditional convenience store operators are trying to diversify. Video rentals are one example of attempts to broaden offerings at convenience stores, but increased foodservice is another.

Table 2.31 shows a breakdown of sales of the typical convenience store. Multiplying the sales per store for fast food by 69,200 stores produces fast-food sales of $1.1 billion. The

Table 2.30

Foodservice Sales at Grocery and Convenience Stores

Year	Total Sales ($ million)	% Change
1970	188.828	
1971	199.799	5.8
1972	220.618	10.4
1973	248.041	12.4
1974	289.712	16.8
1975	342.729	18.3
1976	408.190	19.1
1977	468.447	14.8
1978	560.263	19.6
1979	691.364	23.4
1980	830.328	20.1
1981	1,032.098	24.3
1982	1,257.180	21.8
1983	1,553.874	23.6
1984	1,954.774	25.8
1985	2,465.722	26.1
1986	2,988.455	21.2
1987	3,421.781	14.5

Compound Annual Growth Rate (%)

1970–87	18.6
1982–87	22.2

Source: "Foodservice Industry: 1987 in Review" and "Foodservice Numbers," Washington, D.C., National Restaurant Association.

Table 2.31

Convenience Store Sales Profile

Item	Sales	% Total
Snacks & groceries	$153,950	21.7
Gasoline	150,000	21.1
Tobacco	121,905	17.2
Soft drinks	91,467	12.9
Alcoholic beverages	75,411	10.6
Deli & sandwiches	42,525	6.0
Car wash	24,000	3.4
Publications	23,247	3.3
Fast food	16,443	2.3
Auto parts & oil	5,897	0.8
Video rentals	4,400	0.6
Total	$709,245	100.0

same calculation for soft drinks indicates total sales of $6.3 billion and for deli and sandwiches, a total of $2.9 billion. All three categories combined produce sales of $10.4 billion annually, close to the figure that McDonald's own research has estimated.

Supermarket Food Bars

Additional competitive inroads have been achieved by the supermarket industry. Table 2.32 indicates the percentage of supermarkets offering various forms of self-service food preparation. While the incidence of such offerings varies widely by region, one observes that in the Middle Atlantic states and around Chicago there is a very high percentage of supermarkets making such services available.

In addition to the expansion of prepared-food offerings by convenience stores and grocery stores, a new kind of entrant in the restaurant industry has cropped up in recent years: the sandwich shop. The largest of these, privately held Subway Sandwiches & Salads, has experienced dramatic growth in recent years, as indicated in Table 2.33.

The chain, which was begun in Milford, Connecticut, by 17-year-old Fred DeLuca in 1965, began franchising in 1974, and by 1976 had 32 stores in operation. Stores in the system rose to 100 by 1979, then exploded to 400 by 1984. Part of the attraction of the concept to franchisees is a very low initial outlay, typically only $55,000, including an initial $7500 franchise fee.

McDonald's has been quick to dismiss the newcomers in the sandwich segment, at least publicly. In response to an analyst's query about the explosion in the number of sandwich chains, Don Lord, McDonald's director of market research, remarked in September 1989

Table 2.32

Supermarkets Offering Food Bars

Area	Supermarkets Offering the Following (%):			
	Self-Service Food Bar	Salad Bar	Soup Bar	Taco Bar
New England	45	45	18	*
Metro New York	19	19	9	1
Middle Atlantic	52	52	45	10
East Central	14	14	12	*
Metro Chicago	44	44	40	14
West Central	28	28	22	7
Southeast	14	14	10	*
Southwest	32	32	26	*
Metro LA	3	3	*	*
Pacific	35	35	22	8
Total U.S.	26	22	19	4

*Less than 1 percent.

Source: Nielsen Marketing Research.

Table 2.33

Growth of Subway Sandwiches and Salads

Category	1986	1987	1988	1989
Number of units % Change	1,178	2,000 69.8	2,900 45.0	3,440 18.6
Sales per store ($000) % Change	NA	172	201 16.9	234 16.4
Total sales ($ million) % Change	$140.0	$344.0 145.7	$582.8 69.4	$805.0 38.1

Source: Nation's Restaurant News, Aug. 8, 1988, and Aug. 7, 1989.

that "It's nothing consequential. It's almost all convenience." This rather cavalier attitude ignores McDonald's own findings that convenience is the single most important factor in selecting a restaurant.

Microwaves

According to a CREST survey in 1987, 62 percent of U.S. households own microwave ovens, compared with only 41 percent that own VCRs. A study by Nielsen Marketing Research found that 81 percent of chain grocery stores with annual sales of $2 million or more had service delis in 1986, in contrast to only 76 percent one year earlier. These delis offered hot poultry (69 percent), cold prepared sandwiches (64 percent), and ribs (48 percent). (NRA 1988 forecast)

Nutritional Issues

According to the *New England Journal of Medicine* (September 14, 1989), between 40 and 55 percent of the calories in fast-food meals are provided by fat. In another analysis, the *Mayo Clinic Nutrition Letter* (June 1989) found that only three breakfast items from the five largest fast-food chains provide less than 30 percent of their calories from fat. Although it is certainly true that fat consumption could be lower, it is not clear that the fast-food chains are the real culprits. Per capita consumption of ice cream has exploded in the 1980s, from 14 quarts annually in 1980 to 23 quarts in 1987. (*New York Times Magazine,* part 2, October 8, 1989)

   Consumer Reports observed, "A steady diet of typical fast-food items would overload you with protein, fat and calories while shortchanging you on vitamins, minerals, and fiber" (June 1988). As indicated in Table 2.34, the levels of saturated fat and sodium tend to be very high for many of the most popular menu items.

   The success of the chains in broadening their menu offerings to include food with less saturated fat, however, has been minimal. One chain, D-Lites, was built on the premise that consumers wanted healthier foods and subsequently filed for bankruptcy.

   Per capita annual consumption of beef has fallen from 78.5 pounds in 1984 to 73.0 pounds in 1988, a 7.0 percent drop. Chicken consumption, on the other hand, increased 23.8 percent over the same time period, from 66.9 to 82.8 pounds.

Cholesterol Concerns

The desire of the American consumer to avoid saturated fat has not made much of an impact on the hamburger chains. According to McDonald's Senior Executive Vice President and Chief Marketing Officer Paul D. Schrage, "We cannot find it [concern over cholesterol] in our research." In late 1989 McDonald's began testing a frozen yogurt dessert with only 1.5 percent fat content, as well as a frozen sorbet with no fat at all.

   The issue of saturated fat and cholesterol may be overblown with respect to certain products. According to McDonald's Executive Vice President and Chief Financial Officer

Table 2.34

Nutritional Content of Popular Menu Items

Nutritional Category	Recommended Daily Intakes*	McDonald's Big Mac	Burger King Whopper	Wendy's Big Classic	KFC 2-piece	McDonald's Fries	Burger King Shake
Calories	2000	572	584	500	460	222	351
Protein (g)	44	25	28	26	34	3	8
Calcium (mg)	1000	202	61	106	132	8	371
Iron (mg)	18	3	4	3	2	1	2
Vitamin A (International units)	5000	251	103	139	24	‡	342
Vitamin C (mg)	60	4	11	12	‡	6	‡
Total fat (g)	78	34	33	28	31	12	10
Saturated fat (g)	26	15	13	11	7	5	5
Sodium (mg)†	3300	794	769	739	619	121	514
Weight (oz)		7	9	8	6	3	11
Price		$1.89	$2.14	$1.92	$2.22	$0.77	$0.99

* Average woman's daily dietary needs.
† Upper limit.
‡ Less than 2 percent of daily quota.

Source: Consumer Reports, June 1988.

Jack M. Greenberg, "an individual could consume 32 orders of our fries daily and still be within USDA guidelines for cholesterol."

PepsiCo's research has found that 33 percent of all Americans wish to avoid cholesterol, compared with 23 percent as recently as 1984, according to John M. Cranor, president of Kentucky Fried Chicken. While 72 percent of all customers like broiled, roasted, or grilled chicken, only 50 percent now like fried chicken. (Multiple responses add to more than 100 percent.) In response to this shift in consumer preferences, Kentucky Fried Chicken launched a test in Las Vegas, Nevada, of char-grilled chicken. The product has achieved 17.5 percent of sales in test units, suggesting that it will be rolled out nationally in 1990 and 1991. A shortage of equipment is the primary reason for even that brief delay.

Chapter 3

Major Fast-Food Segments and Participants

Means of Participation

There are five important ways of participating in the chain restaurant industry, along with two much less prevalent methods. First, a firm may own and operate its own restaurants. This most basic approach to the restaurant business is practiced by every publicly held fast-food operator. Second, a firm may serve as a franchisor, licensing franchisees to operate restaurants designed to duplicate the format developed by the franchisor. Typically franchisors charge their franchisees a small initial fee to join the system, then collect an ongoing royalty based on the sales of the franchisee.

Third, the firm that has elected to engage in franchising may decide to lease facilities to its franchisees. This practice, which is largely confined to the largest fast-food hamburger franchisors, has its roots in the original deal that McDonald's Corporation founder Ray Kroc made with the McDonald brothers. Fourth, a franchisor may elect to sell food products to its franchisees. In some cases the franchisor confines this activity to only a very limited number of proprietary products: for example, Kentucky Fried Chicken requires that its franchisees purchase its secret seasoning package of eleven herbs and spices and Pizza Hut insists that its franchisees purchase its spice mixture. In other cases the franchisor derives the major part of his or her income from the sale of products to franchisees. Examples include TCBY, which sells frozen yogurt mix to its franchisees and, for many years, Howard Johnson, which sold a wide assortment of food products to its franchisees.

The final important way in which chains participate is by means of joint ventures. This method, which in some sense is a hybrid between franchising and company ownership, is most prevalent in foreign markets. The ownership of 50 percent of a restaurant chain by local nationals is virtually a legal requirement in some countries such as Japan and, until

Table 3.1

Means of Participation

	Company-Owned	Franchise	Lease to Franchisee	Joint Venture	Sell Product to Franchisee	Sell Commissary Equipment to Franchisee
Arby's	x	x				
Burger King	x	x	x			x
Captain D's	x	x				
Carl's	x	x				
Chi-Chi's	x	x				
Chili's	x	x		x		
Church's	x	x				
Cracker Barrel	x					
Dairy Queen	x	x				
Domino's	x					
Dunkin' Donuts	x	x			x	
Friendly Ice Cream	x					
Hardee's	x	x				
Jack in the Box	x					
Kentucky Fried	x	x		x		
Little Caesar's	x					
Long John Silver	x	x			x	
McDonald's	x	x	x	x		
Pizza Hut	x	x		x	x	
Popeye's	x	x				
Rally's	x	x				
Red Lobster	x	x				
Roy Rogers	x	x				
Ryan's	x	x				
Sbarro's	x	x				
Shoney's	x	x				x
Sizzler	x	x				
Subway Sandwiches		x				
Taco Bell	x	x				
TCBY	x	x			x	
Wendy's	x	x				
White Castle	x					

recently, Mexico, and even in other cases may provide a sounder foundation for site procurement, labor relations, and legal maneuvering than would 100 percent ownership by an American parent.

Less widespread are two other means of participation: selling equipment to franchisees, and the maintenance of commissaries or other distribution and food-processing centers for either company-owned or franchised stores or both.

Table 3.1 indicates the ways in which the firms discussed in this book have chosen to direct their operations. As can be seen, all important chain restaurant companies operate their own stores, even in cases where franchising may be of vastly greater importance in the overall scheme of the company's profitability.

The Economics of Franchising

In theory, pure franchising should be the most profitable means of participating in the restaurant industry, at least in terms of return on investment. To have franchisees secure their own financing for land and building, then pay a royalty of, say, 4.0 percent of sales to the franchisor creates an income stream for the franchisor with virtually no capital outlay.

It is for this reason that in the very early stages of a restaurant chain's development, when a high percentage of income is derived from franchisees, return on equity for the franchisor can be inordinately high. Wendy's, for example, enjoyed a return on equity in excess of 90 percent annually in the mid-1970s, while McDonald's earned a staggering 120 percent on equity in 1963. The relative importance of company-owned stores, franchised units, and joint ventures is illustrated in Table 3.2.

Note that joint ventures are significant only to three chains, Kentucky Fried Chicken, McDonald's, and Pizza Hut, that operate in foreign markets in a major way. Note, too, that only four chains of the group discussed in this book do not franchise at all. Finally, observe that, on average, franchised stores for the typical chain are equal to slightly more than twice the number of company-owned units.

No clear conclusions can be drawn about the effectiveness of pure company ownership compared with franchising. At one time observers believed that company ownership conferred upon a system better controls and a higher quality of profitability. The collapse of Gino's and Victoria Station, both of which operated company-owned units exclusively, calls this supposition into question, however. Further, the poor performance of Friendly Ice Cream and Steak & Ale provides further proof that company ownership does not insulate a chain from operating difficulties.

Franchising Income Stable

Indeed, franchising can provide a degree of stability that company ownership does not. The reason for this is that, in the event of a sales decline throughout a restaurant's system, franchising profits will fall only in line with the drop in sales. Profit margins are so high in franchising that there is very little leverage when revenues decline. Company store operations, however, have fixed costs that may, at least in the very short run, be equal to more than 50

Table 3.2

Number of Units in System (Worldwide Totals)

	Company-Owned	Franchise	Joint Venture	Total	Date
Arby's	208	2,144	0	2,352	Sep 89
Burger King	817	4,761	0	5,578	May 88
Captain D's	247	341	0	588	Oct 88
Carl's	406	76	0	482	Jan 89
Chi-Chi's	134	70	0	204	July 88
Chili's	137	27	10	174	July 89
Church's	1,100	378	0	1,478	Dec 88
Cracker Barrel	66	0	0	66	July 88
Dairy Queen	5	4,551	0	4,556	Nov 88
Domino's	1,223	3,670	0	4,893	May 89
Dunkin' Donuts	16	1,748	0	1,764	Oct 88
Friendly Ice Cream	840	0	0	840	Dec 88
Hardee's	1,038	2,072	0	3,110	Dec 88
Jack in the Box	628	304	0	932	July 88
Kentucky Fried	1,571	5,782	408	7,761	Dec 88
Little Caesar's	498	1,682	0	2,180	Dec 88
Long John Silver	979	490	0	1,469	Jun 88
McDonald's	2,600	7,110	803	10,513	Dec 88
Pizza Hut	2,984	3,461	217	6,662	Dec 88
Popeye's	130	585	0	715	Oct 88
Rally's	61	87	0	148	July 89
Red Lobster	402	0	0	402	May 88
Roy Rogers	394	238	0	632	Sep 89
Ryan's	100	27	0	127	Mar 89
Sbarro's	235	83	0	318	Jan 89
Shoney's	363	273	0	636	Oct 88
Sizzler	187	417	0	604	Oct 88
Subway Sandwiches	12	3,488	0	3,500	Sep 89
Taco Bell	1,716	1,214	0	2,930	Dec 88
TCBY	115	1,060	0	1,175	Nov 88
Wendy's	1,173	2,589	0	3,762	Dec 88
White Castle	235	0	0	235	Dec 88
Total	20,412	46,584	1438	68,434	

percent of sales. As a result, the impact on profitability of a shortfall in sales is magnified for company operations.

This contrast between the two forms of restaurant operation focuses attention on two regular points of contention between franchisors and franchisees: new products and pricing. Franchisors will occasionally introduce new products that contribute sales but not profits. A particularly contentious example was the insistence by Wendy's in the early 1980s that franchisees begin serving breakfast. The program was never profitable, and franchisees bitterly resented being forced to offer a product that not only lost money but also increased their royalty payments to the parent company. In response to a protest by one Wendy's franchisee group that later filed for bankruptcy, Wendy's chairman Robert L. Barney replied, "Tell 'em to put the [expletive deleted] breakfast in or take the sign down!"

Less pervasive but still sometimes troubling can be differences in pricing strategy. Generally franchisees, all else equal, charge higher menu prices than do the parent companies. The franchisee wants profits *now,* while the franchisor may be more interested in building long-term market penetration. In the summer of 1989, McDonald's began cutting prices aggressively in California, partly in response to Taco Bell's new, deep discount approach, and partly to make Rally's expansion difficult. Yet franchisees cannot be forced to lower their prices for the good of the chain, thereby creating a strategic quandary for the franchisor. Indeed, some industry observers believe that McDonald's acceleration of its efforts to introduce pizza has been in order to boost franchisees' profits, thereby making them more amenable to occasional competitive price cutting.

One other element of the relationship between franchisors and franchisees is noteworthy. Sometimes franchisors with a strong regional base of company-owned units will elect to go the franchising or joint venture route in markets where they are not entirely optimistic about their prospects.

Church's Expansion

A case in point is Church's Fried Chicken, which prospered in the southwest and middle west with company stores. In fact, 39 percent of the chain's stores are in Louisiana and Texas alone, with another 10 percent in the three cities of Chicago (40 stores), St. Louis (25 stores), and Detroit (25 stores). The chain had its strongest position in inner cities and its Texas heartland.

When it came time to expand into the northeast, however, the chain chose to franchise. In fact, Church's never achieved much success in the northeast, so the company's caution was warranted. Nevertheless, the reluctance of a chain to put its own capital into a new market area is almost always a sign of incipient problems with expansion. In similar fashion, Wendy's insistence on developing most European markets with franchisees rather than the company ownership or joint venture approach of McDonald's was a sign of the company's lack of commitment to the European market.

Unit Level Economics for Franchisee

The McDonald's franchisee pays an initial $22,500 fee, along with a $15,000 security deposit that the company keeps for the full twenty-year term of the license. The total cost to the franchisee of the equipment package, working capital, and the fees to McDonald's averages about $575,000. The franchisee then pays McDonald's an ongoing rent of 8.5 percent of sales (or more, subject to a complex escalation formula), along with a 3.5 percent royalty. (The royalty had been held at 3.0 percent for many years, but was raised in early 1986.)

Typically the franchisee may borrow 60 to 75 percent of the total investment. Because of the stability and visibility of McDonald's results, the chain's franchisees typically can borrow at 200 basis points lower costs than do the franchisees of most other chains. After paying him- or herself a draw in the area of $50,000 per year, the franchised operator will achieve profits at the store level of 6 to 10 percent on annual volume of about $1,600,000.

Profitability to Franchisee

In the case of the franchisee who invests $200,000 in cash and borrows $375,000 at 10.0 percent, the profit, after interest expense on a store with 10.0 percent operating margin would be $122,500 on the $200,000 cash outlay. If the margin were as low as 6.0 percent, the operating profit would be $58,500, still an adequate return on a $200,000 outlay.

To accommodate promising young recruits who may not have accumulated the net worth required to equip a store, McDonald's has developed a program called the Business Facilities Lease (BFL) system. In this case, the aspiring franchisee has an initial capital outlay of $65,000, with McDonald's retaining ownership of the equipment and leasing it to the new franchisee, who has an option to buy the equipment from profit as time passes.

McDonald's employs 300 field consultants in 36 regions to oversee its franchising operation.

Territorial versus Site-Only Franchising

Several successful chains of the 1970s, including Pizza Hut, Wendy's, Long John Silver, and Burger King, licensed areas rather than specific sites to franchisees. The franchisor would collect an area franchise fee, then an additional fee for each store actually opened, followed by the usual ongoing royalty arrangement. This practice is still sometimes followed today, with Rally's using the area franchising system.

This method has several drawbacks, however. The first is that in periods of tight money, franchisees may not meet their development schedules, yet still tie up enormous territory that might be developed by better-financed licensees. The second problem is that franchisees will sometimes open stores at only the very best locations, preferring to risk their capital at only the sites that promise the very best returns. While such a practice may maximize the franchisee's return on investment in percentage terms, it leads to fewer stores being opened than the chain could support.

McDonald's normally licenses only a single address rather than a territory. Its early experiments with licensing areas in Washington, D.C.; Paris, France; and Canada all led to unsatisfactory market development, with McDonald's in each case having to buy out the licensee or, in the case of Paris, having to resort to litigation to regain control of the market.

McDonald's Approach to Franchising

In response to the rising cost of constructing new stores, McDonald's has begun to alter its rental agreements with its licensees to compensate for unusually expensive sites. Rather than the standard 8.5 percent of sales that has been the McDonald's standard rental for two decades, a unit with land and building cost of $865,000 or more will cost the franchisee 10.0 percent of sales, while one with a land and building cost of $1,000,000 or more will cost the licensee 11.0 percent of sales.

Further, McDonald's has begun to put in escalation clauses that cause the percentage of sales to be paid to increase over time. That is, the rental will increase with inflation, which had always been the case with McDonald's rental arrangements since its earliest days, but the rate as a percentage of sales rises, too. Some of the recent deals McDonald's has struck with licensees call for fees and rent as a percent of sales to be 12.5 percent of sales in the first four years of the licensing term, 13.25 percent in the next three years, and 13.5 percent in years 8 through 20. At present, only 235 or 4 percent of U.S. stores have such escalators. However, 18 percent of the new stores opened in 1988 contained such escalation provisions.

McDonald's Approach to Individual Franchisees

McDonald's continues to stress the role of the individual franchisee within the system. In late 1989 more than one-third of McDonald's franchisees had only one store, while 75 percent had three stores or less. Only fifty-two franchisees had more than ten stores, and the average within the franchised system was three stores per licensee.

McDonald's continues to attract new applicants in droves. In 1988 the company received 20,000 requests for franchising information, which resulted in the submission of 2000 applications. From this pool 200 applicants were selected to enter the company's training program. This program involves eighteen months of training without pay at McDonald's stores.

In 1988 139 new licensees in the United States and an additional 70 in foreign markets were invited to join the McDonald's system. Of the chain's 340 new stores opened in the United States in 1988, 200 were opened by existing franchisees, 95 by the company, and 45 by new franchisees.

McDonald's Unique Approach

When Ray Kroc signed his original deal with the McDonald brothers, it provided for him to franchise McDonald's restaurants nationwide for ten years while paying the McDonald brothers 0.5 percent of sales. Kroc was not permitted to charge the franchisees more than 1.9 percent of sales. As a middleman, in effect, Kroc's revenues per restaurant could not exceed 1.4 percent of sales.

The explosion of McDonald's stores in the late 1950s yielded Kroc's fledgling company very little profit; by the end of 1960 there were 225 franchised units, 3 company-owned stores (which lost money), and the company was near bankruptcy. Harry Sonneborn, a former vice president of Tastee-Freeze came to Kroc in 1956 for a meager salary of $100 per week and instituted the real estate leasing plan that saved the company. "Harry alone put in the policy that salvaged this company and made it a big-leaguer," said Kroc. "His idea is really what made McDonald's rich." (Love, p. 153)

Sonneborn's insight was that, while Kroc was severely restricted in his ability to earn a satisfactory return from the franchisees because of the razor-thin margin imposed by the McDonald brothers deal, there was an opportunity to provide the franchisees with financing for their stores. Thus was born the practice, which continues to this day, of McDonald's becoming landlord to its licensees.

Kroc's company (Franchise Realty Corporation, which was the new entity that Sonneborn created) would lease property from its owners, then sublet to McDonald's franchisees.

Franchisees were charged either 5.0 percent of sales or 40 percent above McDonald's own rental cost on leased property. The real estate financing concept that Sonneborn brought to McDonald's was the financial salvation of the company in the early days, but it also had unforeseen benefits down the road. First, it provided financing for franchised operators in a nascent industry where none might otherwise have existed. Second, it guaranteed McDonald's complete control over site selection. Third, it ensured that Kroc's vision of quality service, cleanliness, and value would be observed. In short, the system provided control.

McDonald's Real Estate Values

The final advantage that the real estate financing scheme provided was huge underlying profits on owned real estate. In the early 1960s McDonald's, whenever possible, began purchasing sites with mortgage financing so that it could eventually own the underlying real estate. It followed this practice whether the restaurant to be operated on the site was destined to be a franchised or, as became more common in the 1970s, a company-operated store.

The end result was that at December 31, 1988, McDonald's and its affiliates owned 6320 of its restaurant real estate locations, or 60 percent of the total. Even this impressive figure is somewhat distorted by the company's recent concentration on foreign store openings, which often, by virtue of their center city locations, are not available for purchase but must be rented. In the United States alone, McDonald's owned 68 percent of its sites at year-end 1988.

The precise value of these assets is impossible to calculate. One approach, however, would be to mark the value of the properties to current replacement cost. Land on McDonald's books at year-end 1988 was valued at $1656 million, while buildings and improvements on owned land were valued at $3447 million before accumulated depreciation of $1772 million.

The current price of the average McDonald's land parcel is $415,000. Multiplying that figure by the 6320 sites that the company owns produces a figure of $2623 million for the current value of McDonald's land holdings, compared with the $1656 million carried on the firm's books. This difference of nearly $1 billion represents the appreciation in McDonald's land holdings over the company's lifetime.

This calculation is admittedly crude, inasmuch as it gives no recognition to the fact that McDonald's sites are larger now than they were twenty years ago. Nor does it adjust for the fact that many sites purchased now are in foreign markets with far higher land costs. However, it provides some perspective on the size of the McDonald's real estate empire and the capital gains derived from Sonneborn's strategy.

Economics of License Renewal

The actions of franchisors with regard to their franchisees in recent years is reflective of the more difficult operating climate of the 1980s. Franchisors have increasingly turned away

Table 3.3

Changes in Franchised Restaurant Ownership

Year	Repurchased for Company Ownership	Converted to Franchisee Ownership	Ratio of Repurchase to Franchise
1973	533	175	3.05
1974	477	198	2.41
1975	311	184	1.69
1976	280	413	0.68
1977	305	425	0.72
1978	321	312	1.03
1979	484	579	0.84
1980	394	498	0.79
1981	489	426	1.15
1982	475	389	1.22
1983	279	352	0.79
1984	328	339	0.97
1985	322	622	0.52
1986	429	866	0.50

Source: National Restaurant Association, "Franchise Restaurants, A Statistical Appendix to Foodservice Trends," Washington, D.C., March 1988.

from owning their own stores in the more difficult environment of the late 1980s. Table 3.3 shows the number of franchised restaurants acquired by franchisors from franchisees, as well as the number of company-operated units that have been sold to franchisees.

Note that in the mid-1970s many more stores were purchased from franchisees than were sold to them. Such a practice was routinely followed, for example by Wendy's and Jerrico, which used their high-priced stock to reacquire franchisees, thereby both enriching their franchisees (and encouraging new ones to join the system) and accelerating their corporate profit growth. By the mid-1980s, however, an explosion of refranchising activity occurred, with franchisors trying to unload unprofitable units to more efficient franchisees. By mid-1989, Wendy's, for example, was attempting to sell all of its company-owned units to groups of franchisees, some of which were currently Wendy's franchisees and some of which were not.

Royalty Forgiveness

In order to provide a motive to franchisees to upgrade their stores, even McDonald's sometimes resorts to incentive schemes. If a franchisee cannot otherwise be induced to install a playground, for example, McDonald's will pay for the installation. Then, if the facility increases sales volumes by $100,000 annually, the licensee repays McDonald's over a five-year period. If sales do not meet the target, the franchisee pays nothing.

Economics of Refranchising

Some shuffling of ownership within the McDonald's system takes place. In 1988 a total of 252 stores were bought by franchisees either from the company or from other franchisees. In addition, 93 new franchisees bought stores either from the company or from existing franchisees.

Segment Analysis

Table 3.4 indicates the number of franchise participants by segment since the early 1970s. The total number of players grew at a more rapid rate during the 1970s than the 1980s, reflecting to some degree the increasing barriers to entry created by the most dominant chains. More striking than the aggregate data, however, are the number of participants within each segment.

The number of participants in the hamburger segment actually peaked more than a decade ago and has shown a slight decline since that time. The net number of firms competing in the hamburger business was well-established by the early 1970s. In terms of new entries, then, the hamburger industry appears virtually closed. As we shall see, however, these net numbers mask the development of new entrants coupled with the winding down of older factors in the segment.

Table 3.4

Number of Franchise Participants by Segment

Year	Hamburger	Pizza	Chicken	Mexican	Seafood	Sandwich	Other*	Total
1973	104	30	21	14	11	6	59	245
1974	98	36	24	15	13	8	65	259
1975	97	46	28	17	17	7	81	293
1976	96	48	29	19	15	19	89	315
1977	109	60	27	23	14	25	92	350
1978	117	66	31	29	11	33	101	388
1979	112	73	32	28	11	33	110	399
1980	110	83	35	32	12	34	119	425
1981	107	94	30	33	13	39	124	440
1982	102	106	32	33	14	46	125	458
1983	98	111	34	39	11	50	123	466
1984	105	104	33	36	12	51	124	465
1985	105	102	30	36	14	53	130	470
1986	111	105	33	36	17	57	129	488
Compound Annual Growth Rate (%)								
1973–86	0.5	10.1	3.5	7.5	3.4	18.9	6.2	5.4
1981–86	0.7	2.2	1.9	1.8	5.5	7.9	0.8	2.1

*Includes steak, full-menu, and pancake restaurants.

Contrast the experience within the pizza segment, where the number of players more than tripled between 1973 and 1983. In this segment, the stability derived from chain dominance came much later than in the hamburger segment, but now seems to be well-established.

The chicken and Mexican segments demonstrate similar patterns to the pizza industry, albeit with somewhat lower growth rates. In each case the number of participants grew steadily in the 1970s, but peaked in the early 1980s and has shown a modest decline since that time. Interestingly, the seafood and sandwich segments continue to show comparatively rapid growth in the number of players. The explanation for this is straightforward. In neither segment has a dominant chain emerged, hence newcomers can enter without being subjected to the threats of saturation and media advertising dominance that characterize the more mature segments.

Segment Growth Not Key to Profits

Identifying segments with the greatest growth potential is by no means sufficient as a means for predicting success or failure of individual operators. Each segment will almost invariably have participants that are floundering as well as those that are thriving. For example, in the 1970s Church's Fried Chicken was one of the nation's fastest growing and most profitable companies in *any* business at the same time that Kentucky Fried Chicken was floundering. Denny's coffee shops were consistently growing at a rate in excess of 20 percent annually while Howard Johnson was closing units. Wendy's quadrupled the size of its system during that same period that Burger Chef veered toward bankruptcy. More recently, Wendy's has been forced to retrench while Rally's explodes across the landscape, and Chili's prospers while Steak & Ale is sold at distress prices. With little fanfare White Castle continues to prosper even as Burger King's earnings erode.

The segment in which a chain operates has much to do with the backdrop in terms of competition, particularly within regions, but the dynamics of individual operators and the life cycle of individual entrants remains far more important. Moreover, finding a segment that cries out for rapid development provides no assurance that such development can actually be accomplished. In the early 1980s, for instance, the management of Chart House, which was, among other things, a highly successful franchisee of Burger King, hit upon the idea of finding a barbecue chain and expanding it nationally. Knowing that the prospects of developing their own concept ran up against heavy odds, Chart House acquired a successful regional chain, Luther's in Houston, and attempted to expand it nationally. The barbecue segment, which remains wildly popular in markets as diverse as New York City and rural Texas, has virtually no chain participation. Yet the problems of uniformity of product, training, site selection, and supervision of the preparation of a complex product defied even the best franchise operators in the industry. All attempts to expand Luther's failed. Similarly, when Donald Smith left PepsiCo after a meteoric rise at McDonald's followed by a stint as chief executive at Burger King, he identified the Chinese fast-food market as an obvious one to exploit. Yet even this gifted operating manager proved incapable of solving the problem of adapting the concept that he bought to national expansion.

Table 3.5

Franchised Hamburger Restaurants*

Year	Number of Stores	% Change	Sales per Store ($)	% Change	Total Sales ($000)	% Change
1973	21,375		228,449		4,883,094	
1974	22,069	3.2	266,411	16.6	5,879,428	20.4
1975	22,810	3.4	296,357	11.2	6,759,903	15.0
1976	24,064	5.5	333,719	12.6	8,030,623	18.8
1977	24,822	3.1	366,644	9.9	9,100,843	13.3
1978	26,038	4.9	417,192	13.8	10,862,837	19.4
1979	27,310	4.9	466,517	11.8	12,740,586	17.3
1980	27,027	−1.0	519,014	11.3	14,027,398	10.1
1981	26,945	−0.3	531,738	2.5	14,327,705	2.1
1982	27,285	1.3	618,028	16.2	16,862,890	17.7
1983	28,270	3.6	670,245	8.4	18,947,837	12.4
1984	29,305	3.7	752,225	12.2	22,043,955	16.3
1985	30,563	4.3	765,875	1.8	23,407,433	6.2
1986	31,511	3.1	798,403	4.2	25,158,486	7.5
1987	33,031	4.8	825,202	3.4	27,257,232	8.3
1988	35,105	6.3	854,560	3.6	29,999,331	10.1
Compound Annual Growth Rate (%)						
1973–88		3.4		9.2		12.9
1983–88		4.4		5.0		9.6

*Includes roast beef and hot dog restaurants.

Source: National Restaurant Association, "Franchise Restaurants, A Statistical Appendix to Foodservice Trends," Washington, D.C., March 1988.

Major Players

Growth in Hamburger Segment

Table 3.5 shows the growth of franchised hamburger restaurants (including both company-operated and franchised units) since 1973. Note the decline in the number of stores during the 1980–81 period, which coincided with a recession and the lingering effects of an OPEC oil embargo. Observe, too, the far more rapid gains in sales per store during the late 1970s (partially due to inflation) than has recently been the case. Finally, note the slower rate of overall sales growth in recent years. Identifiable chains account for about 90 percent of the sales of this segment of the overall foodservice industry and will be addressed below.

Two Major Players Dominate

In examining the principal players in the fast-food market, one inevitably confronts the increasing dominance of two corporate entities: PepsiCo and McDonald's. PepsiCo, which owns Pizza Hut and Taco Bell (both acquired in 1977) and Kentucky Fried Chicken (acquired in 1986) is the world's largest restaurant company in terms of number of units, with 17,353 units in operation as of December 31, 1988. Worldwide sales by the three

PepsiCo-owned concepts in 1988 totaled $10.0 billion. McDonald's achieved systemwide sales in 1988 of $16.1 billion in its 10,513 outlets.

Each of PepsiCo's three concepts is dominant in its market segment, ranging from Pizza Hut's 20 percent share of the pizza market in 1988 to Taco Bell's nearly 70 percent share of the fast-food Mexican market. The company has considered (and rejected) the possibility of buying a smaller hamburger chain in order to compete with McDonald's. Instead, its goal is to buy only chains where segment domination is feasible. To that end, it reportedly engaged in bidding for Jerrico, the owner of the Long John Silver seafood chain that was ultimately acquired by Castle Harlan, Inc., in the autumn of 1989. It has even studied the acquisition of McDonald's!

McDonald's Overwhelming Importance

McDonald's size alone dictates its overwhelming importance in virtually every aspect of fast food. The chain is, for example, the world's second largest purchaser of chicken (behind Kentucky Fried Chicken, of course). PepsiCo's internal research has projected pizza sales for McDonald's of $2 billion, which would make it the third largest factor in pizza (or perhaps the second, depending upon the impact on Domino's, the current number 2).

The most vulnerable spot that either of these giants has may lie in their relationships with franchisees. PepsiCo, in particular, has altered its licensing arrangement in recent years, raising franchise fees now on franchising agreements still in force, with the threat of raising them still more in the future when the license expires if the franchisee does not agree to the earlier increase.

Table 3.6 shows the domestic systemwide sales (including franchised stores as well as company-operated units) for the eleven largest fast-food hamburger companies. Note that McDonald's alone accounts for just under half the sales of this segment, and has grown at a slightly more rapid pace than the overall market segment for the past two years. These eleven chains accounted for 40 percent of the U.S. fast-food sales, as estimated by the National Restaurant Association.

Table 3.6

Systemwide Sales for Hamburger Chains ($ million)

Chain	1987	1988	% Change	1989	% Change
McDonald's (Domestic)	10,576	11,380	7.6	12,360	8.6
Burger King	4,590	4,840	5.4	5,110	5.6
Hardee's	2,600	2,810	8.1	3,040	8.2
Wendy's	2,700	2,720	0.7	2,860	5.1
Jack-in-the-Box	655	775	18.3	875	12.9
Roy Rogers	525	575	9.5	620	7.8
Carl's Jr.	345	399	15.7	481	20.6
Sonic Drive-In	306	341	11.4	390	14.4
Whataburger	260	310	19.2	340	9.7
White Castle	283	283	0.0	299	5.7
Krystal	184	178	−3.3	184	3.4
Total	23,024	24,611	6.9	26,559	7.9

Table 3.7

Number of Hamburger Chain Units

Chain	1987	1988	% Change	1989	% Change
McDonald's (Domestic)	7,567	7,907	4.5	8,276	4.7
Burger King	4,701	5,020	6.8	5,361	6.8
Wendy's (Domestic)	3,582	3,521	−1.7	3,697	5.0
Hardee's	2,912	3,110	6.8	3,327	7.0
Jack-in-the-Box	897	966	7.7	1,031	6.7
Sonic Drive-In	955	980	2.6	1,000	2.0
Roy Rogers	556	606	9.0	660	8.9
Carl's Jr.	436	443	1.6	482	8.8
Whataburger	445	470	5.6	480	2.1
White Castle	229	235	2.6	250	6.4
Krystal	243	232	−4.5	233	0.4
Total	22,523	23,490	4.3	24,797	5.6

Burger King is owned by the Pillsbury Company, which in turn has been owned since 1988 by a British conglomerate, Grand Metropolitan P.L.C. The chain has been a revolving door for managers. The company has had eight presidents and six chairmen in the twenty-two years since Pillsbury acquired it. (*New York Times,* Nov. 14, 1988, p. D4*)* Following a resurgence in the late 1970s and early 1980s under the leadership of former McDonald's chief operating officer Donald Smith, Burger King's profitability has languished in recent years.

Wendy's, too, is a distressed situation, with its net income having plunged from $76 million in 1985 to a loss of $5 million one year later. Its stock price fell by more than 70 percent between 1986 and 1989, and as of late 1989 sells at a price below where it was more than a decade earlier. Wendy's number of company-owned stores actually declined from 1986 through 1989. The number of units in each of the eleven hamburger chains is summarized in Table 3.7. Note that all but two of the chains continue to expand their number of stores at a moderate pace.

Table 3.8 ranks the same eleven hamburger chains according to sales per store. Note the overwhelmingly high sales per store of McDonald's compared with its competitors. Observe, too, that the chain with the second highest level of sales per store is White Castle, the original home of the fast-food hamburger ("Home of the Slider") and a chain that is an anachronism in that it does no franchising, has limited advertising, and only a modest appetite for expansion. This reluctance to expand, in turn, is dictated by the company's refusal to borrow funds. Although the privately held chain does not disclose its financial results, it is reputed to be among the most profitable of any of the fast-food chains in percentage terms.

Growth of Chicken Segment

Table 3.9 shows the growth of the franchised chicken segment of the restaurant industry since 1973. As in the hamburger segment, the growth in number of units has been relatively

Table 3.8

Sales per Store for Hamburger Chain ($ 000)

Chain	1987	1988	% Change	1989	% Change
McDonald's	1502	1596	6.3	1600	0.3
White Castle	1260	1240	−1.6	1250	0.8
Burger King	1020	1000	−2.0	1050	5.0
Carl's Jr.	772	940	21.8	1000	6.4
Roy Rogers	900	935	3.9	1000	7.0
Jack-in-the-Box	797	903	13.3	1000	10.7
Hardee's	877	920	4.9	964	4.8
Whataburger	800	840	5.0	850	1.2
Wendy's (Domestic)	741	759	2.4	797	5.0
Krystal	765	765	0.0	790	3.3
Sonic Drive-In	321	356	10.9	395	11.0
Unweighted average	887	932	5.1	972	4.3

Table 3.9

Franchised Chicken Restaurants

Year	Number of Stores	% Change	Sales per Store ($)	% Change	Total Sales ($000)	% Change
1973	4927		229,246		1,129,496	
1974	5686	15.4	221,345	−3.4	1,258,617	11.4
1975	5706	0.4	240,779	8.8	1,373,887	9.2
1976	6171	8.1	260,780	8.3	1,609,270	17.1
1977	6437	4.3	324,508	24.4	2,088,861	29.8
1978	6708	4.2	303,222	−6.6	2,034,012	−2.6
1979	7075	5.5	319,154	5.3	2,258,017	11.0
1980	7338	3.7	372,582	16.7	2,734,006	21.1
1981	7388	0.7	383,461	2.9	2,833,007	3.6
1982	7773	5.2	381,160	−0.6	2,947,512	4.0
1983	8147	4.8	419,499	10.1	3,417,658	16.0
1984	8576	5.3	453,727	8.2	3,891,165	13.9
1985	8720	1.7	472,356	4.1	4,118,947	5.9
1986	8968	2.8	487,876	3.3	4,375,275	6.2
1987	9391	4.7	513,426	5.2	4,821,580	10.2
1988	9888	5.3	550,425	7.2	5,442,603	12.9
Compound Annual Growth Rate (%)						
1973–88		4.8		6.0		11.1
1983–88		3.9		5.6		9.8

Source: National Restaurant Association, "Franchise Restaurants, A Statistical Appendix to Foodservice Trends," Washington, D.C., March 1988.

modest, averaging less than 5 percent annually since the early 1970s. Note that sales per store have been erratic, actually showing declines in the recession years 1974 and 1982, as well as a downturn in 1978.

There are several explanations for the cyclical nature of the chicken business. First, the product is heavily consumed by minority groups, whose unemployment rates tend to rise more sharply than that of the overall population during economic downturns. Also, chicken, far more than hamburgers, tends to be an evening meal. Kentucky Fried Chicken derives 65 percent of its revenue from the dinner business. McDonald's, in contrast, produces only 30 percent of its sales in the evening. (Pizza Hut does 73 percent of its business at night, while Taco Bell does 50 percent.) Hence, its consumption, like that of pizza, is more discretionary in that it is less tied to work, school, or shopping.

Fast-food chicken is overwhelmingly a take-out product. Church's, for example, found that 82 percent of its sales in 1988 were to take-out and drive-through customers, with an average check per transaction of $3.77. Popeye's estimates that 73 percent of its sales are made to take-out or drive-through customers and had an average check per transaction of $4.29 in 1988. As a discretionary, more expensive item than the offerings of the hamburger chains, chicken may be more subject to fluctuations of the economy than are other segments of the fast-food business.

Church's and Popeye's Combine

Table 3.10 shows the systemwide sales for the five largest chicken chains. The sharp decline in Church's sales and the sharp gain in Popeye's revenues require explanation. The Church's chain, which was acquired by privately owned Popeye's in September 1989, will undergo a massive restructuring to close losing restaurants. A total of 332 of Church's 1107 stores will be sold or leased to Popeye's franchisees, while another 227 company-operated stores with unsatisfactory sales levels will be closed.

Popeye's management estimates that these closings alone would, on a pro forma basis, have improved Church's company-operated stores' results from a $4.9 million operating loss to an $8.2 million profit in 1988. Additionally, 203 company-owned units will be sold to Church's franchisees, though this action will not affect the sales or number of units in the

Table 3.10

Systemwide Sales for Chicken Chains ($ million)

Chain	1987	1988	% Change	1989	% Change
Kentucky Fried Chicken	2700	2900	7.4	3000	3.4
Popeye's	460	477	3.7	590	23.7
Church's	534	559	4.7	360	−35.6
Chick-Fil-A	202	230	13.9	268	16.5
El Pollo Loco	115	173	50.4	220	27.2
Total	4011	4339	8.2	4438	2.3

Table 3.11

Number of Chicken Chain Units

Chain	1987	1988	% Change	1989	% Change
Kentucky Fried Chicken	4814	4899	1.8	4997	2.0
Popeye's	675	715	5.9	1030	44.1
Church's	1495	1481	−0.9	1028	−30.6
Chick-Fil-A	363	386	6.3	410	6.2
El Pollo Loco	115	165	43.5	200	21.2
Total	7462	7646	2.5	7665	0.2

system shown in Table 3.11. In this context, it is worth noting that the Notice of Special Meeting of Shareholders to approve the acquisition of Church's by Popeye's (or, more precisely by Popeye's parent corporation, A. Copeland Enterprises, Inc.) points out that of 884 stores operated by Church's on June 30, 1989, the company owned the land and buildings for 584 units and owned the building on leased sites for an additional 191. Part of the scheme for paying for this acquisition is to mortgage these properties, thereby paying down part of the debt of the acquisition.

Slow Growth in Chicken

More important than the shifts within the segment, however, is the overall stagnation of sales in the entire chicken business. This trend is, at first glance, particularly puzzling in light of the continuing gains in chicken consumption at the expense of beef in the total American diet. Beef consumption per capita fell from 79.8 pounds in 1986 to 73.0 pounds in 1988. Poultry consumption, on the other hand, rose from 72.5 pounds per capita in 1986 to 82.8 pounds per capita in 1988.

Why the lack of growth among fast-food chicken chains? The answer, of course, is that *fried* chicken consumption is a victim of the same health concerns that are driving Americans away from red meat. Both El Pollo Loco (which is owned by TW Food Services) and, to a lesser extent, Chick-Fil-A, which offer grilled or broiled poultry products, are enjoying considerable success in this environment.

Indeed, in a presentation made to prospective bond investors in New York on October 19, 1989, the management of TW Food Services, Inc., projected a 25 percent sales growth rate through 1992 for El Pollo Loco. At this same meeting, incidentally, the acquirors of TW disclosed that they, too, intend to refinance certain owned properties in order to reduce acquisition debt.

Table 3.11 shows the modest growth in the overall number of chicken outlets, along with the shift from Church's units to Popeye's stores as a result of the merger discussed above. Note the continuing rapid growth in units by El Pollo Loco. The sales per store of the

Table 3.12

Sales per Store for Chicken Chains ($ 000)

Chain	1987	1988	% Change	1989	% Change
El Pollo Loco	1000	1050	5.0	1100	4.8
Chick-Fil-A	575	622	8.2	662	6.4
Popeye's	710	725	2.1	630	−13.1
Kentucky Fried Chicken	558	597	7.0	600	0.5
Church's	357	378	5.9	350	−7.4
Unweighted average	640	674	5.4	668	−0.9

various players in the chicken business are summarized in Table 3.12. Note the dramatic difference between El Pollo Loco and its fried chicken competitors.

Whether Kentucky Fried Chicken's forays into grilled chicken in 1990 and 1991 will cut into El Pollo Loco's success remains to be seen. It seems likely, however, based on test market results in Las Vegas, that Kentucky Fried Chicken will, at the very least, experience strong initial trial of the product. With no advertising, Kentucky Fried Chicken achieved 4 to 8 percent incremental sales in its Las Vegas test market. The ultimate goal would be to produce grilled chicken sales equal to 30 percent of the entire sales mix, with half of the sales being incremental. The capital cost per store of installing the facilities for broiling the product ranges from $25,000 to $30,000.

Growth of Pizza Segment

The growth of franchised pizza chains has been quite different from that of the more mature hamburger or chicken segments. Table 3.13 summarizes the growth in number of restaurants, sales per restaurant, and total sales of the franchised pizza chains since 1973. Note that the rate of increase in number of stores has averaged well over 10 percent annually in the period under inspection and continues at nearly that same rate today.

Observe, too, the relatively small (and declining) rate of sales growth per store. Unlike the hamburger and chicken segments, however, the slowdown in sales per store probably is less reflective of a decline in sales for comparable stores than of a change in the *kind* of stores being opened. While the typical McDonald's store or Kentucky Fried Chicken store opened today is larger (and considerably more expensive) than those opened a decade ago, the pizza segment is moving more toward smaller, less expensive stores directed at the home delivery market.

Pizza Hut, a relatively late entrant into the delivery business, operated 771 delivery-only units in the United States at the end of 1988, or 13.5 percent of its domestic system total of 5707 units. Little Caesar's, which offers carry-out service, has exploded from 900 stores at the end of 1985 to an estimated 2747 at the end of 1989. Delivery-only units tend to be far smaller than the full-service pizza restaurants that they supplement.

Table 3.13

Franchised Pizza Restaurants

Year	Number of Stores	% Change	Sales per Store ($)	% Change	Total Sales ($000)	% Change
1973	3,364		150,150		505,103	
1974	4,329	28.7	162,953	8.5	705,423	39.7
1975	5,011	15.8	184,467	13.2	924,364	31.0
1976	5,745	14.6	189,997	3.0	1,091,534	18.1
1977	6,759	17.7	209,536	10.3	1,416,254	29.7
1978	7,542	11.6	230,082	9.8	1,735,279	22.5
1979	8,407	11.5	254,742	10.7	2,141,618	23.4
1980	8,914	6.0	275,470	8.1	2,455,542	14.7
1981	9,695	8.8	326,932	18.7	3,169,601	29.1
1982	10,629	9.6	351,874	7.6	3,740,072	18.0
1983	11,852	11.5	392,256	11.5	4,649,022	24.3
1984	12,705	7.2	388,219	−1.0	4,932,329	6.1
1985	14,174	11.6	436,990	12.6	6,193,899	25.6
1986	16,221	14.4	459,866	5.2	7,459,493	20.4
1987	17,739	9.4	458,103	−0.4	8,126,293	8.9
1988	19,912	12.2	459,645	0.3	9,152,448	12.6
Compound Annual Growth Rate (%)						
1973–88		12.6		7.7		21.3
1983–88		10.9		3.2		14.5

Source: National Restaurant Association, "Franchise Restaurants, A Statistical Appendix to Foodservice Trends," Washington, D.C., March 1988.

National Pizza, which is a publicly held franchisee of Pizza Hut, discloses its sales volumes and profitability for its conventional restaurants and its delivery-only units separately. For the thirteen weeks ended June 27, 1989, National Pizza's restaurants achieved sales volumes per store 30 percent higher than the sales per store of delivery units. Food costs, as might be expected, were substantially equal at 25 percent of sales, with labor costs being far lower as a percent of sales (22.7 percent) in the restaurants than in the delivery units, where direct labor was 29.6 percent of sales. As a result, profit margins at the store level were a far higher 26.5 percent of sales for the conventional Pizza Hut units in the National Pizza system than the 18.1 percent of sales in the delivery-only outlets.

The attraction of the delivery units lies in their minimal requirements for facilities. PepsiCo has calculated that the sales per dollar of invested capital in a delivery unit is three times that of a conventional Pizza Hut restaurant. Sites do not need to be in prime locations and can be very inexpensive. To open a Little Caesar's delivery unit, for example, costs the franchisee a $15,000 franchise fee and $120,000 in leasehold improvements. Pizza Hut spends only a small fraction (typically only $250,000 or less) of the cost to open a full Pizza Hut unit (which ranges from $850,000 to 900,000) when it opens a delivery outlet. Hence, the margins may be lower on a delivery unit, but the profitability in terms of return on investment is vastly superior.

Table 3.14

Ethnic Food Demand
($ million)

Year	Italian Foods	% Change	Pizza	% Change	Italian Sauces	% Change	Hispanic Foods	% Change	Oriental Foods	% Change
1976	1068.0		352.6		191.3		373.8		153.0	
1977	1260.4	18.0	420.0	19.1	215.3	12.5	429.0	14.8	171.7	12.2
1978	1346.8	6.9	541.0	28.8	277.5	28.9	490.0	14.2	208.2	21.3
1979	1433.0	6.4	628.1	16.1	342.5	23.4	560.2	14.3	239.6	15.1
1980	1632.0	13.9	660.1	5.1	387.0	13.0	683.5	22.0	289.3	20.7
1981	1815.1	11.2	699.6	6.0	470.6	21.6	830.8	21.6	323.6	11.9
1982	1909.2	5.2	725.5	3.7	514.1	9.2	894.3	7.6	345.6	6.8
1983	2111.2	10.6	740.7	2.1	566.0	10.1	1017.9	13.8	400.7	15.9
1984	2193.7	3.9	759.3	2.5	611.8	8.1	1134.5	11.5	439.4	9.7
1985	2344.9	6.9	795.7	4.8	664.5	8.6	1280.9	12.9	466.0	6.1
1986	2441.8	4.1	842.6	5.9	705.0	6.1	1427.8	11.5	505.5	8.5
1987	2615.2	7.1	897.4	6.5	766.3	8.7	1576.6	10.4	545.4	7.9
1996*	5369.4	105.3	1537.7	71.4	1522.0	98.6	3289.1	108.6	1167.9	114.1

Compound Annual Growth Rate (%)

	Italian Foods		Pizza		Italian Sauces		Hispanic Foods		Oriental Foods	
1976-86	8.6		9.1		13.9		14.3		12.7	
1987-96*	8.3		6.2		7.9		8.5		8.8	

*Estimated values.

Source: Business Trend Analysts, "The Market for Ethnic Foods," Commack N.Y.

Consider a Pizza Hut delivery unit with a cost of $250,000 and annual volume of $550,000. With an 18 percent profit margin, the store's unleveraged return on investment approaches 40 percent. In contrast, a Pizza Hut restaurant with an $850,000 land, building, and equipment cost, even at $800,000 volume (which would be unusually high for a Pizza Hut) and a 27 percent margin at the store level achieves a return of only 25.4 percent. While this would be a well-above-average return in the fast-food industry of the late 1980s, it does not compare favorably with the unit economics of the smaller, less expensive delivery units. As a result, Pizza Hut now spends 20 percent of its capital outlays on delivery-only units.

The growing emphasis on the smaller delivery-only units explains much of the modest growth in sales per store. Note that the rate of total sales growth for the segment is extremely high, nearly five percentage points higher in the late 1980s than the rate of sales growth of either the chicken or hamburger segments. This increase is to a large degree reflective of a growing American acceptance of ethnic foods of all sorts. Table 3.14 shows the increase in demand for selected ethnic foods in supermarkets. Note the consistent pattern of rapid growth for all the markets identified.

Largest Players in Pizza Market

The eight largest factors in the pizza market are shown in Table 3.15. While at first glance the growth of the segment appears healthy, for several of the players the situation is one of profitless prosperity. Domino's, with a close second ranking within the segment, is privately held, so it does not disclose its financial results. However, according to one reliable published estimate (*Business Week,* Sept. 25, 1989, p. 46) the chain earned less than $8 million in net income in 1988 on revenues in excess of $1 billion. This represented a decline from peak net income of less than $16 million on revenue of about $500 million three years earlier.

More disturbing than the decline in profits in the face of exploding revenue growth, though, is the low absolute level of profits. Roughly 75 percent of the Domino's system is

Table 3.15

Systemwide Sales for Pizza Chains ($ million)

Chain	1987	1988	% Change	1989	% Change
Pizza Hut	2200	2800	27.3	3100	10.7
Domino's	1900	2300	21.1	2600	13.0
Little Caesar's	725	908	25.2	1200	32.2
Pizza Inn	310	330	6.5	344	4.2
Chuck E. Cheese	239	261	9.2	278	6.5
Round Table	250	250	0.0	265	6.0
Godfather's	261	245	−6.1	236	−3.7
Sbarro	116	154	32.8	200	29.9
Total	6001	7248	20.8	8223	13.5

franchised. With franchised store sales of $1.8 billion in 1988 at an estimated 4 percent royalty, Domino's royalty income should have been in the area of $75 million.

Since this revenue stream is almost pure profit, the company-owned Domino's stores must have lost a significant amount of money in order to bring overall corporate profitability down to the $8 million level. Indeed, it is the writer's understanding that at least half of the stores in the Domino's company-operated stable actually lose money.

Possible Sale of Domino's

In September 1989 the chain's founder and 97 percent owner, Mr. Thomas S. Monaghan, indicated that he was considering sale of the chain. Speculation in the press put the value of the chain at $350 million or even higher. The most suitable buyers seem to be foreign food companies that would not be deterred by the resulting goodwill amortization from such an acquisition, since accounting practices in many countries do not mandate such amortization.

In addition, however, the acquiror may have to be prepared to pay a still higher price in order to buy back a meaningful number of Domino's franchisees in order to create profitable enterprise. This scenario presupposes, of course, that an acquiror would be willing to buy into a looming confrontation in the pizza business between PepsiCo (worldwide sales in 1988 of $13.0 billion, net income of $762 million, and corporate advertising outlays of $853 million) and McDonald's (system sales worldwide in 1988 of $16.1 billion, net income of $646 million, and worldwide advertising expenditures in excess of $1 billion).

Difficulties for Pizza Operators

Not all of the rest of the pizza segment is prospering, either. Chuck E. Cheese, a combination of pizza parlor and children's entertainment center, went through bankruptcy in the early 1980s. The parent of Pizza Inn, Pantera Corp., filed for Chapter 11 protection on Sept. 22, 1989. Pillsbury recorded an after-tax charge of $141 million in the quarter ended February 1988 "to withdraw from several developmental or marginal restaurant chains, the largest being Godfather's Pizza; . . ." (The Pillsbury Company 1988 Annual Report, p. 2)

Little Caesar's, a privately owned firm in Farmington Hills, Michigan, is growing impressively. Its key is very low cost take-out units in inexpensive locations, with two-for-one specials emphasizing its low prices. So is Sbarro's, an Italian concept that operates principally in mall locations. Sbarro's pizza sales account for about half of its revenues. Its strategy is somewhat different from the other factors in the segment in that it features pizza by the slice rather than the whole pie. With one of the strongest balance sheets in the industry (equity equal to 72 percent of total assets as of July 1989), virtually no debt, and a high 23.3 percent return on beginning stockholders' equity in 1988, Sbarro's may be better equipped than any other pizza chain to weather a continuing escalation of competitive activity.

Pizza Hut's Role

What of the industry leader? Pizza Hut's profits increased 19 percent in 1987, 25 percent in 1988, and an estimated 32 percent in 1989. Plans call for an increase in the number of outlets to over 9000 (including delivery-only units) by 1993. Table 3.16 shows the growth in number of units for the largest competitors in the pizza market. Note the projected sharp slowdown in growth at Domino's, as well as the very rapid rate of expansion at Little Caesar's and Sbarro's.

Table 3.17 shows the sales per store for the various pizza concepts. Note the continuing strong increases at Pizza Hut, far higher than any of its competitors.

Table 3.16

Number of Pizza Chain Units

Chain	1987	1988	% Change	1989	% Change
Pizza Hut	5,394	5,707	5.8	6,050	6.0
Domino's	4,279	4,893	14.3	5,008	2.4
Little Caesar's	1,308	2,180	66.7	2,747	26.0
Pizza Inn	677	666	−1.6	758	13.8
Round Table	520	530	1.9	550	3.8
Godfather's	605	580	−4.1	523	−9.8
Sbarro	190	253	33.2	316	24.9
Chuck E. Cheese	262	258	−1.5	258	0.0
Total	13,235	15,067	13.8	16,210	7.6

Table 3.17

Sales per Unit for Pizza Chains ($ 000)

Chain	1987	1988	% Change	1989	% Change
Chuck E. Cheese	1037	1110	7.0	1187	6.9
Sbarro	605	619	2.3	657	6.1
Pizza Hut	490	520	6.1	572	10.0
Round Table	480	490	2.1	500	2.0
Pizza Inn	430	450	4.7	468	4.0
Domino's	432	439	1.6	441	0.5
Godfather's	410	414	1.0	440	6.3
Little Caesar's	398	421	5.8	428	1.7
Unweighted average	535	558	4.2	587	5.2

Mexican Segment's Growth

Table 3.18 summarizes the growth of franchised Mexican restaurants. The rapid increase in the segment as a whole is reflective of the growth of ethnic foods of all types illustrated in Table 3.15 above. In addition, Hispanics are growing as a percent of the overall population.

This segment is overwhelmingly dominated by a single operator, PepsiCo's Taco Bell. With 2878 units in operation in the United States at year-end 1988, the chain accounted for 56.2 percent of all franchised Mexican fast-food units. With sales in 1988 estimated at $1.6 billion, the chain accounted for half the sales of the segment. More astounding still, the chain's growth has accelerated dramatically off this very high base.

Sales per store in the Taco Bell system for the first nine months of 1989 soared 21 percent, bringing the chain's share of the segment to 65 percent. By year-end 1989, Taco Bell's share of the Mexican segment was projected by PepsiCo's management to be 70 percent. No other factor in the Mexican fast-food segment even approaches Taco Bell's success on a regional basis. Several chains based in Texas, such as privately owned Taco Cabana and its publicly traded clone, Two Pesos, have enjoyed limited success, but only in certain markets. (Taco Cabana successfully sued Two Pesos for copyright enfringement.)

Table 3.18

Franchised Mexican Restaurants

Year	Number of Stores	% Change	Sales per Store ($)	% Change	Total Sales ($000)	% Change
1973	1030		134,379		138,410	
1974	1157	12.3	153,641	14.3	177,763	28.4
1975	1462	26.4	186,448	21.4	272,587	53.3
1976	1652	13.0	187,114	0.4	309,113	13.4
1977	2147	30.0	230,574	23.2	495,043	60.1
1978	2329	8.5	258,641	12.2	602,376	21.7
1979	2477	6.4	280,385	8.4	694,514	15.3
1980	2774	12.0	316,699	13.0	878,523	26.5
1981	3002	8.2	356,331	12.5	1,069,712	21.8
1982	3059	1.9	411,263	15.4	1,258,054	17.6
1983	3469	13.4	484,770	17.9	1,681,668	33.7
1984	3774	8.8	559,911	15.5	2,113,104	25.7
1985	4125	9.3	581,820	3.9	2,400,009	13.6
1986	4460	8.1	647,868	11.4	2,889,490	20.4
1987	4733	6.1	650,535	0.4	3,078,981	6.6
1988	5119	8.2	652,911	0.4	3,342,253	8.6
Compound Annual Growth Rate (%)						
1973–88		11.3		11.1		23.6
1983–88		8.1		6.1		14.7

Source: National Restaurant Association, "Franchise Restaurants, a Statistical Appendix to Foodservice Trends," Washington, D.C., March 1988.

Seafood Industry

The fast-food seafood industry has enjoyed sales growth over the long run comparable to that of the Mexican and pizza industries, as indicated in Table 3.19. Note, however, that the rate of growth in both stores and total sales has slowed significantly in recent years. At first, this slowdown may seem surprising in light of the increase in fish consumption among health-conscious Americans. The drawback is that most of the seafood chains offer primarily deep-fried menu items, which are comparatively high in both calories and saturated fat.

The fast-food seafood segment, like the Mexican segment, is dominated by a single player. Unlike the Mexican segment, however, the dominant factor has not fared particularly well. Long John Silver's Seafood Shoppes, which are owned by Jerrico, Inc., achieved systemwide sales in fiscal 1988 (June) of $753 million, or nearly 45 percent of the sales of the seafood segment. With 1478 stores in operation at December 31, 1988, the chain accounted for 51 percent of all units in the fast-food seafood business.

Yet between 1981 and 1989 the chain showed only minimal profit growth, despite a 62 percent increase in systemwide sales. Essentially the cost to the chain of constantly

Table 3.19

Franchised Seafood Restaurants

Year	Number of Stores	% Change	Sales per Store ($)	% Change	Total Sales ($000)	% Change
1973	540		176,377		95,245	
1974	759	40.6	201,075	14.0	152,616	60.2
1975	1351	78.0	218,853	8.8	295,670	93.7
1976	1831	35.5	240,176	9.7	439,762	48.7
1977	2347	28.2	246,726	2.7	579,067	31.7
1978	2297	−2.1	245,462	−0.5	563,827	−2.6
1979	2383	3.7	324,689	32.3	773,736	37.2
1980	2290	−3.9	343,147	5.7	785,806	1.6
1981	2226	−2.8	399,142	16.3	888,491	13.1
1982	2221	−0.2	409,394	2.6	909,265	2.3
1983	2309	4.0	406,350	−0.7	938,261	3.2
1984	2320	0.5	463,115	14.0	1,074,426	14.5
1985	2423	4.4	500,599	8.1	1,212,951	12.9
1986	2518	3.9	541,585	8.2	1,363,710	12.4
1987	2684	6.6	551,306	1.8	1,479,704	8.5
1988	2917	8.7	579,081	5.0	1,689,180	14.2
Compound Annual Growth Rate (%)						
1973–88		11.9		8.2		21.1
1983–88		4.8		7.3		12.5

Source: National Restaurant Association, "Franchise Restaurants, a Statistical Appendix to Foodservice Trends," Washington, D.C., March 1988.

experimenting unsuccessfully with new menu items to broaden its product offering ate away at the profits of the system. As a result, profit margins at the store level narrowed from 19.5 percent of sales in the late 1970s to 15.5 percent by 1988.

The more successful chain in the segment is Captain D's, owned by Shoney's. With 600 units in place at the end of 1989 and sales per store in 1989 of $806,000 (compared with $540,000 for Long John Silver) Captain D's sales systemwide were $381 million, compared with an estimated $785 million for Long John Silver in that year.

Both seafood chains are heavily concentrated in a limited number of states. At year-end 1988 the Captain D's system included 85 stores in Georgia, 77 in Tennessee, and 59 in Alabama, with another 52 in Texas and 45 in Florida. These 318 stores in five southern states accounted for 54 percent of the units in the system. At June 30, 1988, Long John Silver's 202 stores in Texas, 115 in Ohio, 97 in Indiana, and 93 in Florida accounted for 507 stores, or 34.5 percent of the total. Neither chain had made significant penetration into the northeast or the west. In the case of Captain D's, this was because of a deliberate plan of controlled expansion in the southeast. In Long John Silver's case, the chain tried opening in both California and the northeast, but with very poor results.

Budget Steakhouses

Sales, number of units, and sales per store of budget steakhouses are shown in Tables 3.20 through 3.22. On the face of it, the segment appears unpromising. Americans' consumption of beef is on the decline, three out of the seven largest factors in the segment closed more stores than they opened in 1988, and sales per store for the segment's fastest growing and most profitable entry, Ryan's, declined in 1988.

Table 3.20

Systemwide Sales for Steakhouses ($ million)

Chain	1987	1988	% Change	1989	% Change
Sizzler	633	749	18.3	846	13.0
Ponderosa	651	696	6.9	710	2.0
Bonanza	458	571	24.7	620	8.6
Western Sizzlin	466	488	4.7	500	2.5
Golden Corral	429	456	6.3	465	2.0
Ryan's	185	236	27.6	295	25.0
Golden Corral	222	251	13.1	260	3.6
Total	3044	3447	13.2	3696	7.2

Table 3.21

Number of Steakhouse Units

Chain	1987	1988	% Change	1989	% Change
Ponderosa	661	695	5.1	720	3.6
Bonanza	600	612	2.0	652	6.5
Sizzler	547	587	7.3	628	7.0
Western Sizzlin	594	579	−2.5	550	−5.0
Golden Corral	514	505	−1.8	501	−0.8
Quincy's	215	211	−1.9	220	4.3
Ryan's	95	122	28.4	142	16.4
Total	3226	3311	2.6	3413	3.1

Table 3.22

Sales per Unit for Steakhouses ($ 000)

Chain	1987	1988	% Change	1989	% Change
Ryan's	1950	1930	−1.0	2080	7.8
Sizzler	1230	1360	10.6	1430	5.1
Quincy's	952	1179	23.8	1218	3.3
Ponderosa	985	1001	1.6	986	−1.5
Bonanza	918	940	2.4	975	3.7
Golden Corral	862	888	3.0	943	6.2
Western Sizzlin	790	774	−2.0	909	17.4
Unweighted average	1098	1153	5.0	1220	5.8

Perhaps the most interesting aspect of the budget steakhouses is who owns them. Ponderosa is owned by Metromedia, which in turn is owned by billionaire John Kluge. In September, 1989 Ponderosa announced plans to acquire Bonanza, creating nearly a 34 percent share of the market segment overnight. Moreover, one month earlier Metromedia had announced the acquisition of Steak & Ale from the leveraged buyout group at Citicorp. Clearly, Kluge has a vision of the future of selling beef in the 1990s, and given his splendid investment track record it is difficult to gainsay him. Kluge is, according to *Forbes* magazine, the richest man in America.

Table 3.23

Systemwide Sales Dinner Houses ($ million)

Chain	1987	1988	% Change	1989	% Change
Red Lobster	977	1050	7.5	1200	14.3
Bennigan's	449	455	1.3	459	0.9
Chi-Chi's	410	431	5.1	422	−2.1
T.G.I. Friday's	364	383	5.2	410	7.0
El Torito	402	386	−4.0	400	3.6
Chili's	196	260	32.7	331	27.3
Olive Garden	75	171	128.0	300	75.4
Ground Round	216	259	19.9	300	15.8
Steak & Ale	256	221	−13.7	215	−2.7
Stuart Anderson's Black Angus	187	187	0.0	199	6.4
Houlihan's	164	180	9.8	199	10.6
Total	3696	3983	7.8	4435	11.3

Table 3.23 shows the sales of the largest dinner house chains. While none of these operations serves food that could, even by the most liberal definition, be classified as "fast food," they provide an interesting contrast to the fast-food operators. The most successful are clearly two chains owned by General Mills, Red Lobster seafood restaurants and Olive Garden Italian restaurants. Both enjoy high and rising levels of sales per store, segment domination (at least among chains) and rapid expansion in the number of units in their systems. More than any previous marriage between the cash cows in the packaged foods industry and the capital-hungry, rapidly expanding restaurant chains, General Mills appears to have created an extraordinary success story. General Mills experienced its own difficulties in fast food, having experimented in 1976 with a fast-food offshoot of Red Lobster called Hannahan's, which eventually closed.

Other chains in the dinner house segment provide mixed results. Chili's, under the direction of Steak & Ale founder Norman Brinker, appears to be the most successful entrant in the adult hamburger segment that so many others have tried to capture. Black Angus, El Torito, and Bennigan's are not prospering, however.

Number of units and sales per store are indicated in Tables 3.24 and 3.25, respectively.

Table 3.24

Number of Dinner House Units

Chain	1987	1988	% Change	1989	% Change
Red Lobster	392	402	2.6	441	9.7
Bennigan's	206	214	3.9	222	3.7
Ground Round	190	212	11.6	218	2.8
Chi-Chi's	197	196	−0.5	203	3.6
El Torito	191	178	−6.8	182	2.2
Chili's	114	146	28.1	170	16.4
Steak & Ale	178	162	−9.0	159	−1.9
T.G.I. Friday's	128	133	3.9	153	15.0
Olive Garden	52	92	76.9	144	56.5
Stuart Anderson's Black Angus	85	85	0.0	86	1.2
Houlihan's	62	64	3.2	68	6.3
Total	1795	1884	5.0	2046	8.6

Table 3.25

Sales per Unit for Dinner Houses ($ 000)

Chain	1987	1988	% Change	1989	% Change
T.G.I. Friday's	2900	3000	3.4	3200	6.7
Houlihan's	2690	2850	5.9	2990	4.9
Red Lobster	2450	2650	8.2	2800	5.7
Olive Garden	2500	2600	4.0	2700	3.8
Stuart Anderson's Black Angus	2200	2200	0.0	2300	4.5
Chi-Chi's	2045	2173	6.3	2250	3.5
El Torito	2080	2090	0.5	2220	6.2
Bennigan's	2200	2200	0.0	2100	−4.5
Chili's	1950	2000	2.6	2100	5.0
Ground Round	1150	1300	13.0	1400	7.7
Steak & Ale	1400	1300	−7.1	1300	0.0
Unweighted average	2142	2215	3.4	2305	4.1

Chapter 4

The Economics of Fast-Food Restaurants

Sales Productivity at the Store Level

The first step in evaluating the economics of the chain restaurant industry is to explore profitability at the store level. From there, the analyst can evaluate the impact of individual stores on the income statement of the operator, whether franchisor or franchisee, and proceed to model the corporate income statement. But proper analysis must begin with an understanding of the economics of the individual unit.

Evaluation begins with the measure of sales per store. Such a figure, however, is meaningless without giving consideration to the cost of constructing the unit. Obviously, a 6000-square-foot store costing $1.8 million to construct should generate higher sales than a 600-square-foot building costing $575,000. But how much more?

Table 4.1 illustrates the wide divergence in size of store for fifteen major restaurant chains. The concepts range from the tiny double drive-through units of Rally's to the huge dinner houses operated by Old Spaghetti Warehouse, which are not fast-food units. Among true fast-food operators, McDonald's, with its 3700-square-foot building, generally occupies the largest facilities.

In terms of sales per square foot, a wide range also exists. Table 4.2 shows the sales per square foot for the same group of restaurant chains. Rally's, with its drive-through-only format, has, by design, the highest level of sales per square foot. Generally, the chicken chains and some of the Italian concepts rank lower in this regard.

A still more useful analytical approach is to relate sales levels to the dollars of capital required to build the store: all else equal, a higher ratio suggests a more successful operation. Table 4.3 shows the total cost of building restaurants for twenty-five different restaurant chains, along with their most recent sales volumes and the ratio of sales to

Table 4.1

Square Footage of Restaurant Unit

Chain	Area (ft^2)
Old Spaghetti Warehouse	15,000
Luby's	10,500
Cracker Barrel	9,700
Cooker	7,800
Chili's	6,000
McDonald's	3,700
Hardee's	3,100
Sbarro's	3,000
Carl's Junior	2,800
Burger King	2,500
El Pollo Loco	2,250
Popeye's	2,000
TCBY	1,300
Church's	1,200
Rally's	600
Unweighted average	4,763
Unweighted average, fast food only	2,245

Table 4.2

Sales per Square Foot

Chain	Sales ($)
Rally's	1,530
McDonald's	431
Cooker	410
Chili's	375
Carl's Junior	375
El Pollo Loco	367
Burger King	334
Hardee's	333
Cracker Barrel	254
Popeye's	225
Luby's	224
Sbarro's	219
TCBY	172
Old Spaghetti Warehouse	160
Church's	125
Unweighted average	369

Table 4.3

Sales and Capital Costs of Major Chains

Chain	Cost of Land, Building, & Equipment ($)	Sales per Store ($)	Ratio of Sales to Capital Cost
Chi-Chi's	1,200,000	2,334,000	1.95
Cooker	1,800,000	3,200,000	1.78
Shoney's	1,032,000	1,739,000	1.69
Rally's	575,000	918,000	1.60
Popeye's	435,000	671,000	1.54
Captain D's	580,000	806,000	1.39
Old Spaghetti Warehouse	1,733,000	2,402,713	1.39
Cracker Barrel	1,900,000	2,460,000	1.29
Sizzler	1,450,000	1,800,000	1.24
Chili's	1,850,000	2,250,000	1.22
Ryan's	1,800,000	2,184,000	1.21
Perkins	1,075,000	1,230,000	1.14
Carl Karcher	1,051,000	1,200,000	1.14
McDonald's	1,425,000	1,596,000	1.12
Burger King	960,000	1,002,000	1.04
Bob Evans Farms	1,350,000	1,395,000	1.03
TCBY	218,125	224,000	1.03
Church's Chicken	400,000	375,497	0.94
Wendy's	846,000	793,000	0.94
Homestyle Buffet	1,617,500	1,500,000	0.93
Pancho's	1,400,000	1,200,000	0.86
Taco Bell	825,000	589,000	0.71
Long John Silver	725,000	501,355	0.69
Kentucky Fried Chicken	925,000	597,000	0.65
Pizza Hut	875,000	520,000	0.59

capital cost. These data are based on the results of company-operated stores in the most recently available fiscal year.

Lease Adjustments

This calculation is straightforward for chains that open free-standing units, where the costs of land, building, equipment, and signs are identifiable. More troublesome are cases where the normal economic unit is not a free-standing unit, but a location in a shopping center or urban site where the restaurant operates in leased facilities. The notion of land costs in a case where the concept uses primarily mall locations is not meaningful.

To address this problem, the analyst can utilize a factor that capitalizes a leased unit's rent in order to make it comparable to a free-standing unit. In the accompanying table, then, the typical rental for Sbarro's, Homestyle Buffet, and TCBY has been multiplied by a capitalization factor of 7.5 in order to provide a basis for comparison with the other concepts.

Data Weakness

A caveat is in order in examining the ratios. The data for capital costs are for the most recent available date, as are the sales per store. However, the sales per store for newly opened units may be quite different from the sales for the existing system of restaurants. For example, the ratio of the average sales of all stores in the Kentucky Fried Chicken system to the cost of erecting a new store is .65. A newly constructed Kentucky Fried Chicken store, however, typically achieves annual volumes in excess of $1 million (as do the other two concepts owned by PepsiCo: Taco Bell and Pizza Hut).

Comparing the current cost of contruction with the sales of units that may, in some cases, be more than twenty years old, distorts the comparisons. Unfortunately, chains generally do not make available data on the sales results of new units alone, but rather provide a blended average that includes all stores, old and new.

High Sales Productivity of Dinner Houses

The data in the accompanying table, then, can best serve as an approximation of the relative sales productivity of the concepts involved. Note that the highest sales per dollar of capital invested are either in dinner houses or in double drive-through concepts, the two extreme opposites in terms of the underlying strategy: one tries to offer the customer the best possible dining environment, the other offers no dining environment at all. The presumption, then, is that the attempts to offer indoor seating by the fast-food chains are not economically efficient uses of their capital.

Unit-Level Profitability

Sales per dollar of invested capital is not, by itself, a measure of profitability. Some concepts, by virtue of low food costs, can achieve satisfactory profitability despite low capital turnover. Hence, it is necessary to identify profit margins at the store level as the next step in analyzing unit economics. Table 4.4 ranks twenty-seven restaurant chains according to their profit margins at the store level.

The data in these calculations suffer from an imperfection grounded in the way that various chains finance their stores. A chain that finances its restaurants with corporate debt will normally not assign the interest costs from these borrowings to the individual store, whereas a chain that leases its units normally includes its lease costs in store-level operating expenses. Hence, the profitability at the store level of PepsiCo's units (Taco Bell, Pizza Hut, and Kentucky Fried Chicken) is slightly overstated compared with Sbarro's, which normally leases its units. This is a variation on the problem of comparability already alluded to in analyzing sales-capital ratios.

As in the preceding analysis, all of the data here are based on the results of company-operated stores and thus do *not* include franchise fees in the margin calculation. In

Table 4.4

Store-Level Margins

Chain	Margin (%)
Uno's	25.2
Old Spaghetti Warehouse	21.8
Ryan's	19.2
Sbarro's	18.6
Pizza Hut	18.0
McDonald's	17.7
Cracker Barrel	17.6
Burger King	16.9
Hardee's	16.2
Carl Karcher	15.5
Long John Silver	15.5
Pancho's	15.5
TCBY	15.2
Cooker	15.0
Luby's	15.0
Taco Bell	15.0
Homestyle Buffet	14.7
Chili's	14.0
Sizzler	13.9
Perkins	13.5
Shoney's	13.2
Kentucky Fried Chicken	13.0
Captain D's	12.0
Wendy's	11.0
El Pollo Loco	10.0
Rally's	9.0
Dunkin' Donuts	−3.6

practice, the margins for most franchised operators exceed those of company-owned units, somewhat mitigating the effect of taking a fee out of the franchisee's results.

Observe that margins generally fall within a relatively narrow range, with the dinner house concepts and some of the pizza chains clustered near the top. Note, too, the unsatisfactory results of the Dunkin' Donuts concept. In this case, the results apply only to a relatively small number of stores. The company-owned units in the Dunkin' Donuts system serve more as a laboratory for experimentation for new products than as a true indication of the underlying profitability of the concept. Moreover, in certain cases the company-operated stores may reflect action by the franchisor to reacquire ailing franchised units, again artificially depressing the results.

Overall Profitability Calculations

The sales-capital calculation and the margin calculation can be combined to provide an indication of profit per dollar of invested capital. These data are shown in Table 4.5. Note that this calculation does not precisely equal the cash flow return on invested capital, because the profit margin data include depreciation as a charge against earnings.

Table 4.5

Profit per Dollar of Invested Capital

Chain	Sales/ Capital Cost	Operating Margin (%)	Profit/ Capital Cost (%)
Old Spaghetti Warehouse	1.39	21.8	30.3
Cooker	1.78	15.0	26.7
Ryan's	1.21	19.2	23.2
Cracker Barrel	1.29	17.6	22.7
Shoney's	1.69	13.2	22.3
McDonald's	1.12	17.7	19.8
Carl Karcher	1.14	15.5	17.7
Burger King	1.04	16.9	17.6
Sizzler	1.24	13.9	17.2
Chili's	1.22	14.0	17.1
Captain D's	1.39	12.0	16.7
TCBY	1.03	15.2	15.7
Perkins	1.14	13.5	15.4
Rally's	1.60	9.0	14.4
Homestyle Buffet	0.93	14.7	13.7
Long John Silver	0.69	15.5	10.7
Taco Bell	0.71	15.0	10.7
Pizza Hut	0.59	18.0	10.6
Wendy's	0.94	11.0	10.3
Kentucky Fried Chicken	0.65	13.0	8.5

How have the economics at the store level changed over time? Table 4.6 shows the sales/capital cost ratio for a selected group of chains in the late 1970s and early 1980s compared with their current results. Observe the general deterioration in this series over the past decade, reflecting the need to acquire ever-more-expensive locations in order to maintain sales per store.

Table 4.7 shows the profit margins today compared with those of a decade ago. Here the data show virtually no deterioration, suggesting that pricing policies have been adequate to maintain margins even as capital productivity has flagged.

In analyzing the underlying source of margin stability, we shall see that lower food costs as a percent of sales have generally offset increases in capital and other costs, thereby

Table 4.6

Historical Sales per Dollar of Capital

Chain (Date)	Sales ($)	Capital Cost ($)	Sales/ Capital Cost Decade Ago	Current Sales/ Capital Cost
Burger King (5/81)	748,000	790,000	0.95	1.04
Church's (12/80)	463,000	300,000	1.54	
Hardee's (10/78)	410,000	480,000	0.85	
Jerrico (6/81)	475,000	400,000	1.19	0.69
Kentucky Fried Chicken (6/81)	427,000	475,000	0.90	0.65
McDonald's (12/80)	942,000	650,000	1.45	1.12
Pizza Hut (12/81)	400,000	375,000	1.07	0.59
Wendy's (12/80)	627,100	529,000	1.19	0.94
Unweighted average			1.14	0.84

Table 4.7

Historical Operating Margins

Chain (Date)	Store-Level Margin Decade Ago (%)	Current Store-Level Margin (%)
Burger King (5/81)	10.5	16.9
Church's (12/80)	21.0	
Hardee's (10/78)	8.5	16.2
Long John Silver (6/81)	19.5	15.5
Kentucky Fried Chicken (6/81)	10.0	13.0
McDonald's (12/80)	16.9	17.7
Pizza Hut (12/81)		18.0
Wendy's (12/80)	21.0	11.0
Unweighted average	15.3	15.5

allowing margins to remain constant. The implication of the lower food costs, however, is that the consumer is not being offered as good a price-value relationship now as was true a decade ago.

Table 4.8 shows the growth in sales per store over the past decade. The unusually high growth of Hardee's largely reflects the chain's great success with its breakfast program, which now accounts for 39 percent of total sales, compared with only a minor contribution ten years ago.

Table 4.9 shows the growth in costs of land, building, and equipment for the same group of chains. Note that with the exception of Burger King and Hardee's, all chains have shown faster growth in the cost of constructing a new unit than in growth in sales per store. This point simply further illustrates the trend already indicated in Table 4.6.

Table 4.8

Sales Growth Over Time

Chain (Date)	Sales Decade Ago ($)	Current Sales ($)	Compound Annual Growth (%)
Burger King (5/81)	748,000	1,002,000	4.3
Church's (12/80)	463,000	375,497	−2.3
Hardee's (10/78)	410,000	1,000,000	9.3
Long John Silver (6/81)	475,000	501,355	0.8
Kentucky Fried Chicken (6/81)	427,000	597,000	4.9
McDonald's (12/80)	942,000	1,596,000	6.8
Pizza Hut (12/81)	400,000	520,000	3.8
Wendy's (12/80)	627,100	793,000	3.0
Unweighted average			3.8

Table 4.9

Growth in Cost of Restaurants

Chain (Date)	Capital Cost Decade Ago ($)	Current Capital Cost ($)	Compound Annual Growth (%)
Burger King (5/81)	790,000	960,000	2.8
Church's (12/80)	300,000	400,000	3.2
Hardee's (10/78)	480,000		
Long John Silver (6/81)	400,000	725,000	8.9
Kentucky Fried Chicken (6/81)	475,000	925,000	10.0
McDonald's (12/80)	650,000	1,425,000	10.3
Pizza Hut (12/81)	375,000	875,000	12.9
Wendy's (12/80)	529,000	846,000	6.0
Unweighted average			7.7

Table 4.10

Return on Investment (ROI) Over Time

Chain (Date)	Store-Level ROI Decade Ago (%)	Current Store-Level ROI (%)
Burger King (5/81)	10.0	17.6
Church's (12/80)	32.3	
Hardee's (10/78)	7.2	
Long John Silver (6/81)	23.2	10.7
Kentucky Fried Chicken (6/81)	9.0	8.4
McDonald's (12/80)	24.5	19.8
Pizza Hut (12/81)		10.7
Wendy's (12/80)	25.0	10.3
Unweighted average	18.7	12.9

Table 4.10 compares the profitability of concepts today versus a decade ago. The decline in sales per dollar of invested capital, combined with stable margins, means that overall profitability has eroded significantly.

Drive-Through Windows and Sales Growth

At present, nearly 7000 McDonald's stores have drive-through windows. Sales through the drive-through windows have gradually risen in recent years, totaling 48 percent of sales in 1986, 50 percent in 1987, and 51 percent in 1988 for those stores that have the facility. The obvious attraction of the drive-through, from the standpoint of profitability, is that it requires less square footage in the building to accommodate customers than does the installation of indoor seating. Some observers have hypothesized that the mix of sales through the drive-through windows is less profitable, since customers could order only sandwiches and fries at McDonald's and purchase soft drinks (which carry a higher profit margin for McDonald's) at a vending machine or convenience store. In fact, this is not the case, and the mix of product sold through the windows at McDonald's is similar to that sold inside the restaurants.

Once McDonald's began the installation of indoor seating in its units beginning in 1968, the profitability of such a strategy became an article of faith within the fast-food industry and most of McDonald's competitors began emulating the practice.

Wendy's founder R. David Thomas had a different insight, however.

I thought, "Where is all this business going from the drive-in business? The drive-in used to be real popular and there are more cars on the road but there are less drive-ins." We tried a pick-up window years ago . . . With about 100 different items and it didn't work. It was really a super failure. But I thought, "With a limited menu I don't understand why we can't do it. If it doesn't work, all we do is just never open the window." That was the downside and maybe it cost us $1,500 to open up the pick-up window. (*Endless Shakeout*, p. 87)

Early Success of Wendy's

The success of the drive-through window was so clear at Wendy's that most major factors in the industry emulated it, including McDonald's, Kentucky Fried Chicken, and Burger King, all of which typically generated something over 50 percent of their sales through the drive-through window. The obvious advantage of the drive-through window is the reduced requirements for square footage within the building with an attendant gain in sales per dollar of invested capital. Indeed, part of Wendy's superior profitability in the mid-1970s relative to its competitors certainly reflected the superior sales productivity of the drive-through.

Capacity of Drive-Throughs

The hourly capacity for a drive-through window at McDonald's is 144 cars, or one every 25 seconds. At present, McDonald's is beginning to install dual drive-through windows in many of its stores. These facilities, which are not to be confused with the double drive-through, or drive-in-only concepts discussed below, increase the efficiency of the operation by giving customers the choice of two lanes from which to order, while picking up their food at a single window. The newer facilities increase the hourly capacity of the drive-throughs to 204 cars per hour. As of late 1989, 400 McDonald's stores featured the dual drive-throughs.

The Emergence of Double Drive-Throughs

Not until the mid-1980s, however, did fast-food visionaries conceive of the logical extension of the drive-through concept: making the store completely drive-through and eliminating indoor seating altogether. This was not a return to the McDonald's concept of the early days, since those early McDonald's units required customers to stand in line at a window and wait to be served, then carry the food back to their cars. Here the idea was to serve customers in their cars.

Early Prototypes

Several entrepreneurs, including former Minnie Pearl chairman John Jay Hooker, began to experiment with a 100 percent drive-through model. Hooker's experiment, Hooker Hamburgers, was based on the notion that a drive-through could be combined with a miniature convenience store, offering take-out fast food combined with the fastest-selling items in convenience stores, cigarettes and beer.

Rally's Emergence

Another veteran of an earlier fast-food chain, however, became the most successful developer of the new concept: the double drive-through. In January of 1985, James A.

Table 4.11

Rally's Financial Profile (Fiscal Year ended June 1989)

	1985	1986	1987	1988	1989
Systemwide sales ($ million)	0.128	1.286	9.762	55.201	102.168
% Change		904.7	659.1	465.5	85.1
Number of stores	1	4	22	76	148
% Change		300.0	450.0	245.5	94.7
Sales per store* ($ million)	—	—	0.855	1.012	0.918
% Change				18.4	−9.3

*Stores open one full year.

Patterson, the originator of Long John Silver for Jerrico, opened the first Rally's restaurant in Louisville, Kentucky. By August of 1989 a total of 161 Rally's were operating in 21 states, including 25 in Indiana, 18 in Kentucky, 17 in Florida, and 15 in Louisiana. An additional 13 were open in Ohio and Arizona, 12 in Detroit, and 8 in California, with the remainder scattered throughout the country (see Table 4.11).

The Rally's concept is to generate very high sales per dollar of invested capital by offering customers a hamburger that is priced about 30 percent below that of the major chains. The high food cost as a percent of sales will result in a comparatively low profit margin, but the level of sales per dollar of invested capital allows a satisfactory return on investment. The menu is kept deliberately limited, with the result that the customer is normally served within 45 seconds of pulling up to the drive-through window.

Rally's units are open 12 to 14 hours per day, seven days a week for lunch, dinner, and late-night snacks. Following a reorganization of the system that provided for the acquisition of certain franchisees upon completion of the firm's initial public offering in the fall of 1989, approximately 40 percent of the system's restaurants were company-owned and operated. Plans call for 90 percent of the company's future expansion to be accounted for by franchisees, however.

Management of the company is experienced for a comparatively new operation, with the chairman and CEO of the company being Richard Sherman, former president and chief operating officer of Kentucky Fried Chicken.

James M. Trotter III and William E. Trotter II serve as directors of the company. The Trotter brothers were among the first franchisees of Burger King in 1962 and eventually went on to become principal owners and senior executives of a series of highly profitable publicly held franchisees. Patterson's direct involvement with the company is limited because of a dispute with Wendy's, of which Patterson is a franchisee.

High Sales Productivity

Since a Rally's prototype required less than half of the acreage and one-quarter the building size of the larger hamburger operators, the sales per dollar of capital cost and sales per

Table 4.12

Rally's and McDonald's Compared

	Rally's	McDonald's
Sales per store ($)	918,000	1,596,000
Sales per square foot ($)	1,530	431
Sales per $ of capital ($)	1.60	1.12

square foot are truly staggering. As shown in Table 4.12, Rally's sales per square foot are nearly four times that of McDonald's!

At the same time, the strategy of cutting food prices below that of the established factors produces a food cost nearly 8 percentage points higher than that of McDonald's. As a result, the profit margin at the store level is less than half that of McDonald's. The net effect of the low margin and high turnover is to produce a pretax return on invested capital similar to that of McDonald's, though somewhat below that of some of the other new concepts of the 1980s.

Rally's Franchising Strategy

Franchising is central to Rally's growth strategy, and to that degree the franchisor's strategy of developing high sales per store is, of course, a highly effective one. Rally's system has forty-three franchisees who have cumulatively operated more than 1000 units as franchisees of Burger King, Wendy's, Arby's, Kentucky Fried Chicken, Domino's Pizza, and Long John Silver's.

The Rally's franchising system is one of territorial licensing, with a $5000 nonrefundable fee payable to the franchisor upon agreement for a territorial license, $15,000 upon commencement of construction, and a 4.0 percent royalty coupled with a 4.0 percent advertising requirement. Terms are typically for fifteen years.

In-N-Out Burger's Quality Offering

Ironically, the Rally's approach to drive-throughs, with its emphasis on very fast service and low pricing, while likely to be the model for explosive growth in the 1990s, may not be the most profitable formula. That distinction goes to the original California drive-through, In-N-Out Burger. Opened in 1948, In-N-Out's founder, Harry Snyder, hit upon the idea of having customers order through a two-way speaker rather than be waited on by a carhop.

The In-N-Out system, which today numbers fifty-five restaurants, is in some ways an anachronism in the fast-food world of the 1990s. The menu is extremely limited, including only hamburgers, cheeseburgers, fries, soft drinks, and shakes. Prices average about 15 percent more than at McDonald's, and since every hamburger is cooked to order, each order takes 12 minutes to be served.

So strong is the demand for these slowly prepared sandwiches (the term "fast food" seems almost inappropriate) that In-N-Out stores achieve annual volumes of $1.7 million, or nearly double that of Rally's! The chain's profit margins are probably lower than at

McDonald's, since the chain pays its starting help $6.00 per hour, or one-third more than at McDonald's stores in the same area.

In-N-Out's Profitability

However, the very high capital turnover almost surely means that In-N-Out enjoys the highest level of return on invested capital in the fast-food industry. (Precise data are not available because the company remains privately held by the Snyder family.) (*Forbes*, July 24, 1989)

At least five other double drive-through chains have made it through the initial start-up phase. Central Park, based in Chattanooga, Tennessee, and managed by a former 7-Eleven executive operates more than forty units in Tennessee, Alabama, Georgia, and Arkansas. Fast Track, headquartered in Baton Rouge, operates twenty stores, all but one in Louisiana, and is run by people with backgrounds at McDonald's and Burger King. Zipp's in St. Louis and Snapps in Columbus, Ohio, each operate about ten stores, while Checkers in Mobile, Alabama, has plans for over thirty stores in the near future.

The key for these operators, assuming success of their concepts at the store level, will be to gain access to the public equity markets by taking advantage of the excitement generated by the initial public offering of Rally's, before a shakeout occurs in the segment. (*Nation's Restaurant News*, August 29, 1988)

The risk in the double drive-through segment does not seem to lie with the established competitors striking back. The only weapon available to the older chains would be to cut price, which would no doubt put great pressure on the upstart drive-through specialists but would also serve to destroy the profit margins of the dominant existing players. An analogy might be found in the telephone industry, where the cost to AT&T of cutting price against MCI was always prohibitive because of the inevitable damage to the profits of the Bell system. It proved cheaper, at least in the short run, to allow a new entrant to gain two or three points of market share rather than to destroy margins for the established factor with over 90 percent market share.

The more troublesome considerations are the possibility of environmental legislation, particularly in California, serving to outlaw drive-through operations, as well as questions about the fundamental profitability of the concepts. While the sales-to-capital ratios are most impressive, the profit margins, as discussed above, are not. If greater recognition through critical mass and advertising serve to hold or expand Rally's margins slightly, the chain's expansion prospects are very bright indeed. On the other hand, the current margins are low enough that there is little room for error. A shock in commodity costs, for example, could put far more pressure on an operator with 9 percent margins than one with 18 percent margins.

Further, the profitability calculations shown between McDonald's and Rally's are for company-owned stores only. Once a 4.0 percent royalty fee is subtracted, the return on capital as well as the margin for error for the franchisee are reduced considerably.

The double drive-through segment has been characterized by easy entry and quick exit. The segment, according to McDonald's director of market research, Donald Lord, began in Nashville in 1987, and quickly involved eight different chains. By the fall of 1989, all were out of business. According to a statement in September, 1989 by McDonald's senior executive vice president and chief marketing officer Paul Schrage, "We can't even pick them up on our tracking studies."

McDonald's Response

In response to the marketing challenge raised by the new, inexpensively positioned double drive-through entries, McDonald's has begun to cut prices in selected markets. In Kansas City, for example, two McDonald's stores that bracketed a Rally's unit reportedly cut price and drove the store out of business. The same thing allegedly occurred in stores near New Orleans, though Rally's management denies this.

The important thing is that McDonald's recognizes the challenge. By the summer of 1989, McDonald's had slashed prices on its smallest sandwiches in many California markets from $0.75 (hamburgers) and $0.85 (cheeseburgers) to $0.59 and $0.69, respectively, to meet the challenge from Rally's.

Real Estate and the Economics of Remodeling

McDonald's employs 200 people in its U.S. real estate department, with an additional 100 in its five largest foreign markets. In addition to such obvious criteria as income data and traffic flow, McDonald's utilizes more subtle data, for example, school enrollments, in its site selection process.

Importance of Highway Locations

Locations on major highways, while not traditionally a major focus for McDonald's site selection, have become more important in recent years. McDonald's market research has found that 15 percent of all cars stop every 15 miles on U.S. highways, providing an active market for stores located on major roads. In this context, it is intriguing that Cracker Barrel Old Country Stores, which operates almost exclusively on interstate highways, has enjoyed growth in profit approaching 25 percent annually over the past five years.

Ownership versus Leasing

In 1988 McDonald's owned 6320 or 60 percent of its sites, up from 4494, or 58 percent, five years earlier. This percentage is widely different, however, in different regions. McDonald's owns 68 percent of its sites in the United States, while owning a mere 35 percent in foreign markets.

McDonald's Foreign Real Estate Strategy

The company's strategy for foreign markets normally involves initially opening stores in urban locations, where the real estate cannot be purchased. The reason for this is to gain maximum exposure at what the company refers to as "billboard locations." Only as the chain spreads gradually to the suburbs can sites be purchased readily.

Trends in Land Costs

Part of the deterioration in profitability of the large, traditional fast-food operators in the 1980s has been a result of inflation in land and building costs without an attendant increase in sales per store. Table 4.13 shows the cost of real estate for McDonald's units opened since 1971. Note the relatively benign level of inflation in land cost in the early 1970s; between 1971 and 1978, for example, the rate of increase was only 3.5 percent annually. The experience for the 1980s has involved a far higher level of increase. More importantly, as we shall see, McDonald's sales per store in the 1970s grew more rapidly than did the inflation in its building costs. The opposite has occurred in the 1980s.

One result has been that McDonald's income statement in recent years has been penalized by higher capital (i.e., rent and depreciation) charges. The depreciation charge does not directly reflect higher real estate costs, since of course land is not depreciated.

Table 4.13

McDonald's Land Costs

Year	Land Costs per Unit ($ 000)	% Change
1971	101	
1972	98	−3.0
1973	101	3.1
1974	121	19.8
1975	121	0.0
1976	115	−5.0
1977	123	7.0
1978	127	3.3
1979	135	6.3
1980	142	5.2
1981	155	9.2
1982	163	5.2
1983	187	14.7
1983 (new series)	230	
1984	258	12.2
1985	318	23.3
1986	323	1.6
1987	357	10.5
1988	415	16.2

Compound Annual Growth Rate (%)

1971–88		8.7
1971–83		5.3
1983–88		12.5

Note: Data prior to 1975 include Canadian and U.S. stores. Subsequent data are U.S. stores only. "New series" in 1983 includes, for the first time, large or unusual sites.

What has happened is that in order to open new stores at sales levels comparable to those of existing units, McDonald's is being forced into far more expensive sites.

Economics of Remodeling

Among the most successful tools for building sales via remodeling, McDonald's has found, is the construction of playgrounds for children. The most recent development is the "soft playground," which is actually a variation of a concept originally introduced in the late 1970s by Pizza Time Theaters. In this playground the child is free to jump, crawl, and play ball in an enclosed, safe area that is, to all practical effects, childproof.

The cost of installation of such a playground in an existing McDonald's unit averages $50,000. Incremental traffic produced by the facility is typically 7.0 percent. On a sales increase of $110,000, the incremental profits, assuming that labor costs are entirely variable, would be $47,000 (food, paper, and labor costs at McDonald's company-operated stores averaged 56.7 percent of sales in 1988).

In fact, labor costs are fixed to some degree, so the marginal profitability is probably even higher. Clearly, the return on the investment in remodeling for McDonald's, in those stores that can accommodate the playground, approaches 100 percent. This kind of improvement in profitability can sometimes be achieved simply through refurbishment and remodeling of units. In Phoenix, for example, Denny's spent an average of $165,000 per store to remodel twenty-three restaurants. Average unit volume increased between 8 and 9 percent in the market.

Store Relocations

The economic rewards for relocating stores in nearby sites with better locations can be enormous. Between 1983 and 1988 McDonald's relocated sixty stores. These units, in the aggregate, recorded sales increases of 45 percent, or $27 million. Some of the individual store's results were far more dramatic. A unit in Mansfield, Ohio, for example, was achieving annual volume of $835,000, far below the chain's average. In the first year after relocation, the store's volume was $1,854,000, rose to $1,943,000 the second year, and reached $2,045,000 in the third.

Even rebuilding newer facilities on the same site can often provide very positive returns. Between 1983 and 1988 McDonald's rebuilt 122 stores on existing sites. In the first year after rebuilding, these stores averaged 28 percent higher volumes than before. An older McDonald's store in Topeka, Kansas, for example, had been constructed in 1967. The facility suffered from limited parking and inadequate space to install a drive-through window. McDonald's elected to spend $160,000 on additional land and $302,000 on leasehold improvements, including installation of a drive-through. The store achieved a 34 percent gain in volume the first year after the expansion, followed by a 16 percent increase in the second year and a 4 percent gain in the third. By 1988, the store was achieving above-average sales of $1.8 million annually.

So compelling are the investments in remodeling that McDonald's has ramped up the rate of rebuilding from twenty in 1985 to sixty-two in 1988 to a projected level of eighty-five in 1989. In 1988 McDonald's spent $400 million in remodeling existing units. This figure is in addition to amounts spent by its franchisees in their stores.

Investments in Automation

By late 1989 McDonald's had installed electric clam-shell grills in 3400 of its 11,000 restaurants. These units allowed burgers to cook on both sides at once, thereby improving speed of delivery. Not content with this tool, however, McDonald's began to experiment with clam-shells that were gas-powered, in order to reduce energy costs. McDonald's found that the installation of its in-store processing computer system cut 40 hours off the weekly paperwork of its store managers.

Labor Costs

The central argument of this book is that a growing labor shortage has forced fast-food chains to raise prices in order to offset rising labor costs. This pricing practice, in turn, has caused the relative value to the consumer of eating out to deteriorate. This erosion in perceived value, in turn, has caused restaurant patrons to dine out less frequently. Finally, the shrinkage in the market has accelerated an overstored or saturated condition.

Size of Labor Force

The restaurant industry is notable in three respects as an employer: it is among the largest employers of any industry, has a young demographic profile, and it pays the least. Table 4.14 shows the total number of employees for the ten largest nonagricultural industries

Table 4.14

Total Employment of Ten Largest Nonagricultural Industries

Industry	Total Employees (000)			CAGR* 1980–87 (%)
	1980	1985	1987	
Health services	5278	6299	6828	3.7
Eating & drinking places	4626	5709	6127	4.1
Food stores	2384	2775	2957	3.1
Special trade contractors	2246	2628	2904	3.7
General merchandise stores	2245	2324	2432	1.1
Electrical equipment mfg.	2091	2197	2084	0.0
Transportation equipment mfg.	1900	1980	2048	1.1
Machinery mfg.	2494	2174	2023	−2.9
Banking	1571	1706	1734	1.4
Food processing	1708	1603	1624	−0.7

*Compound annual growth rate.

ranked by total employment. Definitional questions abound in this area, but the health services category includes 1,288,000 persons engaged in nursing at personal care facilities in addition to 3,154,000 persons employed at hospitals. If the nurses at personal care facilities were to be grouped separately, the restaurant industry would be the nation's largest employer.

Low Compensation

With reference to compensation, there is little ambiguity. As indicated in Table 4.15, employees at eating and drinking places are paid considerably less than are the employees of any other nonagricultural industry. This is not to say that the industry is necessarily exploitative: many of its employees are students and other young people experiencing their first jobs. Further, many foodservice workers are working part-time. As shown in Table 4.16, the average work week is less than 26 hours at fast-food restaurants. The same table shows the growth in employment in the foodservice industry since 1970.

Note that average hours worked per employee have declined, while the growth in number of employees has been faster than the real growth of restaurant sales. Clearly, then, turnover has accelerated, creating productivity problems.

The growth of employment in franchised restaurants alone (as opposed to all foodservice) is illustrated in Table 4.17. The comparatively low level of wages in foodservice is not race-related, incidentally: the mix of blacks, Asians, and Hispanics who work in the restaurant industry closely approximates their participation rate in the total labor force.

Table 4.15

Wage Rates in Ten Lowest-Paying Industries ($ per hour)

Industry	1980	1985	1987
Eating & drinking places	3.69	4.33	4.42
Apparel stores	4.30	5.25	5.56
Apparel manufacturing	4.56	5.73	5.93
Leather & leather products	4.58	5.83	6.08
General merchandise stores	4.77	5.92	6.48
Amusement, recreation services	5.52	6.94	6.95
Food stores	6.24	7.35	6.95
Textile mill products	5.07	6.7	7.17
Furniture & furnishing stores	5.53	7.13	7.49
Banking	4.94	6.84	7.51

Source: U.S. Bureau of Labor Statistics, "Employment and Earnings," published monthly.

Table 4.16

Employment and Earnings for Eating and Drinking Places

Year	Total Employment (000)	% Change	Average Hourly Earnings ($)	% Change	Average Weekly Hours	% Change
1970	2,574.6		1.86		31.2	
1971	2,700.4	4.9	1.96	5.4	30.9	−1.0
1972	2,860.2	5.9	2.07	5.6	30.4	−1.6
1973	3,053.8	6.8	2.18	5.3	29.9	−1.6
1974	3,231.2	5.8	2.37	8.7	29.5	−1.3
1975	3,379.5	4.6	2.55	7.6	29.1	−1.4
1976	3,656.2	8.2	2.69	5.5	28.5	−2.1
1977	3,948.6	8.0	2.93	8.9	27.9	−2.1
1978	4,277.2	8.3	3.22	9.9	27.1	−2.9
1979	4,513.1	5.5	3.45	7.1	26.3	−3.0
1980	4,625.8	2.5	3.69	7.0	26.1	−0.8
1981	4,749.5	2.7	3.95	7.0	26.1	0.0
1982	4,831.2	1.7	4.09	3.5	26.2	0.4
1983	5,041.8	4.4	4.27	4.4	26.3	0.4
1984	5,403.3	7.2	4.33	1.4	26.3	0.0
1985	5,692.1	5.3	4.36	0.7	25.8	−1.9

Source: Bureau of Labor Statistics, "Employment and Earnings," published monthly.

Table 4.17

Franchise Restaurant Employment

Year	Total Employment	% Change
1973	744,469	
1974	806,807	8.4
1975	893,468	10.7
1976	1,064,618	19.2
1977	1,230,081	15.5
1978	1,367,637	11.2
1979	1,497,283	9.5
1980	1,612,479	7.7
1981	1,664,170	3.2
1982	1,815,086	9.1
1983	1,954,646	7.7
1984	2,182,143	11.6
1985	2,441,947	11.9
1986	2,453,621	0.5

Source: National Restaurant Association, "Franchise Restaurants, a Statistical Appendix to Foodservice Trends," Washington, D.C., March 1988.

Demographics of the Labor Force

Typical employees of foodservice firms are young, and the average age of the typical employee is declining over time. In 1980, according to Bureau of the Census, 53 percent of the males employed in the restaurant industry were less than 25 years old, while 49 percent of the women employed in the industry were 25 years old or younger. A decade earlier, the median age of male workers in the industry was 32.7 years and 36.8 years for females. By 1984, according to the same source, 33.9 percent of all male foodservice employees were 19 years old or less. At McDonald's, 56 percent of the crew members are teen-agers, 27 percent are age 20 to 29, and only 17 percent are 30 or older.

Labor Costs for Individual Concepts

Labor costs relative to sales show considerable variation among restaurant concepts. Table 4.18 shows recent data for 21 different chains. Note that the two extremes are occupied by a dinner house that goes out of its way to provide an unusually high level of service (Cooker) and a frozen yogurt concept, TCBY.

Table 4.18

Labor Cost as a Percent of Sales for Chain Restaurants

Chain	Labor Cost as % Sales
Cooker	36.6
Perkins	35.0
Shoney's	33.7
Church's	32.3
Cracker Barrel	30.0
Burger King	28.0
Pancho's	27.5
Taco Bell	27.0
Pizza Hut	27.0
Luby's	27.0
Uno's	26.7
Carl Karcher	26.1
Homestyle Buffet	25.6
Kentucky Fried Chicken	25.5
Wendy's	24.9
Ryan's	23.7
Chili's	23.0
McDonald's	22.3
Sbarro's	22.0
Captain D's	18.5
TCBY	16.0

Table 4.19

Labor Costs Over Time

Chain	Labor as % Sales, Decade Ago	Labor as % Sales, Current
Burger King	25.0	28.0
Hardee's	25.0	
Kentucky Fried Chicken	23.0	25.5
Long John Silver	21.0	
McDonald's	22.5	22.3
Pizza Hut	24.0	27.0
Taco Bell	18.0	27.0
Wendy's	17.0	24.9
Unweighted average	21.9	25.8

Labor Costs in Hamburger Segment

Within the hamburger segment, the comparatively low level of labor costs at McDonald's is noteworthy, as is the high level of labor costs relative to sales at Burger King. Table 4.19 illustrates the remarkable shift in labor costs that has occurred over the past ten years. The overall increase of approximately 4 percentage points in the unweighted average cost includes a slight decrease in McDonald's labor costs. Note the enormous increases in labor costs at Wendy's and Taco Bell.

Minimum Wage Law

The minimum wage laws are not the culprit in rising labor costs. The free market has determined that, with a declining number of young people in a full-employment economy, upward pressure on wage rates in the fast-food industry is inevitable. Table 4.20 shows the history of minimum wage since 1950. Note that the last legislated increase was in 1981.

New Minimum Wage Law

At this writing, an increase in the minimum wage to $3.80 per hour in 1990 and $4.25 per hour in 1991 appears likely. However, as indicated in Table 4.21, minimum wage has already lagged far behind the average of all wages. This phenomenon has not prevented the fast-food industry from experiencing a severe labor cost squeeze.

Reduction in Turnover Is Critical

McDonald's finds a strong link between the quality of its labor force at the store level and the sales of a given restaurant. An improvement of one grade on the company's store-level grading system translates to $136,000 higher sales (or more than 8 percent) at a McDonald's restaurant.

Table 4.20

History of Minimum Wage Rates

Date	Hourly Rate for Employees Covered under Laws Prior to 1966 ($)	% Change	Hourly Rate for Employees Covered under 1966 Amendments & Later ($)	% Change
Jan. 25, 1950	0.75			
Mar. 1, 1956	1.00	33.3		
Sept. 3, 1961	1.15	15.0		
Sept. 3, 1963	1.25	8.7		
Feb. 1, 1967	1.40	12.0	1.00	
Feb. 1, 1968	1.60	14.3	1.15	15.0
Feb. 1, 1969			1.30	13.0
Feb. 1, 1970			1.45	11.5
Feb. 1, 1971			1.60	10.3
May 1, 1974	2.00	25.0	1.90	18.7
Jan. 1, 1975	2.10	5.0	2.00	5.3
Jan. 1, 1976	2.30	9.5	2.20	10.0
Jan. 1, 1977			2.30	4.5
Jan. 1, 1978	2.65	15.2	2.65	15.2
Jan. 1, 1979	2.90	9.4	2.90	9.4
Jan. 1, 1980	3.10	6.9	3.10	6.9
Jan. 1, 1981	3.35	8.1	3.35	8.1

Compound Annual Growth Rate (%)

1967–81	6.4		9.0	
1976–81	7.8		8.8	
1950–81	4.9		NM*	

*NM — not meaningful.

Source: U.S. Department of Labor.

Table 4.21

Minimum Wage Relative to All Wages

Year	Minimum Wage as % Average Wages*
1950	54
1956	52
1967	50
1971	46
1980	44
1988	33

*Minimum wage as a percent of gross average hourly earnings of production workers in manufacturing.

Source: U.S. Department of Labor, Employment Standards Administration, "Minimum Wage and Maximum Hour Standards under the Fair Labor Standards Act."

As discussed by McDonald's chairman Michael Quinlan, reducing turnover is a key priority for the chain, and in fact, McDonald's has improved its turnover of hourly workers in recent years. Five years ago, turnover averaged 180 percent per year. By mid-1989, that figure had fallen to 130 percent, still very high, but a remarkable improvement. The figure, as McDonald's calculates, has an upward bias in the sense that if a youngster who works at a McDonald's store near home goes off to college and works at a McDonald's near the campus, he or she is counted as an employee who quit as well as a new employee, though in reality that person has never left the McDonald's system.

Labor Profile of a McDonald's Unit

The typical McDonald's store has sixty employees and a $350,000 payroll for its $1.6 million in annual sales volume. In late 1989, McDonald's average hourly crew rate was $4.60 per hour, well above the national minimum wage of $3.35 per hour, and also above fourteen of the fifteen higher state minimum wage rates in effect.

In suburban Chicago, McDonald's typically starts its crew workers at an hourly rate of $4.00 per hour, with reviews after three months. Raises at the review period are based on grades, with an acceptable crew person usually receiving a raise of 10 to 15 cents per hour every three months, a good crew person receiving a raise of 15 to 20 cents, and the outstanding employee receiving a 20- to 25-cent increase. At the end of a year, then, the successful employee can earn $4.75 per hour.

Economics of Management

Managers in a McDonald's company-owned store in 1989 averaged an annual salary of $28,000. In addition, a profit-sharing plan contributed an additional 14 to 14.5 percent to the manager's compensation. Managers were also entitled to stock options in certain cases. Further, a manager with five years' tenure was entitled to a company car with all expenses paid except for gas and oil. According to McDonald's senior vice president Stanley L. Stein, McDonald's management turnover has remained approximately constant for the past five years.

Best Chains Run by Operators

The best fast-food chains are run not by marketing people or financial planners but by hands-on operators. Over half of the top management of McDonald's Corporation (including three of the four most senior officers) have held store manager positions.

Managing Food Costs

Restaurant chains have raised prices in response to rising labor costs, not rising food costs. As a result, the value of eating out has deteriorated compared with eating at home.

Table 4.22

Food Costs and Inflation, Year-to-Year Changes (%)

Year	CPI	Food at Home	Food Away from Home	NRA Food Cost Index	All Food PPI*
1971	4.3	2.4	5.2	NA	1.7
1972	3.3	4.5	4.0	7.0	5.5
1973	6.2	16.3	7.8	20.8	20.6
1974	11.0	14.9	12.7	10.0	18.7
1975	9.1	8.3	9.3	9.0	6.7
1976	5.8	2.1	6.8	−1.5	−3.8
1977	6.5	6.0	7.6	5.8	4.4
1978	7.7	10.5	9.0	11.2	10.5
1979	11.3	10.8	11.2	12.2	9.5
1980	13.5	8.0	9.9	5.0	8.0
1981	9.6	7.3	9.0	3.0	3.1
1982	6.8	3.4	5.3	2.5	1.2
1983	3.2	1.1	4.4	0.7	1.1
1984	4.2	3.7	4.2	5.0	4.8
1985	3.6	1.4	3.9	−2.2	−1.8

*Producer Price Index.

Source: Bureau of Labor Statistics and National Restaurant Association.

Table 4.23

Food Cost as Percent of Sales

Chain	Food Cost as % Sales
Ryan's	43.8
Rally's	40.8
Buffets, Inc.	40.0
Homestyle Buffet	39.2
TCBY	38.0
Long John Silver	37.4
Church's	36.6
Captain D's	36.5
Popeye's	36.1
Sizzler	35.1
McDonald's	34.4
Shoney's	33.7
Carl Karcher	33.7
Dunkin' Donuts	32.5
Wendy's	32.0
Burger King	32.0
Kentucky Fried Chicken	31.0
Chi-Chi's	30.9
Taco Bell	30.0
Cracker Barrel	30.0
Cooker	30.0
Chili's	29.0
Pancho's	27.5
Perkins	27.0
Luby's	26.3
Old Spaghetti Warehouse	25.5
Sbarro's	25.2
Pizza Hut	25.0
Uno's	24.4

Price Gains versus Food Inflation

Table 4.22 shows the increase in the price of food prepared at home since 1971, along with the increase in the price of food consumed at restaurants. The table also presents National Restaurant Association data on the cost of food to restaurant operators. For the last seven years in a row, restaurant prices have risen faster than the cost of eating at home. Moreover, for five of the last six years, the price of food consumed away from home has risen more rapidly than the food cost index of restaurant operators.

Table 4.23 shows food costs as a percent of sales in the most recent fiscal year for a sample of twenty-nine chain restaurant companies. Note the relatively high food costs for the chains that offer all-you-can-eat buffets, that is, Ryan's, Buffets, Inc., and Homestyle Buffet.

Rally's also demonstrates a very high food cost as a percent of sales, as the chain deliberately prices its product 30 percent below that of the major hamburger chains. The four chains with the highest food costs, then, are the ones that have consciously tried to offer consumers the best value for their money in terms of quantity of food.

Low Food Costs for Pizza Chains

At the opposite extreme are the chains that offer either pizza or pasta or both. Clearly, the food costs for these kinds of carbohydrate-based restaurants are quite different from what the hamburger and chicken concepts offer. The Mexican chains, Chi-Chi's and Taco Bell, feature food costs that average higher than the Italian concepts, while the hamburger chains are higher still.

Most striking is the decline in food costs over time as a percent of sales. Table 4.24 shows food costs relative to sales in the most current year as well as a decade ago for eight major chains. Note that in every case save that of Taco Bell (where costs have stayed flat), food costs have dropped relative to sales. Clearly, the consumer's dollar at these chains is purchasing less food than it did a decade ago relative to the cost of food eaten at home.

Table 4.25 traces cost of sales as a percent of sales for the entire fast-food industry since 1970. Note that cost of sales as a percent of sales rose throughout the 1970s, reaching a peak of 36.3 percent of sales in 1978 and 1979.

Since that time, food cost as a percent of sales has slipped, suggesting that the customer's dollar is buying less food. The decade of prosperity for the growing fast-food industry, when consumers received ever-improving value for their expenditures, has given way to a time when chains, plagued by labor cost pressures, have been forced to raise prices to offset labor cost increases. As a result, customers are eating out less often than they would have, which in turn has exacerbated the problem of saturation.

Table 4.24

Food Costs Over Time

Chain	Food Cost as % Sales, Decade Ago	Food Cost as % Sales, Current
Burger King	39.0	32.0
Hardee's	37.5	
Kentucky Fried Chicken	41.0	31.0
Long John Silver	39.5	37.4
McDonald's	40.2	34.4
Pizza Hut	30.0	25.0
Taco Bell	30.0	30.0
Wendy's	40.0	32.0
Unweighted average	37.2	31.7

Table 4.25

**Sales and Food Costs of Fast-Food Restaurants
($000)**

Year	Fast-Food Sales	% Change	Fast-Food Sales as Cost	% Sales
1970	6,190		1,873	30.26
1971	7,011	13.3	2,121	30.25
1972	8,037	14.6	2,504	31.16
1973	9,684	20.5	3,295	34.03
1974	11,365	17.4	4,072	35.83
1975	13,597	19.6	4,891	35.97
1976	16,346	20.2	5,879	35.97
1977	19,358	18.4	6,963	35.97
1978	22,285	15.1	8,080	36.26
1979	25,902	16.2	9,393	36.26
1980	28,699	10.8	10,296	35.88
1981	32,202	12.2	11,262	34.97
1982	35,357	9.8	12,195	34.49
1983	39,494	11.7	13,428	34.00
1984	43,719	10.7	14,950	34.20
1985	47,191	7.9	15,395	32.62
1986	52,509	11.3	16,925	32.23
1987	57,234	9.0	18,448	32.23
1988	60,425	5.6	19,643	32.51

Compound Annual Growth Rate (%)

1970–88	13.5	
1970–80	16.6	
1980–88	9.8	
1983–88	8.9	

Source: National Restaurant Association.

Chapter 5

Market Saturation

Defining Saturation

Few subjects are as critical to an understanding of the fast-food industry as the issue of saturation. The very term "saturation" is ambiguous and requires some precise definition. The concept of a fully saturated market need not mean that no new stores can be opened in that market. Moreover, the concept of a saturated market does not simply mean that new stores will cannibalize the sales of existing ones. Surely even in the least-saturated markets there is *some* cannibalization. Rather, saturation, by our definition, means that new stores will operate at levels of sales (and, by extension, of profitability) below those of existing ones operated by a given chain nationally or in a region.

Satisfactory Volumes at New Stores

On the face of it, saturation is not yet a problem. McDonald's, for example, continues to open new stores at sales levels slightly above those of its existing restaurants, while Pizza Hut, Kentucky Fried Chicken, and Taco Bell are all opening stores at sales levels nearly double those of their existing units.

Such a phenomenon is more surprising than it may first appear. Even if saturation were not yet a problem, it would not be unreasonable to assume that the best sites would have already been selected and that, as a result, new stores would occupy less advantageously located plots of land. Part of the explanation for the continuing progress in opening new sites at high volumes is that trade patterns are ever-changing. The service highway of ten years ago may be rendered less important by the opening of a new shopping center in a different location or the closing or relocation of a factory. An additional explanation lies in the cumulative impact of the marketing programs of the largest chains. A new Burger King or McDonald's store benefits to some degree from the fact that its brand name is simply better known today than it was a decade ago.

Rising Construction Costs

As we have seen, the cost of new stores continues to outstrip the gains in sales volumes of most chains, suggesting that the location of new restaurants on very expensive, prime real estate may be one reason for the continuing high sales volumes of the new stores. Put another way, without resorting to unusually expensive sites, it might well be that new stores would open at volumes below those of existing ones. Moreover, the fact that new stores continue to open at volumes equal or greater than those of existing ones says nothing about the ultimate size of the market. Few would deny that the fast-food market will someday become overstored or saturated. The critical question is *when*.

Store Openings and Population

The soundest methodology for analyzing the issue of saturation is to relate current store-opening patterns to population. The analyst can determine how many residents are required to support a fast-food unit, then make projections of how many units can be supported in a state, a region, or nationally in order to blanket the area with the maximum possible number of units.

The analysis that follows is based on population and store openings by state. Arguably, Standard Metropolitan Statistical Areas (SMSAs) would be a better unit of measurement of a trading area. Alternatively, the use of Area of Dominant Influence (ADIs), which is the usual definition of a market for media purposes, particularly television, might be a sounder method for precisely defining a market. Unfortunately, location of individual restaurant units divided along such lines is generally unavailable.

Certain chains, including Burger King, Wendy's, Hardee's, and White Castle, readily make available to the public a complete listing of stores broken down by state. Others, such as McDonald's, are less cooperative in this regard, and the analyst must tally the locations of individual restaurants from the directories of store locations that McDonald's makes available to consumers. Inasmuch as the chain currently operates more than 8000 stores in the United States, this is a most time-consuming enterprise.

Structure of the Analysis

The analysis of saturation is in ten parts:

1. An examination of McDonald's store-opening pattern over time on a state-by-state basis
2. McDonald's store levels on a per capita basis
3. McDonald's potential store openings in the future by state
4. The eight largest hamburger chains' store levels on a state-by-state basis
5. The eight largest chains' units on a per capita basis in each state
6. Estimated dollar sales for the eight largest chains per state
7. Sales for the eight largest chains as a percent of eating and drinking sales in each state
8. Estimated per capita sales in each state for the eight largest chains
9. Overall potential for new store openings
10. Potential store openings by state

McDonald's Company Store Openings in the United States

Table 5.1 shows the total number of McDonald's restaurants open in each of the fifty states and the District of Columbia in year-end 1973, 1978, 1983, and early 1988 (at this writing, year-end 1988 data were not yet available). But merely cataloging numbers of locations does not, by itself, tell the observer much, if anything, about the issue of saturation. In order to address that issue, population and total restaurant sales must be introduced into the analysis. By relating the number of restaurants to population, one can begin to draw conclusions about the number of inhabitants required to support a fast-food restaurant. By exploring the dollar size of the restaurant market, the analyst can also explore the portion of the total market for food consumed away from home that the chains can capture.

Note that between 1983 and 1988 McDonald's opened stores in each of the fifty states. The rate of new openings was quite different, however, ranging from a modest gain of less than 10 percent in states such as Utah, South Dakota, and Indiana, to an increase of more than 40 percent in Alaska, Arkansas, Hawaii, Oklahoma, Texas, and Wyoming. States where the rate of gain was less than 15 percent include such major industrial states as New

Table 5.1

Increase in McDonald's Units Over Time

State	1973	1978	1983	1988	State	1973	1978	1983	1988
Alabama	36	62	83	107	Montana	7	9	12	19
Alaska	4	6	8	24	Nebraska	12	24	36	49
Arizona	22	52	82	102	Nevada	12	21	30	43
Arkansas	12	32	45	67	New Hampshire	20	29	30	37
California	313	456	546	684	New Jersey	77	121	151	177
Colorado	36	56	94	110	New Mexico	9	27	38	44
Connecticut	51	71	85	109	New York	198	384	405	448
Delaware	9	14	18	23	North Carolina	43	129	185	215
D.C.	13	18	21	27	North Dakota	4	10	12	18
Florida	156	237	339	450	Ohio	166	274	348	418
Georgia	79	136	168	201	Oklahoma	22	43	66	102
Hawaii	24	37	36	51	Oregon	20	37	50	68
Idaho	6	14	17	21	Pennsylvania	127	244	299	338
Illinois	165	277	380	435	Rhode Island	13	19	22	27
Indiana	77	151	196	211	South Carolina	24	58	83	106
Iowa	27	43	71	81	South Dakota	9	13	15	16
Kansas	20	43	61	81	Tennessee	40	78	112	150
Kentucky	27	65	88	115	Texas	99	183	300	442
Louisiana	28	66	91	129	Utah	11	20	37	38
Maine	27	33	42	52	Vermont	6	10	13	16
Maryland	63	103	128	148	Virginia	77	154	192	218
Massachusetts	89	129	154	170	Washington	31	73	102	121
Michigan	126	238	294	329	West Virginia	8	24	39	50
Minnesota	42	77	114	130	Wisconsin	60	106	144	159
Mississippi	15	41	55	72	Wyoming	2	7	11	17
Missouri	58	100	146	184					
					Total U.S.	2622	4654	6094	7449

York, Pennsylvania, Massachusetts, and Michigan. Interestingly, economic downturn in the oil patch does not appear to have been much of a deterrent to new store openings, as Louisiana, Texas, and Oklahoma all registered major increases in new stores.

McDonald's Expansion by State

Table 5.2 ranks the states according to the rate of McDonald's expansion in the period from 1983 to 1988. The compound annual growth rate ranged from a high of 24.6 percent in Alaska to a low of 1.3 percent in South Dakota. Note that the Great Plains states, the Gulf Coast, and South-Central states generally experienced the most rapid growth in new McDonald's stores: Oklahoma, Arkansas, Texas, Louisiana, Nebraska, Kansas, Florida, Mississippi, and Alabama all experienced an increase in the number of McDonald's stores well above the national average.

Table 5.2

McDonald's Growth in Units Ranked by State (1983–88)

State	CAGR* 1983–88 (%)	State	CAGR* 1983–88 (%)
Alaska	24.6	Maine	4.4
Montana	9.6	Idaho	4.3
Oklahoma	9.1	New Hampshire	4.3
Wyoming	9.1	Vermont	4.2
North Dakota	8.4	Rhode Island	4.2
Arkansas	8.3	Ohio	3.7
Texas	8.1	Georgia	3.7
Nevada	7.5	Washington	3.5
Louisiana	7.2	New Jersey	3.2
Hawaii	7.2	Colorado	3.2
Nebraska	6.4	North Carolina	3.1
Oregon	6.3	New Mexico	3.0
Tennessee	6.0	Maryland	2.9
Kansas	5.8	Illinois	2.7
Florida	5.8	Iowa	2.7
Mississippi	5.5	Minnesota	2.7
Kentucky	5.5	Virginia	2.6
Alabama	5.2	Pennsylvania	2.5
D.C.	5.2	Michigan	2.3
Connecticut	5.1	New York	2.0
West Virginia	5.1	Wisconsin	2.0
Delaware	5.0	Massachusetts	2.0
South Carolina	5.0	Indiana	1.5
Missouri	4.7	South Dakota	1.3
California	4.6	Utah	0.5
Arizona	4.5		
		Total U.S.	4.1

*Compound annual growth rate.

At the other extreme, the Northeast industrial and Great Lakes states were among the areas with the lowest rates of expansion. Indiana, Massachusetts, Wisconsin, New York, Michigan, Pennsylvania, Minnesota, and Illinois accounted for eight of the eleven states with the lowest rates of growth, with nearby Iowa, South Dakota, and Virginia comprising the balance.

Indiana Bellwether State for Saturation Analysis

The low rate of expansion in Indiana is particularly noteworthy for, as will be seen, this state has been among the most saturated of any in the country for over a decade. The recent low level of McDonald's expansion there suggests that a limit may have been reached in terms of saturation.

This geographical expansion pattern was not so pronounced in the preceding decade. Table 5.3 shows the annual rate of expansion for McDonald's by state in the ten years ended

Table 5.3

McDonald's Growth in Units Ranked by State (1973–83)

State	CAGR* 1973–83 (%)	State	CAGR* 1973–83 (%)
Wyoming	18.6	Virginia	9.6
West Virginia	17.2	Wisconsin	9.1
North Carolina	15.7	Pennsylvania	8.9
New Mexico	15.5	Michigan	8.8
Arkansas	14.1	Alabama	8.7
Arizona	14.1	Illinois	8.7
Mississippi	13.9	Florida	8.1
South Carolina	13.2	Vermont	8.0
Utah	12.9	Georgia	7.8
Washington	12.6	Ohio	7.7
Kentucky	12.5	New York	7.4
Louisiana	12.5	Maryland	7.3
Kansas	11.8	Alaska	7.2
Texas	11.7	Delaware	7.2
Nebraska	11.6	New Jersey	7.0
North Dakota	11.6	California	5.7
Oklahoma	11.6	Massachusetts	5.6
Idaho	11.0	Montana	5.5
Tennessee	10.8	Rhode Island	5.4
Minnesota	10.5	South Dakota	5.2
Iowa	10.2	Connecticut	5.2
Colorado	10.1	D.C.	4.9
Indiana	9.8	Maine	4.5
Missouri	9.7	New Hampshire	4.1
Oregon	9.6	Hawaii	4.1
Nevada	9.6		
		Total U.S.	8.8

*Compound annual growth rate.

1983. During this era the rate of expansion was low in the Northeast, particularly New England, but also lagged in California and was slightly below average in Florida. The pattern of rapid expansion in Arkansas, Texas, Oklahoma, Nebraska, and Kansas was certainly present during the 1973–83 period, but the southeastern states, particularly the Carolinas, Tennessee, Kentucky, West Virginia, and, to a lesser extent, Virginia, all figured heavily in the company's expansion.

Minimum Population Required

How many people are required to support a McDonald's store? Table 5.4 shows the number of McDonald's stores in each state in early 1988 and the year-end population for 1987, as well as the population per store at that date. Table 5.5 presents the same data, but ranks the states according to the level of population per McDonald's store. Note that nationally there is one McDonald's store for every 33,000 people, while the chain's penetration is considerably higher in a number of states. At the extreme, note that there is one McDonald's store for every 21,349 people in Hawaii and one for every 23,877 inhabitants or less in Alaska, Maine, Washington, D.C., and Nevada.

A subsequent analysis will show that each of these four states and the District of Columbia rank in the top nine states in terms of per capita spending on tourism. Put another way, these states clearly benefit from spending on food consumed away from home by people who are not members of the indigenous population.

Penetration of Industrial Midwest

The same cannot be said for the next most heavily penetrated states, however: Ohio, Indiana, and Illinois. Each ranks among the nation's lowest in terms of per capita spending on tourism, and each has one McDonald's store for every 27,000 inhabitants or less.

As already indicated in Table 5.4, each of these states has, in recent years, experienced some of the slowest rates of new store openings of any states in the country. It may well be, then, that one McDonald's store for every 26,000 to 27,000 residents is, at least in nontourist areas, the most that can be achieved.

Saturation in the Hamburger Segment

Hamburger Competition by State

McDonald's does not operate in a vacuum, however. In order to expand the analysis, it is necessary to introduce a broader array of fast-food competitors. Table 5.6 shows the number of fast-food hamburger units in 1988 for the eight largest fast-food hamburger chains. While only three of the chains, McDonald's, Burger King, and Wendy's, can be said to be national chains, each of the others represents a major competitive factor in certain regions.

Jack-in-the-Box, for example, has more stores in California than does either Burger King or Wendy's. Hardee's operates more stores in Georgia than does McDonald's, and in the

Table 5.4

McDonald's 1988 Saturation Level

State	Number of Stores, 1988	Population 12/31/87 (000)	Population per Store (000)
Alabama	107	4,137.1	38.664
Alaska	24	545.7	22.738
Arizona	102	3,441.1	33.736
Arkansas	67	2,420.0	36.119
California	684	27,939.0	40.846
Colorado	110	3,346.3	30.421
Connecticut	109	3,242.5	29.748
Delaware	23	642.5	27.935
D.C.	27	623.3	23.085
Florida	450	12,163.9	27.031
Georgia	201	6,295.2	31.319
Hawaii	51	1,088.8	21.349
Idaho	21	1,033.9	49.233
Illinois	435	11,657.6	26.799
Indiana	211	5,570.8	26.402
Iowa	81	2,860.7	35.317
Kansas	81	2,495.0	30.802
Kentucky	115	3,771.5	32.796
Louisiana	129	4,517.8	35.022
Maine	52	1,191.8	22.919
Maryland	148	4,562.6	30.828
Massachusetts	170	5,884.1	34.612
Michigan	329	9,262.9	28.155
Minnesota	130	4,292.3	33.018
Mississippi	72	2,676.2	37.169
Missouri	184	5,173.6	28.117
Montana	19	832.1	43.795
Nebraska	49	1,616.8	32.996
Nevada	43	1,026.7	23.877
New Hampshire	37	1,060.1	28.651
New Jersey	177	7,728.6	43.664
New Mexico	44	1,525.0	34.659
New York	448	17,964.0	40.098
North Carolina	215	6,463.6	30.063
North Dakota	18	694.3	38.572
Ohio	418	10,834.9	25.921
Oklahoma	102	3,344.4	32.788
Oregon	68	2,738.4	40.271
Pennsylvania	338	11,973.4	35.424
Rhode Island	27	990.0	36.667
South Carolina	106	3,458.4	32.626
South Dakota	16	721.9	45.119
Tennessee	150	4,899.5	32.663
Texas	442	16,888.0	38.208
Utah	38	1,712.4	45.063
Vermont	16	550.3	34.394
Virginia	218	5,943.2	27.262
Washington	121	4,548.9	37.594
West Virginia	50	1,934.6	38.692
Wisconsin	159	4,836.6	30.419
Wyoming	17	500.4	29.435
Total U.S.	7,449	245,623	32.974

Table 5.5

McDonald's 1988 Saturation Level Ranked by State

State	Number of Stores, 1988	Population 12/31/87 (000)	Population per Store (000)
Hawaii	51	1,088.8	21.349
Alaska	24	545.7	22.738
Maine	52	1,191.8	22.919
D.C.	27	623.3	23.085
Nevada	43	1,026.7	23.877
Ohio	418	10,834.9	25.921
Indiana	211	5,570.8	26.402
Illinois	435	11,657.6	26.799
Florida	450	12,163.9	27.031
Virginia	218	5,943.2	27.262
Delaware	23	642.5	27.935
Missouri	184	5,173.6	28.117
Michigan	329	9,262.9	28.155
New Hampshire	37	1,060.1	28.651
Wyoming	17	500.4	29.435
Connecticut	109	3,242.5	29.748
North Carolina	215	6,463.6	30.063
Wisconsin	159	4,836.6	30.419
Colorado	110	3,346.3	30.421
Kansas	81	2,495.0	30.802
Maryland	148	4,562.6	30.828
Georgia	201	6,295.2	31.319
South Carolina	106	3,458.4	32.626
Tennessee	150	4,899.5	32.663
Oklahoma	102	3,344.4	32.788
Kentucky	115	3,771.5	32.796
Nebraska	49	1,616.8	32.996
Minnesota	130	4,292.3	33.018
Arizona	102	3,441.1	33.736
Vermont	16	550.3	34.394
Massachusetts	170	5,884.1	34.612
New Mexico	44	1,525.0	34.659
Louisiana	129	4,517.8	35.022
Iowa	81	2,860.7	35.317
Pennsylvania	338	11,973.4	35.424
Arkansas	67	2,420.0	36.119
Rhode Island	27	990.0	36.667
Mississippi	72	2,676.2	37.169
Washington	121	4,548.9	37.594
Texas	442	16,888.0	38.208
North Dakota	18	694.3	38.572
Alabama	107	4,137.1	38.664
West Virginia	50	1,934.6	38.692
New York	448	17,964.0	40.098
Oregon	68	2,738.4	40.271
California	684	27,939.0	40.846
New Jersey	177	7,728.6	43.664
Montana	19	832.1	43.795
Utah	38	1,712.4	45.063
South Dakota	16	721.9	45.119
Idaho	21	1,033.9	49.233
Total U.S.	7,449	245,623	32.974

Table 5.6

Domestic Fast-Food Hamburger Units, 1988

State	McDonald's	Burger King	Hardee's	Wendy's	Jack-in-the-Box	Carl's Junior	White Castle	Roy Rogers	Total for 8 Chains
Alabama	107	81	143	62					393
Alaska	24	9		9					42
Arizona	102	82	9	53	86	31			363
Arkansas	67	32	24	33					156
California	684	441	15	251	463	387			2,226
Colorado	110	82		72	15				294
Connecticut	109	66		34				25	234
Delaware	23	12	8	14				13	70
D.C.	27	12	4	4				23	70
Florida	450	356	138	259					1,203
Georgia	201	149	206	156					712
Hawaii	51	29		13	30				123
Idaho	21	11		12	1				45
Illinois	435	220	169	169	5		36	1	1,035
Indiana	211	94	154	125			26		610
Iowa	81	35	107	31					254
Kansas	81	38	54	47			2		222
Kentucky	115	37	81	67			20	3	323
Louisiana	129	93	14	56					292
Maine	52	36		6					94
Maryland	148	72	69	73				133	495
Massachusetts	170	144	1	37				4	356
Michigan	329	224	86	176			25		840

State									Total
Minnesota	130	90	94	34			13		361
Mississippi	72	29	37	43					181
Missouri	184	81	138	83	31		25		542
Montana	19	7	9	10					45
Nebraska	49	36	20	26					131
Nevada	43	18		23	14	16			114
New Hampshire	37	22		13					72
New Jersey	177	158	4	60			17	109	525
New Mexico	44	32	6	18	5				105
New York	448	333	5	139			23	69	1,017
North Carolina	215	149	324	119				2	809
North Dakota	18	7	19	9					53
Ohio	418	215	99	299			37	16	1,084
Oklahoma	102	44	59	46					251
Oregon	68	44		39	1	2			154
Pennsylvania	338	222	72	158				106	896
Rhode Island	27	29	1	8					65
South Carolina	106	89	161	57					413
South Dakota	16	14	17	7					54
Tennessee	150	100	122	125			4		501
Texas	442	287	48	234	235				1,246
Utah	38	21	28	21	3				111
Vermont	16	8	1	5					30
Virginia	218	115	175	117				52	677
Washington	50	20	41	39	38				188
West Virginia	121	73	2	43					239
Wisconsin	159	88	146	39					432
Wyoming	17	8	6	9					40
Total U.S.	7449	4694	2916	3582	927	436	228	556	20,788

117

Table 5.7

Domestic Fast-Food Hamburger Units, 1978

State	McDonald's	Burger King	Hardee's	Burger Chef	Wendy's	Jack-in-the-Box	Total for 6 Chains
Alabama	62	35	71	17	33		218
Alaska	6	4			1		11
Arizona	52	13	10		13	76	164
Arkansas	32	8	6		22		68
California	456	133			60	413	1,062
Colorado	56	35		12	20	17	140
Connecticut	71	31	18		14	1	135
Delaware	14	5	7		1	3	30
D.C.	18	3	2				23
Florida	237	174	34	42	78	27	592
Georgia	136	73	78	35	62		384
Hawaii	37	4			4	10	55
Idaho	14	5			3		22
Illinois	277	160	67	99	51	51	705
Indiana	151	38	9	54	57		309
Iowa	43	16	44	4	14		121
Kansas	43	14	36	2	14	7	116
Kentucky	65	14	19	29	30		157
Louisiana	66	79	4	31	20		200
Maine	33	11			7		51
Maryland	103	28	23	8	20	9	191
Massachusetts	129	53	5	13	12	14	226
Michigan	238	123	25	77	55	20	538
Minnesota	77	37	29	10	11		164
Mississippi	41	16	10	11	21		99
Missouri	100	21	30	46	27	38	262
Montana	9	5	1		3		18
Nebraska	24	17		6	11		58
Nevada	21	4		2	12	10	49
New Hampshire	29	10		2	3	2	46
New Jersey	121	87	9	9	8	13	247
New Mexico	27	9	1		7	2	46
New York	384	214	16		30	38	682
North Carolina	129	47	213	7	43		439
North Dakota	10	5	11		1		27
Ohio	274	108	13	139	157		691
Oklahoma	43	10	12	4	24	10	103
Oregon	37	14			16		67
Pennsylvania	244	102	46	26	49	5	472
Rhode Island	19	12		11		2	44
South Carolina	58	40	99	4	29		230
South Dakota	13	9	4				26
Tennessee	78	42	41	16	54		231
Texas	183	107	1	32	80	198	601
Utah	20	5			5		30
Vermont	10	2		1			13
Virginia	154	63	85	24	26	28	380
Washington	73	8		2	13	29	125
West Virginia	24	2	6	42	21		95
Wisconsin	106	18	32	19	9		184
Wyoming	7	4			1		12
Total U.S.	4654	2077	1117	837	1251	1023	10,959

Carolinas not only operates far more units than McDonald's, but also operates more stores than Wendy's and Burger King combined. Carl Karcher operates more stores in California than does Wendy's, while Roy Rogers has a far greater presence in Maryland than does any hamburger operator other than McDonald's.

A snapshot of stores in operation is only a first step in analyzing penetration levels. How have store openings changed over time? Table 5.7 shows the number of stores in operation in each state a decade ago. The sample is slightly different for several reasons: data for White Castle, Roy Rogers, and Carl Karcher are not readily available from the late 1970s. Moreover, Burger Chef, which was purchased by Hardee's in 1982, and has had virtually all of its stores converted to the Hardee's format, is included in the 1978 listing because it represented a major presence in several midwestern states a decade ago.

Several elements of individual companies' histories of expansion are noteworthy. First, Jack-in-the-Box operates fewer units today than it did a decade ago, though it has expanded its number of units in its home state of California. It has disappeared in such important states as Massachusetts, Michigan, and New York, preferring to concentrate on areas where it has a major marketing presence.

Table 5.8 shows the percentage increase in the number of fast-food hamburger restaurants in each of the fifty states and the District of Columbia. Table 5.9 ranks states by the rate of increase in the number of fast-food hamburger stores during the past decade.

Western Expansion Fastest

The expansion pattern of the fast-food chains over the last ten years has a pronounced regional pattern, with increases being strongest in western states with relatively small urban populations. Of the twenty states absorbing the greatest increase in fast-food hamburger units, all but three (West Virginia, Vermont, and Tennessee) fit the above description.

Midwest Expansion Less Rapid

At the other end of the listing, industrial states in the Northeast, Middle Atlantic region, and along the Great Lakes, including New York, Illinois, Ohio, Michigan, Massachusetts, New Jersey, and Pennsylvania accounted for all but one (Louisiana) of the thirteen states with the slowest growth rates.

Penetration Levels by State

How heavily penetrated are the individual states? Table 5.10 shows the total number of stores for each of the eight chains from Table 5.6 and calculates the population per store. Table 5.11 ranks the states according to the number of residents per store, with the most heavily saturated states at the top of the list. Note that the national average is one store for every 11,816 people.

Table 5.8

Expansion for Five Largest Hamburger Chains

State	Number of Units 1978	Number of Units 1988	Increase 1978–88 (%)
Alabama	218	393	80.3
Alaska	11	42	281.8
Arizona	164	332	102.4
Arkansas	68	156	129.4
California	1,062	1,839	73.2
Colorado	140	294	110.0
Connecticut	135	209	54.8
Delaware	30	57	90.0
D.C.	23	47	104.3
Florida	592	1,203	103.2
Georgia	384	712	85.4
Hawaii	55	123	123.6
Idaho	22	45	104.5
Illinois	705	998	41.6
Indiana	309	584	89.0
Iowa	121	254	109.9
Kansas	116	220	89.7
Kentucky	157	300	91.1
Louisiana	200	292	46.0
Maine	51	94	84.3
Maryland	191	362	89.5
Massachusetts	226	352	55.8
Michigan	538	815	51.5
Minnesota	164	348	112.2
Mississippi	99	181	82.8
Missouri	262	517	97.3
Montana	18	45	150.0
Nebraska	58	131	125.9
Nevada	49	98	100.0
New Hampshire	46	72	56.5
New Jersey	247	399	61.5
New Mexico	46	105	128.3
New York	682	925	35.6
North Carolina	439	807	83.8
North Dakota	27	53	96.3
Ohio	691	1,031	49.2
Oklahoma	103	251	143.7
Oregon	67	152	126.9
Pennsylvania	472	790	67.4
Rhode Island	44	65	47.7
South Carolina	230	413	79.6
South Dakota	26	54	107.7
Tennessee	231	497	115.2
Texas	601	1,246	107.3
Utah	30	111	270.0
Vermont	13	30	130.8
Virginia	380	625	64.5
Washington	125	188	50.4
West Virginia	95	239	151.6
Wisconsin	184	432	134.8
Wyoming	12	40	233.3
Total U.S.	10,959	19,568	78.6

Table 5.9

Expansion for Five Largest Hamburger Chains Ranked

State	Number of Units 1978	Number of Units 1988	Increase 1978-88 (%)
Alaska	11	42	281.8
Utah	30	111	270.0
Wyoming	12	40	233.3
West Virginia	95	239	151.6
Montana	18	45	150.0
Oklahoma	103	251	143.7
Wisconsin	184	432	134.8
Vermont	13	30	130.8
Arkansas	68	156	129.4
New Mexico	46	105	128.3
Oregon	67	152	126.9
Nebraska	58	131	125.9
Hawaii	55	123	123.6
Tennessee	231	497	115.2
Minnesota	164	348	112.2
Colorado	140	294	110.0
Iowa	121	254	109.9
South Dakota	26	54	107.7
Texas	601	1,246	107.3
Idaho	22	45	104.5
D.C.	23	47	104.3
Florida	592	1,203	103.2
Arizona	164	332	102.4
Nevada	49	98	100.0
Missouri	262	517	97.3
North Dakota	27	53	96.3
Kentucky	157	300	91.1
Delaware	30	57	90.0
Kansas	116	220	89.7
Maryland	191	362	89.5
Indiana	309	584	89.0
Georgia	384	712	85.4
Maine	51	94	84.3
North Carolina	439	807	83.8
Mississippi	99	181	82.8
Alabama	218	393	80.3
South Carolina	230	413	79.6
California	1,062	1,839	73.2
Pennsylvania	472	790	67.4
Virginia	380	625	64.5
New Jersey	247	399	61.5
New Hampshire	46	72	56.5
Massachusetts	226	352	55.8
Connecticut	135	209	54.8
Michigan	538	815	51.5
Washington	125	188	50.4
Ohio	691	1,031	49.2
Rhode Island	44	65	47.7
Louisiana	200	292	46.0
Illinois	705	998	41.6
New York	682	925	35.6
Total U.S.	10,959	19,568	78.6

Table 5.10

Saturation Levels by State

State	Total Chain Units	Population per Store
Alabama	393	10,527
Alaska	42	12,993
Arizona	363	9,480
Arkansas	156	15,513
California	2,226	12,551
Colorado	294	11,382
Connecticut	234	13,857
Delaware	70	9,179
D.C.	70	8,904
Florida	1,203	10,111
Georgia	712	8,842
Hawaii	123	8,852
Idaho	45	22,976
Illinois	1,035	11,263
Indiana	610	9,132
Iowa	254	11,263
Kansas	222	11,239
Kentucky	323	11,676
Louisiana	292	15,472
Maine	94	12,679
Maryland	495	9,217
Massachusetts	356	16,528
Michigan	840	11,027
Minnesota	361	11,890
Mississippi	181	14,786
Missouri	542	9,545
Montana	45	18,491
Nebraska	131	12,342
Nevada	114	9,006
New Hampshire	72	14,724
New Jersey	525	14,721
New Mexico	105	14,524
New York	1,017	17,664
North Carolina	809	7,990
North Dakota	53	13,100
Ohio	1,084	9,995
Oklahoma	251	13,324
Oregon	154	17,782
Pennsylvania	896	13,363
Rhode Island	65	15,231
South Carolina	413	8,374
South Dakota	54	13,369
Tennessee	501	9,779
Texas	1,246	13,554
Utah	111	15,427
Vermont	30	18,343
Virginia	677	8,779
Washington	188	24,196
West Virginia	239	8,095
Wisconsin	432	11,196
Wyoming	40	12,510
Total U.S.	20,788	11,816

Table 5.11

Saturation Levels by State Ranked

State	Population	Total Chain Units	Population per Store (000)
North Carolina	6,463.6	809	7.990
West Virginia	1,934.6	239	8.095
South Carolina	3,458.4	413	8.374
Virginia	5,943.2	677	8.779
Georgia	6,295.2	712	8.842
Hawaii	1,088.8	123	8.852
D.C.	623.3	70	8.904
Nevada	1,026.7	114	9.006
Indiana	5,570.8	610	9.132
Delaware	642.5	70	9.179
Maryland	4,562.6	495	9.217
Arizona	3,441.1	363	9.480
Missouri	5,173.6	542	9.545
Tennessee	4,899.5	501	9.779
Ohio	10,834.9	1,084	9.995
Florida	12,163.9	1,203	10.111
Alabama	4,137.1	393	10.527
Michigan	9,262.9	840	11.027
Wisconsin	4,836.6	432	11.196
Kansas	2,495.0	222	11.239
Iowa	2,860.7	254	11.263
Illinois	11,657.6	1,035	11.263
Colorado	3,346.3	294	11.382
Kentucky	3,771.5	323	11.676
Minnesota	4,292.3	361	11.890
Nebraska	1,616.8	131	12.342
Wyoming	500.4	40	12.510
California	27,939.0	2,226	12.551
Maine	1,191.8	94	12.679
Alaska	545.7	42	12.993
North Dakota	694.3	53	13.100
Oklahoma	3,344.4	251	13.324
Pennsylvania	11,973.4	896	13.363
South Dakota	721.9	54	13.369
Texas	16,888.0	1,246	13.554
Connecticut	3,242.5	234	13.857
New Mexico	1,525.0	105	14.524
New Jersey	7,728.6	525	14.721
New Hampshire	1,060.1	72	14.724
Mississippi	2,676.2	181	14.786
Rhode Island	990.0	65	15.231
Utah	1,712.4	111	15.427
Louisiana	4,517.8	292	15.472
Arkansas	2,420.0	156	15.513
Massachusetts	5,884.1	356	16.528
New York	17,964.0	1,017	17.664
Oregon	2,738.4	154	17.782
Vermont	550.3	30	18.343
Montana	832.1	45	18.491
Idaho	1,033.9	45	22.976
Washington	4,548.9	188	24.196
Total U.S.	245,623	20,788	11.816

Most Saturated States

The most heavily saturated states are five states along the north-south automobile route between the Northeast and Florida. They are also states that have a very strong regional competitor, Hardee's, with a major stake. Looking beyond states that benefit heavily from tourism (Hawaii, the District of Columbia, and Nevada), and excepting more states that lie on the north-south auto route along the East Coast, one finds Indiana, Arizona, and Missouri are heavily saturated.

In each of these states, the eight chains have opened one store for every 9000 to 10,000 residents, or a per capita level of store openings roughly one-third above the national average. Taken by themselves, these data would suggest that the United States could absorb a one-third increase in the total number of fast-food hamburger units before achieving the level of penetration already achieved in these three states.

Regional Saturation Patterns

Sales Levels for Chains by State

Simply combining the number of units involved in order to calculate per capita store-opening levels has one obvious drawback, however. The individual chains involved have different sales levels per store, ranging from $800,000 per store at Wendy's to a level twice that high at McDonald's. Table 5.12 shows the result of multiplying the number of stores of each chain by its average annual sales volumes in order to estimate the dollar sales per state of each of the chains. This methodology is inexact, because the chains' results are by no means uniform from state to state or region to region.

Burger King, for example, has sales per store that actually exceed those of McDonald's in New Hampshire, while McDonald's itself achieves well-above-average results in California and below-par results in Pennsylvania. Wendy's, on the other hand, suffers badly in California. With all of the caveats, however, Table 5.12 can provide another angle on the issue of market penetration.

Table 5.13 shows the sales of the eight hamburger chains and their share of restaurant sales in each state. Estimated per capita sales by the eight chains are summarized in Table 5.14. Sales of the chains achieve their highest share of total restaurant expenditures in Southeast and Gulf Coast states, accounting for more than 20 percent of total restaurant sales in Alabama, Arkansas, Delaware, Georgia, Indiana, Mississippi, Missouri, North Carolina, South Carolina, Tennessee, and Virginia, while capturing a staggering 41.8 percent of restaurant dollars spent in West Virginia.

Share of the food consumed away from home dollar held by the chains is generally lowest in the Northwest and Northeast, accounting for less than 12 percent of restaurant sales in Alaska, California, Connecticut, the District of Columbia, Hawaii, Idaho, Massachusetts, Montana, New Hampshire, New York, Oregon, Rhode Island, Vermont, and Washington.

The relatively low share held by the hamburger chains in the Northeast may be some-what distorted in this analysis by the omission of Friendly Ice Cream, a strong regional

Table 5.12

Estimated Hamburger Chain Sales by State, 1988 ($000)

State	McDonald's	Burger King	Hardee's	Wendy's	Jack-in-the-Box	Carl's Junior	White Castle	Roy Rogers	Total for 8 Chains
Alabama	170,772	82,377	125,411	47,058	0	0	0	0	425,618
Alaska	38,304	9,153	0	6,831	0	0	0	0	54,288
Arizona	162,792	83,394	7,893	40,227	71,638	29,140	0	0	395,084
Arkansas	106,932	32,544	21,048	25,047	0	0	0	0	185,571
California	1,091,664	448,497	0	190,509	385,679	363,780	0	0	2,480,129
Colorado	175,560	83,394	13,155	54,648	12,495	0	0	0	339,252
Connecticut	173,964	67,122	0	25,806	0	0	0	25,000	291,892
Delaware	36,708	12,204	7,016	10,626	0	0	0	13,000	79,554
D.C.	43,092	12,204	3,508	3,036	0	0	0	23,000	84,840
Florida	718,200	362,052	121,026	196,581	0	0	0	0	1,397,859
Georgia	320,796	151,533	180,662	118,404	0	0	0	0	771,395
Hawaii	81,396	29,493	0	9,867	24,990	0	0	0	145,746
Idaho	33,516	11,187	0	9,108	833	0	0	0	54,644
Illinois	694,260	223,740	148,213	128,271	4,165	0	50,400	1,000	1,250,049
Indiana	336,756	95,598	135,058	94,875	0	0	36,400	0	698,687
Iowa	129,276	35,595	93,839	23,529	0	0	0	0	282,239
Kansas	129,276	38,646	47,358	35,673	0	0	2,800	0	253,753
Kentucky	183,540	37,629	71,037	50,853	0	0	28,000	3,000	374,059
Louisiana	205,884	94,581	12,278	42,504	0	0	0	0	355,247
Maine	82,992	36,612	0	4,554	0	0	0	0	124,158
Maryland	236,208	73,224	60,513	55,407	0	0	0	133,000	558,352
Massachusetts	271,320	146,448	877	28,083	0	0	0	4,000	450,728

State									
Michigan	525,084	227,808	75,422	133,584	0	0	35,000	0	996,898
Minnesota	207,480	91,530	82,438	25,806	0	0	18,200	0	425,454
Mississippi	114,912	29,493	32,449	32,637	0	0	0	0	209,491
Missouri	293,664	82,377	121,026	62,997	25,823	0	35,000	0	620,887
Montana	30,324	7,119	7,893	7,590	0	0	0	0	52,926
Nebraska	78,204	36,612	17,540	19,734	0	0	0	0	152,090
Nevada	68,628	18,306	0	17,457	11,662	15,040	0	0	131,093
New Hampshire	59,052	22,374		9,867	0	0	0	0	91,293
New Jersey	282,492	160,686	3,508	45,540	0	0	23,800	109,000	625,026
New Mexico	70,224	32,544	5,262	13,662	4,165	0	0	0	125,857
New York	715,008	338,661	4,385	105,501	0	0	32,200	69,000	1,264,755
North Carolina	343,140	151,533	284,148	90,321	0	0	0	2,000	871,142
North Dakota	28,728	7,119	16,663	6,831	0	0	0	0	59,341
Ohio	667,128	218,655	86,823	226,941	0	0	51,800	16,000	1,267,347
Oklahoma	162,792	44,748	51,743	34,914	0	0	0	0	294,197
Oregon	108,528	44,748	0	29,601	833	1,880	0	0	185,590
Pennsylvania	539,448	225,774	63,144	119,922	0	0	0	106,000	1,054,288
Rhode Island	43,092	29,493	877	6,072	0	0	0	0	79,534
South Carolina	169,176	90,513	141,197	43,263	0	0	0	0	444,149
South Dakota	25,536	14,238	14,909	5,313	0	0	0	0	59,996
Tennessee	239,400	101,700	106,994	94,875	0	0	5,600	0	548,569
Texas	705,432	291,879	42,096	177,606	195,755	0	0	0	1,412,768
Utah	60,648	21,357	24,556	15,939	2,499	0	0	0	124,999
Vermont	25,536	8,136	877	3,795	0	0	0	0	38,344
Virginia	347,928	116,955	153,475	88,803	0	0	0	52,000	759,161
Washington	79,800	20,340	35,957	29,601	31,654	0	0	0	197,352
West Virginia	193,116	74,241	1,754	32,637	0	0	0	0	301,748
Wisconsin	253,764	89,496	128,042	29,601	0	0	0	0	500,903
Wyoming	27,132	8,136	5,262	6,831	0	0	0	0	47,361
Total U.S.	11,888,604	4,773,798	2,557,332	2,718,738	772,191	409,840	319,200	556,000	23,995,703

Table 5.13				Table 5.14	

Hamburger Chains' Share of Eating and Drinking Place Sales

Per Capita Sales by State

State	Sales of 8 Chains ($000)	Sales as % Eating & Drinking Sales		State	Per Capita Sales of 8 Chains
Alabama	425,618	27.2		Alabama	103
Alaska	54,288	10.1		Alaska	99
Arizona	395,084	19.1		Arizona	115
Arkansas	185,571	20.9		Arkansas	77
California	2,480,129	11.8		California	89
Colorado	339,252	13.9		Colorado	101
Connecticut	291,892	11.2		Connecticut	90
Delaware	79,554	20.6		Delaware	124
D.C.	84,840	11.5		D.C.	136
Florida	1,397,859	16.6		Florida	115
Georgia	771,395	20.5		Georgia	123
Hawaii	145,746	10.8		Hawaii	134
Idaho	54,644	12.0		Idaho	53
Illinois	1,250,049	18.3		Illinois	107
Indiana	698,687	21.9		Indiana	125
Iowa	282,239	18.8		Iowa	99
Kansas	253,753	19.9		Kansas	102
Kentucky	374,059	19.9		Kentucky	99
Louisiana	355,247	15.6		Louisiana	79
Maine	124,158	15.8		Maine	104
Maryland	558,352	19.2		Maryland	122
Massachusetts	450,728	8.3		Massachusetts	77
Michigan	996,898	18.6		Michigan	108
Minnesota	425,454	15.7		Minnesota	99
Mississippi	209,491	24.9		Mississippi	78
Missouri	620,887	20.6		Missouri	120
Montana	52,926	11.4		Montana	64
Nebraska	152,090	15.6		Nebraska	94
Nevada	131,093	17.3		Nevada	128
New Hampshire	91,293	11.6		New Hampshire	86
New Jersey	625,026	13.8		New Jersey	81
New Mexico	125,857	14.7		New Mexico	83
New York	1,264,755	11.5		New York	70
North Carolina	871,142	26.1		North Carolina	135
North Dakota	59,341	17.1		North Dakota	85
Ohio	1,267,347	19.5		Ohio	117
Oklahoma	294,197	16.2		Oklahoma	88
Oregon	185,590	10.7		Oregon	68
Pennsylvania	1,054,288	16.8		Pennsylvania	88
Rhode Island	79,534	11.0		Rhode Island	80
South Carolina	444,149	25.4		South Carolina	128
South Dakota	59,996	15.6		South Dakota	83
Tennessee	548,569	23.1		Tennessee	112
Texas	1,412,768	14.0		Texas	84
Utah	124,999	19.7		Utah	73
Vermont	38,344	9.4		Vermont	70
Virginia	759,161	22.1		Virginia	128
Washington	197,352	6.4		Washington	43
West Virginia	301,748	41.8		West Virginia	156
Wisconsin	500,903	17.0		Wisconsin	104
Wyoming	47,361	12.6		Wyoming	95
Total U.S.	23,995,703	15.9		Total U.S.	98

competitor in the Northeast. While not strictly a fast-food hamburger entry, Friendly does offer inexpensive hamburgers and does have a strong presence: the chain has more stores in Massachusetts than McDonald's. No such distortion exists in the Northwest, however.

Finally, Table 5.15 ranks the states according to estimated hamburger sales per capita. Note that the national average is $98 per capita annually. Observe, too, that the pattern that has emerged in other attempts to measure saturation recurs. Specifically, the southeastern states experience high levels of fast-food sales per capita, as do a limited number of states that benefit from tourism. Of states not characterized by the above attributes, Indiana, Ohio, and Missouri again show up as the most heavily saturated states. Their levels of per capita fast-food hamburger consumption appear to be 20 to 25 percent above the national average. Again, the analysis suggests that expansion of the number of fast-food units by one-quarter to one-third could be achieved before the entire country would be brought to the level of saturation currently being achieved in a number of representative, that is, nontourist, states.

Table 5.15

Hamburger Chains' per Capita Sales, 1988

State	Per Capita Sales of 8 Chains ($)	State	Per Capita Sales of 8 Chains ($)
West Virginia	156	Iowa	99
D.C.	136	Wyoming	95
North Carolina	135	Nebraska	94
Hawaii	134	Connecticut	90
South Carolina	128	California	89
Virginia	128	Pennsylvania	88
Nevada	128	Oklahoma	88
Indiana	125	New Hampshire	86
Delaware	124	North Dakota	85
Georgia	123	Texas	84
Maryland	122	South Dakota	83
Missouri	120	New Mexico	83
Ohio	117	New Jersey	81
Florida	115	Rhode Island	80
Arizona	115	Louisiana	79
Tennessee	112	Mississippi	78
Michigan	108	Arkansas	77
Illinois	107	Massachusetts	77
Maine	104	Utah	73
Wisconsin	104	New York	70
Alabama	103	Vermont	70
Kansas	102	Oregon	68
Colorado	101	Montana	64
Alaska	99	Idaho	53
Kentucky	99	Washington	43
Minnesota	99		
		Total U.S.	98

Table 5.16

Domestic Travel Expenditures by State, 1986

State	Expenditure ($ million)	1987 Pop. (000)	Per Capita Spending
Nevada	7,280	1,026.7	7,091
Hawaii	3,039	1,088.8	2,791
Vermont	1,337	550.3	2,430
D.C.	1,283	623.3	2,058
New Jersey	12,971	7,728.6	1,678
Florida	20,350	12,163.9	1,673
New Hampshire	1,710	1,060.1	1,613
Alaska	866	545.7	1,587
Maine	1,879	1,191.8	1,577
Colorado	5,175	3,346.3	1,546
Wyoming	771	500.4	1,541
Arizona	4,815	3,441.1	1,399
Minnesota	5,178	4,292.3	1,206
California	33,658	27,939.0	1,205
New Mexico	1,810	1,525.0	1,187
Utah	1,939	1,712.4	1,132
South Carolina	3,895	3,458.4	1,126
Delaware	709	642.5	1,104
Maryland	4,766	4,562.6	1,045
Virginia	6,073	5,943.2	1,022
Massachusetts	5,896	5,884.1	1,002
Idaho	1,012	1,033.9	979
Missouri	4,970	5,173.6	961
North Carolina	6,079	6,463.6	940
New York	16,775	17,964.0	934
Washington	4,233	4,548.9	931
Texas	15,691	16,888.0	929
Oregon	2,484	2,738.4	907
North Dakota	621	694.3	894
Connecticut	2,806	3,242.5	865
Wisconsin	4,175	4,836.6	863
Montana	717	832.1	862
Pennsylvania	10,105	11,973.4	844
Georgia	5,247	6,295.2	833
Tennessee	4,081	4,899.5	833
Michigan	7,625	9,262.9	823
Oklahoma	2,743	3,344.4	820
South Dakota	592	721.9	820
Illinois	9,554	11,657.6	820
Louisiana	3,596	4,517.8	796
Kansas	1,965	2,495.0	788
Arkansas	1,873	2,420.0	774
Nebraska	1,247	1,616.8	771
West Virginia	1,417	1,934.6	732
Iowa	1,966	2,860.7	687
Ohio	6,897	10,834.9	637
Kentucky	2,293	3,771.5	608
Indiana	3,083	5,570.8	553
Mississippi	1,351	2,676.2	505
Rhode Island	494	990.0	499
Alabama	1,866	4,137.1	451
Total U.S.	252,958	245,622.7	1,030

At the beginning of this analysis, the reader's attention was directed to McDonald's pattern of above-average store openings in the Gulf Coast states, the South-Central region, and the Great Plains states. The low levels of penetration achieved in Mississippi, Texas, and Oklahoma suggest that these remain fruitful areas. Arkansas and Mississippi also have low per capita levels of hamburger consumption, but the chains already hold an inordinately high share of the food consumed away from home market in those states. Most promising of all are states in the Northwest where the hamburger chains have low per capita sales and also hold a very low share of the restaurant market in those states.

Note that the entire thrust of the argument on saturation rests on two assumptions. First, the analyst must presume that the chains are rational and exercise some control over their store openings. If chains open stores in markets where they are achieving well-below-average results, the observer must conclude that they would be better off opening new stores in less densely saturated markets. On the other hand, the analysis also can only provide a floor, or lower limit, for the number of stores that can eventually be opened. It may be, for example, that more stores can be opened in Indiana until there is one for every 5000 people. If so, the ultimate size of the market would be far larger than it currently appears. In this context, it is particularly noteworthy that McDonald's has elected to slow its rate of openings in Indiana, suggesting that the limit of penetration per capita is in fact being approached.

As a final tool in the analysis of identifying saturated and understored markets, Table 5.16 shows the level of spending for domestic tourism in each state. The data are ranked by the per capita spending in each state. For clarification, note that the spending figures are the dollars spent *in* each state, not *by* the residents of each state. Tourism appears to overstate the size of the indigenous hamburger market in such states as Nevada, Vermont, Washington, D.C., and perhaps, to a lesser extent Florida and Virginia.

McDonald's Views on Saturation

McDonald's management remains sanguine on the issue of market saturation, pointing out that there are 1400 counties in the United States with no McDonald's stores at all. Certainly there are markets where, after a hiatus, the company is reaccelerating its rate of store openings. In the New York area, for example, McDonald's currently operates 183 stores. Through the first nine months of 1989, the system opened 5 new stores in the market, with annualized sales of $11.0 million, or $2.2 million per restaurant, well above the McDonald's domestic system average of $1.6 million.

McDonald's chief executive officer Michael R. Quinlan told security analysts in September 1989, "Discounting is the heaviest I have ever seen. We are looking at an overload situation right now. It certainly hasn't backed us off of new expansion. Whatever discounting we've done over the last year and a half hasn't hurt our margins." Indeed, McDonald's managed to improve its margins in late 1989 even in the face of heavy discounting.

"We're turning up the flame on dealing," said chief marketing officer Paul Schrage at the same meeting. "We don't like to discount. We prefer to disguise our discounting with games and contests so as not to cheapen the brand."

Interestingly, McDonald's managed to prosper even in the difficult environment described by Quinlan. Profits in company-owned restaurants in the quarter ended September 1989 rose 18.4 percent, a greater increase than in most recent years for the company despite a decline in traffic counts estimated at 7 percent per store. Management attributes the strong profit performance to a determination not to cut price even in the face of fierce discounting by its competitors.

Shoney's Recapitalization

One approach to the issue of overstoring is to examine what the best-managed companies in the industry themselves seem to believe. The key is to explore how they are spending their dollars, not what their public pronouncements are. Through the three months ended February 14, 1988, Shoney's Inc. had recorded 115 consecutive record quarters in earnings per share, a record exceeding even that of McDonald's. The firm's expansion was rapid and steady: for the fiscal year ended October 25, 1987, Shoney's had opened 57 company-operated stores, bringing the total to 652. Plans were announced to open an additional 65 in the coming year. The company had recently completed its twenty-ninth consecutive year of higher profits, achieving its highest pretax profit margin in fifteen years.

The recurring industry pattern of lower food costs was clearly present even in this exceedingly well-run company: food costs averaged 42.0 percent of sales in 1979 and had fallen to 38.1 percent by fiscal 1987. Labor costs were not significantly changed over the period, falling from 22.9 percent in 1979 to 22.0 percent in 1987.

On March 6, 1988, the management of Shoney's announced a dramatic $730 million plan to recapitalize the company. Holders of Shoney's 36.5 million common shares were to receive a special one-time dividend of $16.00 per share in cash, a $4.00 principal amount in subordinated debentures, and retain the same number of shares in the company.

Management Incentives

Management would receive an additional one million shares of stock in the company under option plans. Growth was to be curtailed to 26 new units in the next year in order to allow the newly indebted, recapitalized company to use its cash flow to repay debt. Part of the rationale behind this move was the strength in the company's financial position, coupled with unrealized gains in real estate. The firm owned 438 restaurant properties at the end of fiscal 1987, and had total long-term debt of only $19.7 million, equal to less than 6 percent of its total stockholders' equity of $301 million.

But surely another reason, beyond the fact that Shoney's financial muscle would allow it, was the management's belief that growth prospects had diminished. Indeed, pretax income for the quarter ended February 1988 rose only 4.7 percent, well below the company's recent experience.

Chapter 6

Marketing and Product Development

Interview with Michael R. Quinlan, CEO of McDonald's

Michael R. Quinlan is the chairman and chief executive officer of McDonald's Corporation. The following interview was conducted at the company's headquarters in Oak Brook, Illinois, in the spring of 1988.

R. Emerson: Legend has it that you started in the mailroom. Could you speak to that?

Quinlan: A very simple story. It was 1963, I was a sophomore at Loyola University in Chicago, totally out of money and was talking to my roommate one day about how I had to get a job, pronto, or I was going to have to do something like drop out of school for awhile. He said, "Why don't you go see my mother." "That's nice, but who's she?" "June Martino, she works at McDonald's." [Mrs. Martino was Ray Kroc's secretary. She eventually rose to the position of corporate treasurer. More significantly, she owned 10 percent of the stock in the company when Kroc was unable to pay her salary and offered her stock in lieu of cash.] "Okay, I know a little bit about McDonald's, but what can she do for me?" "I don't know: go see her." So next day I went down, got on the El on the north side here of Chicago, and went down to see her. I went through these gorgeous offices with teak floors and Persian rugs and finally got into her office after going through two secretaries. And she said, "Oh, hi, honey, how are you?" First words out of her mouth. And I said, "Hi, Mrs. Martino," and she said, "Well, Johnnie says you need a job," and I said "Well, yes, I do," and she said, "You can start tomorrow." I said, "Wouldn't you like to hear a little something about me or tell me a little something about McDonald's?" and she said, "Oh, we'll get to that later. You start tomorrow at $2.00 an hour. I'll call the personnel officer right now and fix it up."

And that was it. Boom. That was November '63. Just blind luck. I really knew nothing about the company. I had eaten there a few times. I had no opinions about it one way or the other. I had been working at odd jobs since I was 10 or 11 years old. It could have been Burger King, it could have been Henry's, it could have been Pillsbury, could have been anybody. I needed a job and I needed it fast. That was it.

RE: It's a long way from the mailroom to becoming chief of operations.

Early Career with McDonald's

Q: I had a succession of jobs in the early days. I was fortunate to come into the company when it was very small and in an environment where everyone was literally doing seventeen different things simply because there was nobody else to do them. And in the years between 1966 and 1969 I was fortunate in that I got involved in a number of different jobs and really did a whole slug of different things for McDonald's and got a lot of experience. The last two of those years I worked for Ed Schmitt, at which time he was the regional vp [Mr. Schmitt went on to become president of McDonald's Corp.] for the old Midwest region. Ed took an interest in me and made sure that I was able to do as much as I was capable of doing. He just put the blocks to me and whatever I could bite off I did. I learned a whole lot about the company in those four years, and then went into operations in 1970.

But not as a novice, Bob, I knew a lot about about the business even by that time. I frankly found the company to be fascinating. It was very fast-paced, there was no bureaucracy to speak of, saw the Kroc/Sonneborn rift, thought that was kind of interesting, and became aware of the balance of power between operations and finance and real estate back when Ray was looking for a president before [Fred L.] Turner took over. These things made a big impression on me at a very early age. So in 1970 I went into operations, spent the better part of a year in restaurant operations, then immediately went into the field and I give Ed Schmitt credit for this again. He made sure that I had good training in operations and then I moved through three different operations-oriented jobs in the space of probably two years. By that time I really knew as much about the business as anybody else around other than the officers of the company at that time. And so, we opened up a new district in St. Louis.

I opened that up for the company in late 1972 and then went out to Washington just six or seven months later and took over the Mid-Atlantic region, took over from [Donald] Smith, by the way. And inherited a very large, unwieldy region with a whole lot of things that needed fixing and needed improving.

So the three years I spent out there were also very rewarding because I was enmeshed in some serious, heavy-duty problem-solving, and as you know the best way to learn something is to have to go through it and fix it yourself. So that was it. I would say that from 1970 through late 1976 I was involved either in operations or in general management all of that time. And it came to me very naturally.

RE: The company has always grown its own managers, except for finance specialists like chief financial officer Jack Greenberg . . .

Q: Except for finance, treasury, tax, legal, some marketing people.

RE: You've always grown your own marketing and operations people. Was there a problem with losing those people in the early days? Did you get raided a lot? Obviously, Smith was raided. [Donald Smith left McDonald's as chief operating officer in 1977 to become president of Burger King. Quinlan became his successor.]

Q: That's one guy. Never has so much been written about one individual. But, yeah we lost a few. Competition picked off a few. And some elected to go to the competition and a few elected to go into other businesses.

    More often than not, they would go to the competition and I observed this during those years. Those were the years when a lot of the chains were being founded. Like a Hardee's was founded and Burger King was starting to get big time. We lost a couple to Hardee's and one to Carrol's and, of course, Smith went to Burger King. A couple of other regional managers left. One went to Shakey's. We probably lost seven or eight what we would call high-level people at that time.

RE: A lot of the chains, like Wendy's, went through a period when some of the senior people found they could make more money as franchisees than as managers. Did that ever happen here?

Q: Senior management?

RE: Say, like you were in 1975?

Q: No. In the early years for McDonald's we had some time when some people who for whatever reason decided that their career wasn't going the way they would have liked it to, maybe we helped them decide, got into the business of being licensees, some for the right reasons, some frankly for the wrong reasons. So we went through a period where we lost some people. Very few high-level people, though. You have to remember back then we were more in the embryo stages of the McOpCo system [McDonald's program of company-owned stores] and just getting going and the company-owned restaurants weren't making a huge amount of money and, of course, we were growing so fast that anybody with any talent was moving up in the organization at a fairly rapid pace so that there wasn't a stagnant environment there that would cause people to say, "Well, gee, my best opportunity is to leave and become a licensee," although some did.

RE: It's always been one of my pet theories about this business that the growing chains are the only ones that can keep good people because of the need for advancement. At a given level people aren't paid that well in this business. But as long as you're expanding there is always the promise of advancement.

Q: Yeah.

RE: That's why chains like Kentucky Fried Chicken and Howard Johnson have such poor operations, because they aren't expanding their system.

Q: You lack the stimulus and the challenge and the change of growth, I suppose . . .

RE: There's no way for a guy to get ahead in a mature chain.

Q: For the past seven or eight years we've had a very active program of McDonald's people leaving the employ of the company to become licensees of McDonald's. Very few have left to become licensees of other companies.

RE: Is this the BFL program?

Q: Not necessarily the BFL program. Sometimes they go in on a conventional basis. It depends on the amount of disposable cash they have at the time they leave. But it's a different kind of program today. Now that we are so big you've got such an enormous sample of people to draw from. A lot of times people will say, "Well, gee, I've had enough of the travel or maybe I'm a square peg in a round hole or I've learned enough about the licensing end of the business where I've decided I'd like to be my own boss so to speak. I like that end of the business as opposed to the corporate or the company side." But it's a very orderly succession. We've been very lucky. I think I can say over the past five years we've been able to match the needs of the company with the desires of some of the people within the company and we've been able to do some very positive licensing to company employees over the last four or five years. We probably have an average of thirty people per year that leave the employ of the McDonald's Corporation and become McDonald's licensees. And they've been doing very well with it. I'm just pleased as hell with it.

RE: What about the fat cats with fifty stores? Is motivating them a problem?

Q: No, I don't really think so. It's funny, you look at the continuum over the years and you see all the various subgenerations of McDonald's licensees come into the system and today I think that the good operators are still good and highly motivated regardless of the number of stores they have. Some are getting older and some leave the business. There's a bit more turnover today than there was ten years ago in the licensee community. Maybe not on a percentage basis but on a numbers basis. . . .

State of the Industry Today

Q: As you well know, the business today is a hell of a lot harder to run than it was ten years ago. It's more complicated, it's faster-paced. Competition is tougher. The marketplace is tougher, breakevens are much higher. But then, to balance that, you've got a lot of the young lions coming up and you've got second generations coming up and getting involved in the business and some of them are just dynamite. They're real strong people. To answer your question and then I'll get off of it: I don't see great evidence of the fat-cat syndrome where people are sitting on their heels. I think they're still aggressive, they're driving, they want to achieve, they want to do more and more and more all the time and they have an awful lot of pride. We're drivers, too, from our side of the business.

RE: What happens to a 65-year-old franchisee who's been with the chain for twenty years and has thirty or forty stores. What happens when he retires? He can't force you to buy him out . . .

Q: True.

RE: In reality, what happens?

Q: The fellows you are talking about are a minute sample of the McDonald's system. But if I could rephrase the question. If John Smith is 65 years old, has been with the system for twenty-three years, and does not have a second generation to help him in the business or if he does not have someone who's come up who can really help him run that operation in the right way, sometimes they'll consolidate a little bit, they'll sell off a couple of their restaurants and go to a smaller base, sometimes they'll sell to other operators, and sometimes they'll sell to the company. It's kind of a potpourri of all three.

Generally speaking, if it's time for someone to leave the system, there's not a whole lot of disagreement between the company and the operator. It's generally obvious to both, and most of the times it's a positive thing as opposed to a negative thing. And then they can sell either to us or to another licensee, as long as we approve. It doesn't happen that frequently that a licensee sells out to one of his employees. The licensees supply a lot of new licensees to the system, employees that they've had for a long time.

Labor Conditions

RE: The whole question of changes in the labor force. How severe is the labor shortage?

Q: It's really a mixed bag. There are areas of the country where it's painfully obvious there's a labor shortage. Just to highlight some of them, obviously the Northeast, some areas of New York, North Atlanta, Palm County in Florida, your real high-growth areas where there's low unemployment, where industry is running at a record clip, particularly the service industry, and there it's tough, although to me the far tougher challenge is keeping the people, not recruiting them. Stopping turnover and cutting that down is the key to solving this problem. There's no question about it, though, it's having an inflationary impact on our industry and it's going to, I think, accelerate the demise of weaker companies and I think it's going to happen pretty quickly.

RE: Will labor pressure be felt less at fast-food chains with lower labor costs than at coffee shops with higher labor content relative to sales?

Coming Shakeout

Q: It's going to result in a little bit of further segmentation of the market. I think the small-time mom and pop that can somehow get in with a low breakeven and operate well on a low-volume basis, I think they'll be alright in isolated locations, more neighborhood shops, or urban locations. The middle-of-the-road guys are the ones that are going to get ground up because the competition for good commercial property and construction costs is continuing to escalate, and the key is going to be you've got to operate more efficiently with your labor force. You just can't afford to churn people constantly. There are areas in Boston, for example, where if you don't treat people right the first day they're gone, they'll just go right down the street because somebody else is offering more, and it's open season in some of those areas. But that's not the rule, that's the exception.

I mean, I can take you up in Minneapolis or Indianapolis or Milwaukee and I could go on and on and on, and it's not a hell of a lot different than it was five years ago. It's just that you have to be a little bit better in terms of people practices to keep the people that you have. It's a problem for us, but I don't see it as a really big problem. I hear some of the horror stories going around and some of the competitors that we have and it shocks me. We're not without sin, we're not without problems, but you've gotta take better care of the young people today. Now that's the young population. Certainly the trend is gonna be toward more older workers.

I don't necessarily call them senior citizens, maybe they are, maybe they aren't. But that pool is obviously getting stronger as time goes on and we're actively involved in recruiting older people—there's no question about it. As a percentage of the crew, it's not major yet by any means: it's less than 10 percent.

Site Costs

RE: You talked about continuing inflation in real estate costs. Why, with savings and loans, gas stations, and some fast-food operators closing their outlets, do costs still go up for prime property? I would think there might be less competition for sites today, or at least more availability.

Q: I don't think so, Bob. There are more users out there in the marketplace. If you look at any area you'll see a tremendous turnover rate if you take it over a two-year period of time. Tremendous turnover in the number of businesses that go in and out of a given trading area. But for people like us, our needs are pretty specific in terms of the size of the facility and the placement of the facility in the traffic flow, probably more particular than a lot of other people that are in there in the commercial sector looking for a convenient-type location. You know, we can't operate on less than 40,000 square feet on a free-stander or we're choking off our volume.

Plus, I'll tell you one more thing. In my opinion, one of the things that is imperative for success from this point on is to be absolutely sure that you buy *the* best location. Not second best, not third best, but *the* best. I've seen it so many times, and to buy the best, you know the property owners know what the value of their land is and they know how their placement is in terms of convenience and ingress and egress, traffic flow and all that stuff, convenience to traffic generators, and those sites are getting harder and harder to get.

There's progressively more competition for the Grade A locations and obviously less of them as time goes on. Ergo, cost goes up. That doesn't bother me as long as we've made the decision: we're going to pay the piper. And we're going to do that because we've found out that by paying for it and getting the Grade A, the volume comes right along with it. But for somebody that doesn't have the same kind of volume-generating capacity, unless their margins are significantly larger than ours, it's tough to make a buck out there, it really is.

RE: Are the stores that you're opening now operating at volumes as high as those of your stores opened two or three years ago, adjusted for price increases?

Q: A little higher.

RE: They are a little higher?

Q: Uh-huh.

RE: So if you took that figure as the litmus test for overstoring or saturation, then you're not at that point yet?

Q: I don't see it, not for us. Now, for the industry in general I'm not sure that I'd be willing to say that.

RE: I'm intrigued with the demographics of the customer base. No one has cracked the upscale market. In 1983 Wall Street funded a lot of them: there was Fuddruckers and Chili's and yet most of these have become the answer to trivia questions: "Do you remember x?" Is there a way for you to crack that market? The customer who's too old to eat at McDonald's, or wants a beer with his hamburger?

Q: No, we're not going to go into the alcohol business. I think there are some opportunities in the dinner segment of the business that we haven't cracked yet. In the lunch segment, no, and frankly needing quick turnover and wanting quick turnover and with the enormous popularity of the drive-through segment of the business, I don't see any big opportunities for McDonald's to crack the upscale—nor do I want them, frankly, in the lunch business. But in the dinner business that's another story. I think if I were a betting man, which apparently I am according to the *Business Week* article, I would bet you that the next big successes that McDonald's has over the next five years will be more in the dinner segment of the market.

RE: I'm still waiting for the return of McRib.

Q: We just had it back a couple of months ago.

RE: You've been so slow with new products, testing them so methodically, yet introducing very few new products. Are you going to change that?

Q: If you look at the last five years, I can prove to you that we've been a hell of a lot more aggressive in testing products than we ever were prior to that time. Just look at our list of failures. It's harder to get something that sticks. It's easy to get something that gives you a quick blast.

Steak sandwich, very successful right out of the box. McRib was very successful right out of the box, versions 1, 2, 3, 4, and 5 of the chicken sandwich had; versions 1 through 9 of the McFeast or the McDLT. We've learned that you need to be patient, because . . . you have to understand, in a high-turnover business like ours, for us to put something in and have it stick to the menu, it's got to do several things. It's got to add transaction counts, it's got to add profit. And it cannot be injurious to the overall ability of the restaurant to operate as well as it was operating before. And that's why we fooled around so long with the biscuits, for example. We played with those for four years before we finally settled on going with fresh-made biscuits as opposed to preprocessed quick-frozen biscuits that could be thawed and baked off in the store. Same thing with the salads. We played with the salads for lord knows how many years and I'm not willing for a product that might add 2 percent to my sales short-run, net, not willing to risk the basic equation that we have that's working so well thus far. It's just a lousy trade.

RE: Does it make any sense to have rolling, temporary introductions of new products? Just to get that quick blast you described?

Q: No, but on a promotional basis we've actually changed our marketing strategy in the last three or four years, if you look at what we've done there have been three or four different occasions, basically one a year, where we will put in one of our old products on a six-week burst basis.

RE: Including my favorite, the double cheeseburger.

Q: Double cheeseburger is one, bacon double cheese, a knock-off of that, and McRib has come back a couple of times. You just haven't seen it. And cheddar melt. And I believe in that philosophy, I like it and I think it's a good marketing tool.

RE: Will the dinner business require a new product?

Q: I think it will. I think that the American taste and eating habits are getting so segmented now, I think at least for us it will take some new products to sell significantly more than what we're currently selling at dinnertime.

RE: Do you regard McNuggets as part of the core menu now? They're here to stay?

Q: Yes.

RE: There was speculation that you created supply problems for yourselves because of your huge volume requirements for chicken.

Q: No, we're in a grow-out program with chicken. Chicken is not the same kind of commodity that beef is in terms of supply problems. You can come up to speed very fast in terms of chicken supply versus chicken needs. . . .

Dinner Business

Q: . . . So, we're doing alright in the dinner business segment right now, but I just think there's more potential there. I'm convinced that convenience and quality is the way to go and so we're gonna be focusing our efforts on that segment in the years to come.

RE: In evaluating QSR, NRA surveys have found that customers give the industry good marks for speed of service and convenience, along with low marks for food quality. However, that didn't seem to bother customers because their expectations were also low with regard to food quality. But what surprised me was that consumers also gave the industry poor marks for price/value, in other words they did not feel that they were getting much food for their money. If you had asked me, "Why do people go to Burger King or McDonald's?" I would have answered, "Well, it's cheap." I would have assumed that good price/value would have ranked right up there with convenience and speed of service. But apparently that isn't the real motivation at all. Consumers seem to feel they get a better deal at coffee houses or at upscale restaurants.

Price/Value Relationships

Q: Well, if I compare our price/value today with what it was six years ago, I don't see any deterioration. If you look at the trends in packaged goods in supermarkets, for example — you look at what you pay for some of those entrees — they're really pretty expensive for what you get. I'm not knocking them, they make some very good products, but I think that some of it, Bob, might be people's propensity to remember what things were . . .

RE: The $0.15 burger?

Q: Even me. To me, a Chevy ought to cost $4500. They don't. I don't think any car is a good value today. Maybe they are. I can go on . . . a suit. It's ridiculous what suits cost today. And yet, I still buy them because I need them. It doesn't cut down my purchasing at all. I think when people's incomes go up they don't relate the price/value today to what it might have been years ago. That's Mike Quinlan's theory, and I could be all wet.

RE: I remember Fred Turner's remark to analysts eight years ago that "Brown-bagging peanut butter is still the only thing cheaper than McDonald's." [Laughter]

Q: We keep an eye on it and it ticks me off when we have to increase prices and we try to hold the lid on as much as we can. I think we're doing about as good a job as we did ten years ago in that area.

RE: *My picture of the industry ten years ago was one of companies growing through new unit openings. An increasing percentage of the capital outlays these days seem to be devoted to reinvestment in existing stores.*

Q: If you want my views on McDonald's, you have to remember, Bob, that we have never, at least in recent history, we have never been forced to make a capital allocation, do this as opposed to doing that. We've been very fortunate in that regard. However, I can look at a change in how we are deploying ourselves today. The reinvestment requirements per restaurant are certainly much heavier today than they were ten years ago. . . .

Refurbishing

Q: . . . Now, part of that is because of the aging of the system. Part of it also is the changing taste of the consumer. They want more from us and we're gonna give 'em more. Decors change. The ambiance that the customer expects changes for the in-store experience.

The drive-through has become so important to our business today we've been forced to increase our capacity and are still being forced to increase our capacity through that side of the restaurant to take advantage of the volume potential that's there. Then the last thing is in the back of the house—as our product line has expanded our storage requirements, the changeover time, our cooking requirements change, and we've just found that it takes a progressively more intensive approach on the reinvestment side to keep the restaurants in top shape. I don't think that's going to change in the near future. If anything, I see it accelerating.

RE: *Can there ever come a time when a whole bunch of stores, say 2000 stores, all have to be refurbished suddenly? Where it would require a major slug of capital to bring the system up to modern standards? Or is it more gradual than that?*

Q: I don't see it too much for McDonald's. That's because there's so much intense pressure put on both for ourselves and with the licensees. We try to do it on a gradual basis year after year. I think you're gonna see it just keep going. We'll do something of a relatively major size to 600 to 700 of our restaurants every year from this point on.

Saturation

RE: *The question of saturation we've already talked about a little bit from the point of view of new restaurant volumes. Are there any major markets where you're finding you can't squeeze any more in?*

Q: No, in fact I'm the other way. With the tools we have available it's obvious to me that we are nowhere near saturation.

In fact, we're as far away from it as I would have said if we had sat here five years ago—I'm more bullish now on our ability to open new restaurants profitably. It requires better analysis and better tools of analysis for the market. We're fortunate that we have them. It used to be easier.

There's no question about, when I was out picking real estate, I thought I was pretty darned good at it and I guess I was by those standards of twelve or thirteen years ago. Today I'd have to be better because the restaurants are all closer together and the locations are much more costly. There's not as much room for error. So you have to be better at your analysis of where your sites can go.

RE: I took a McDonald's store directory and looked at the number of stores by state and I looked at the most saturated states on a per capita basis, whether it was Indiana or Georgia or the Carolinas . . . it's obvious that you still continue to open there . . .

Q: Oh, sure.

RE: So it isn't like you've ground to a halt . . .

Q: The demographics are constantly changing, oozing and ebbing and flowing in each one of the marketplaces and I think that's the beauty of our regional office system. The people that are picking real estate today live right close to those markets.

And they know where a shopping center is going and they know where a housing development is going and they know when a center is going to close up and where a highway is going to be rerouted; because they live there, they're part of the cities or part of the town and that's going to continue.

RE: Is your profitability comparable nationally by region?

Q: There are significant differences by geographical area. How do you define "significant?" Is 10 percent significant? Is 17 percent?

RE: Well, say 10 percent . . .

Regional Differences

Q: There are areas that are better than others. There are areas where it's tough for us to open and make profits.

Any area where the volume is so-so and the costs are high.

You can't charge three bucks for a Big Mac. In Manhattan it's approaching that. But if you go to Binghamton, New York, for example, there's a limit to what you can do so you've gotta be really, really careful. There's other areas where the usage per capita is much higher in relation to the costs of opening a location and those are obviously the ones where we do the best.

RE: So there are variations . . .

Q: There are variations in growth rate that we look at every year and obviously although our site selection is made by our people out on the line we certainly do impact on it here. We're constantly trying to tinker with the dials a little bit and try to heavy up in advance of the demand in the areas where the population growth is projected to be the highest. But I will reiterate that all areas of the country other than—How many stores can you put in Billings, Montana? You put a couple in . . . or Whitefish, Montana, there's 4000 people there—but in your metro areas if you keep a sharp eye on the changing traffic patterns and housing patterns and the changing demographic patterns, traffic generators . . . It includes, "Can you knock somebody else out? Can you dominate another little segment more than you have?"

Closing Stores

RE: It's been rare for you to close stores. Is it conceivable that in the future you'd see some closing of a few hundred stores?

Q: Certainly not to that level although really for the last four years or so, since you wrote the last book what eight or nine years ago . . .

RE: Nine years ago . . .

Q: It used to be a mortal sin for us to close a location. It was kind of a badge: "We never close" and then we closed one in Decatur, Illinois. That was the first one and then we went five years before we closed another one—other than condemnations—Today, we are absolutely willing to walk away if we're in the wrong market.

RE: I got letters from people saying I remember they closed one in Ft. Lauderdale, there was one on the Lynnway in Lynn, Mass . . .

Q: Most of the time . . . 98 out of 100 times . . . it's a relocation as opposed to an actual closing. In Manhattan it's different: if you move three blocks you're in another world. But in most of the cases if you get out of your big metro centers it's a case of moving it a half a mile down the road or sometimes even 300 yards down the road.

Foreign Markets

RE: The move into foreign markets took a very long time and Wall Street was impatient, but now you and maybe KFC seem to be the only U.S. operators successfully entrenched overseas. Your foreign operations are not as profitable yet on a per store basis . . .

Q: You could argue that several different ways. In terms of return on assets, not yet. In terms of return on investment, maybe not yet but they're coming fast. My contention is that in some of the foreign markets the returns will actually exceed what they are here in the U.S. Time will tell. These markets are all in various stages of maturation.

If I take the conglomerate picture of our overseas operation, if I just look at the last two years, it's obvious that all the years of investment are really starting to pay off for us now. Some of these countries are just popping like crazy right now.

RE: The whole question of operating in Europe with advertising restrictions?

Q: It's a problem in terms of us not being able to market in the traditional "most-cost-efficient sense." However, if there's nobody else in the marketplace using that vehicle to market then you're all on the same level and it forces us to a different type of marketing. But it works. We're into more cinemas and billboards and bus stops and local store marketing and things of that nature.

RE: As you think about the company twenty years from now, isn't it inevitable that you'll eventually be more profitable overseas? There is no Burger King or Wendy's to compete with you. There are no regional chains.

Q: We've got a pretty big lead . . . on just about [everyone].

RE: The analogy that occurs to me is Coca Cola 15 or 20 years ago.

Q: I've spent an awful lot of time overseas in the last three years or so and to me the key is getting into the country and operating in such a fashion that the local people appreciate us for what we are and try to be a part of the community. And I really do mean that. We spend an enormous amount of time in community involvement over there and local store marketing. And the countries are run by locals. They're not all out of Oak Brook, Illinois. The Aussies run the Australian company and the Brits run the British company and the Germans run the German company and on and on it goes. . . .

Local Management Overseas

Q: . . . We really have become part of the local scene in almost all of these countries and that's the way it's got to be. Even though I'm a Yank and if I go to McDonald's in Singapore or I go to McDonald's in Taiwan or if I go to McDonald's in Holland I really feel that we are a part of those countries. People know us, it's not the Yankee company over there. You know, it's us. Same thing in Caracas. You go to Caracas and look at all the stuff we've got going on. We're there . . . we're a part of the city of Caracas, Venezuela. People love us. But you have to work at that. You don't have the built up reservoir of — I like to say it's goodwill it took us so many years to generate here.

RE: Have the supply problems been resolved in most of the major countries?

Q: No, they have not been resolved. But we're a hell of a lot further along the continuum in terms of getting a product that matches what I call the McDonald's spec for what a bun should be and what a meat patty should be and what have you. We're not as far along as I'd like to be, but compared to three years ago we're light years along the continuum. We're getting pretty close in most of the countries. Some of the countries, Bob, the raw material just isn't there.

RE: We had touched on media levels. It seems to me that the fast-food industry is becoming more like packaged foods. Lots of media behind brand names that make the cost of entry prohibitive for new entrants. Shelf-space dominance isn't exactly the right analogy but . . .

Q: I know exactly what you mean.

RE: Will you reach a point where the noise level becomes so high that you'll bring ad dollars down as a percent of sales? Like what Anheuser-Busch is doing this year, bringing their ad dollars down not in absolute terms but at least as a percent of sales?

Q: I'd like to reach that level, although I'll tell you something. I'm still convinced that heavy penetration in the media with the GRPs [gross rating points, a measure of media effectiveness] and what have you is the answer to keeping our face before the public. There's also a significantly greater level of competition in our segment of the industry than in A-B's industry, for example. There really aren't that many national players in the beer business. That's a very interesting business, too. But I don't see it letting up for awhile. Although I'd like to get to the day in a few years when we can lessen the amount as a percentage of sales that we spend on marketing.

RE: Is it possible you'd spend less on TV and give more of it away in coupons or games?

Q: No, because most of that is all television-driven anyway. It's very intensive to television whether you're couponing or discounting or running a game or any of that stuff. It's media-intensive, no question about it. I can see maybe a shift down the road toward more truly store-by-store local marketing effort as a percentage of the total than we do today.

RE: If I can get one more Marvin Gardens card, I never have to work again.

Q: Somebody was on here the other day, it wasn't Marvin Gardens, it was #61 . . .

RE: It was one of the yellow ones [laughter] . . . There's so little going on in new competitors, but there is one segment that interests me. The buffet people like Ryan's or Buffets Inc. give up high food costs of 45 percent . . .

Q: Uh-huh.

RE: And make it up with enormous sales turnover, much higher even than you get . . .

Q: They run a much bigger check, too, than we do. Much bigger, and no drive-through business. It's almost becoming a separate segment of the industry. That's not a new segment, though. I mean, how long was Ponderosa around? How long was Bonanza around? It's the same thing, right?

RE: I suppose.

Q: I think if they want to go national, though, they're going to have to get on TV. They're going to have to get into that fight and they haven't to my knowledge been doing that.

RE: No. They haven't spent a nickel on advertising. As Ryan's management said, "Bob, the only way to understand this is to come down and see the miracle in action."

Q: They put out a good product, you know, but it's a very localized type of thing. If you look at what we're doing in some of the real estate locations, the long-distance-travel locations, and the more specialty-oriented locations, we're trying to keep up the ability to market to somebody in Minnesota so that when they get to Florida we get them just the same way. I'm convinced that's the right way to go for us or we'd stop doing that. Those local operations, I don't see how they can do it. They're going to be forced to compete more and more in the local marketplace. I don't know how wide a trading area they can attract their business from, so I don't really know about their expansion capability.

RE: Is the prospect of your company doing an acquisition a dead issue?

Q: Oh, no, it's not dead. But I've learned in the past couple of years what enormous potential we have on top of what we're doing where our returns are still good. What's our return on assets now: 18.4 percent? . . . Think of the returns when we increase sales 1 percent—real sales, forget the inflation—it's an enormous business. I mean, we're doing what, $8 billion? It's more than that; it'll be $10 billion in the United States before you know it. A 10 percent increase is a billion dollar business! A 1 percent increase is a $100 million business. . . . What am I going to get out there for me to deploy? The money is not necessarily a problem— but for me to deploy the assets in terms of management time and attention to something? If I put that into our business in product development and research and equipment research to make the restaurants more efficient and what have you, I think I can get a lot better payout now from McDonald's than I can from going into something else. Frankly, without the risk. You tell me how big Jiffy-Lube is going to be. I don't know. None of us knows. Tell me how big Marriott Courtyard or Holiday Inn Courtyard is going to be, all of that stuff. It might turn out to be the next McDonald's. I don't know. We talked about dinner. We haven't done as much as we're capable of doing in that segment. So that's all still to come. I'd rather put our money and our resources there, short term, than going out on the street and trying to buy something else. I think there's *that* much additional potential for McDonald's.

RE: Is there anything that worries you? When I first started following McDonald's in 1974, it was a very controversial company. People worried about saturation, a worm scare could knock the stock down 10 percent, Briloff's article on accounting could knock the stock . . . [Abraham J. Briloff, Professor of Accounting at the City University of New York published an article in the July 8, 1974, issue of Barron's *entitled "You Deserve a Break," that was highly critical of McDonald's accounting practices.]*

Q: Yeah, that was a five-pointer in a day, wasn't it?

RE: But now, if anything, it's the other way. There's a blue-chip quality to McDonald's, almost a monotonous predictability. Is there anything you worry about?

Q: I worry about the changing tastes of the consumer. If you want to know what I'm personally worried about, there's nothing that I look at as a life-threatening thing. It's not cancer in the beef. Now there are stories that there are cancer inhibitors in cooked beef as opposed to cancer causers in cooked beef. Cholesterol, saturated fats, unsaturated fats. You know, we can alter the menu to accommodate that long term, and we'll have to, I'm sure, as time goes on because people's tastes are changing. But I think we can go with the flow on that. Frankly, the biggest challenge we'll have longer term is keeping the spirit of overachieving alive in the McD system as it was when Kroc was around to crack the whip and drive us all to try to overachieve every day.

I'm not saying we can't do it, but if there's one thing we've got to keep the pedal to the metal on it's the attitude on the part of the McDonald's system of never being satisfied with anything. That's different about us, I really believe that.

RE: So it's still possible for someone to come up through the mail room and aspire to your job?

Q: My son had his chance, he's going to go out and work for us. I don't know how he's going to do.

RE: My son was excited to learn that I was going to come out and meet the man who owns McDonald's.

Q: I wish.

(End of interview.)

McDonald's Need for New Products

By one measure, McDonald's profitability has remained similar over time, that is, its return on assets relative to its cost of long-term debt. (Table 6.1). Note that the gap between return on assets and borrowing cost has widened slightly over the past twenty years.

Table 6.1

McDonald's Profitability and Borrowing Costs

Year	Return on Assets (%)	Long-Term Debt Cost (%)
1971	15.9	10.0
1981	20.7	13.0
1988	17.4	9.0

Source: McDonald's Corp.

Lower Return on Assets

However, by other measures the chain's results, while still impressive by the standards of most retailers, have been under some pressure. McDonald's profits, expressed as a percentage return on assets, fell from 21.2 percent in 1984 to 17.4 percent by 1988.

Reasons for Decline

This deterioration reflects a number of factors. First, the chain has chosen to invest in more of what it calls "billboard locations," highly visible units located on expensive sites. Second, sales have grown slowly given the level of reinvestment that the chain is being forced to make in existing stores. Finally, returns on assets are lower in foreign markets, which are increasing as a percent of the total system.

Margins Steady

Expressed as a percent of sales, on the other hand, McDonald's profitability in company-owned stores has remained remarkably consistent over a long period of time. Table 6.2 shows the principal components of the income statement of McDonald's stores expressed as a percent of sales since 1973. Note the prevalence of profit margins in the 16.5 to 18.5 percent range.

The underlying components of the income statement show considerably varying trends, however. Note the persistent drop in food costs as a percent of sales. Consumers clearly are

Table 6.2

McDonald's Profitability Over Time
(as Percent of Sales)

Year	Food Costs	Labor Costs	Rent	Depreciation	Other Costs	Profit Margin
1973	0.430	0.216	0.015	0.030	0.141	0.168
1974	0.408	0.215	0.014	0.032	0.146	0.185
1975	0.400	0.215	0.013	0.033	0.146	0.193
1976	0.390	0.223	0.012	0.032	0.151	0.192
1977	0.391	0.221	0.012	0.032	0.159	0.185
1978	0.402	0.225	0.013	0.034	0.158	0.168
1979	0.403	0.223	0.013	0.034	0.161	0.166
1980	0.389	0.223	0.013	0.036	0.170	0.165
1981	0.376	0.225	0.012	0.038	0.178	0.170
1982	0.371	0.226	0.012	0.038	0.185	0.169
1983	0.368	0.218	0.013	0.041	0.180	0.180
1984	0.374	0.213	0.014	0.040	0.181	0.179
1985	0.365	0.219	0.014	0.041	0.183	0.179
1986	0.361	0.221	0.016	0.044	0.188	0.178
1987	0.354	0.218	0.015	0.045	0.190	0.170
1988	0.343	0.223	0.016	0.046	0.194	0.178

not getting as much food for their dollar now at McDonald's as they did a decade ago. To some degree, this reflects the growing importance of breakfast, which features items that have a very low food cost, for example, egg dishes.

An additional cause for the drop in food costs relative to sales has been the increase in capital costs: rent and depreciation. We have already seen that McDonald's growth in sales per store, while consistent, has not managed to keep pace with increases in land, building, and equipment costs. The chain has been forced to boost selling prices to offset higher land and building costs.

Labor Costs Consistent

Labor costs have been the most stable component of the income statement, consistently accounting for 22 percent of the sales dollar. On the one hand, absence of pressure from minimum wage increases and the overall wage rate inflation have just about offset the increasing difficulty of attracting workers. The most striking factor in the income statement, perhaps, is the sharp, persistent growth in "all other" expenses relative to sales. This reflects higher insurance and energy costs, and also reflects a gradually higher level of expenditures for marketing.

Rising Advertising Expenditures

Rather than gaining some economies of scale in advertising as it grows larger, McDonald's has elected to increase its marketing as a percent of sales as well as in absolute numbers. This serves to increase pressure on its competitors. However, the recent emergence of the double drive-through concepts with their low-priced, high-food-cost, rapid-turnover strategy suggests that McDonald's may have created an umbrella for new entrants that specifically address the problem of McDonald's prices having become too high.

Brand Recognition

One method for the company to improve its results is to capitalize on its powerful brand recognition. McDonald's has been identified as the fifth-most-powerful brand name in the world, behind Coca Cola, IBM, Sony, and Porsche, but ahead of such giants as Seiko, Honda, Toyota, BMW, and Disney. McDonald's is the second-most-recognized brand in the United States, according to the company's research. "We think like a brand and act like a retailer," said Paul D. Schrage, McDonald's senior executive vice president and chief marketing officer. Certainly the chain's level of brand awareness is unparalleled in foodservice.

The chain's dominance of the children's market is particularly powerful. McDonald's research indicates that three out of four children prefer McDonald's to any other chain. There is in the company's attitude a sense that staying with its proven formula is the wisest course. Why tinker with a formula that has been so successful? "We'll continue to advertise food, folks and fun," said Schrage in September 1989.

Top-of-Mind Awareness

McDonald's achieves top-of-mind awareness more than double that of Burger King. In the quick-service restaurant category, McDonald's top-of-mind awareness is 41 percent. (David B. Green, 1988 annual meeting) The obvious question is, how best to expand sales, playing on the company's existing strengths? A constraint is that, at the peak lunch hour, most McDonald's stores operate at close to capacity. Merely adding new menu items only serves to slow down operations. Unless the new product can significantly raise the average check, there is no point in putting it in the system. One answer is to improve sales at slack periods of the day.

McDonald's Lack of Dinner Sales

McDonald's stores record 30 percent of their sales at dinner. This percentage is far below the 65 percent of sales recorded in the evening by Kentucky Fried Chicken or the 73 percent of sales produced at the dinner hour or later by Pizza Hut. A McDonald's store with annual volume of $1.8 million actually has the physical capacity to accommodate sales of $4.0 million. Hence, the chain, despite its great success, still has enormous underutilized capacity. As a result, there is a strong incentive to introduce new products in order to increase traffic.

New Pizza Tests

By late 1989, McDonald's had begun testing a new pizza product in twenty-four stores in Evansville, Indiana. Several modifications to the test stores had to be made to accommodate the test product. Since the standard McDonald's drive-through window is only 10 inches wide, and the pizza was 14 inches in diameter, modifications had to be made to the drive-through window. Total cost of the ovens in the prototype units as well as modifications to the store itself, averaged between $30,000 and $40,000.

PepsiCo's Estimate of McDonald's Pizza Sales

Preliminary studies by PepsiCo's Pizza Hut estimated that McDonald's might achieve annual pizza sales of $2 billion, or an average of about $250,000 per store. Such a sales level would equate to about 15 percent of a current store's volume. Although some cannibalization would be inevitable, the fact that McDonald's made the product available only after 4 p.m. suggested that cannibalization would be minimal. Moreover, with a 25 percent food cost, nearly 8 points below the rest of the McDonald's menu, any incremental sales would be highly profitable. The impact that McDonald's could make in the pizza segment could be staggering. Perhaps it was no coincidence that within weeks of McDonald's putting pizza into test, Domino's founder Thomas S. Monaghan put his chain up for sale.

Initially, McDonald's pizza has been made with a frozen crust. In response, the chain's competitors have predictably attacked the product for not being fresh. In fact, however, the crust in the test markets is frozen only because it is made centrally in Chicago and shipped to the test markets. Eventually, if brought out nationally, it may well be made fresh in each store.

Impact on Pizza Hut

The test market results, while not necessarily indicative of future sales, were particularly interesting because of the comparatively small impact on Pizza Hut stores in the test market. Pizza Hut units in the area continued to show gains in sales per store in excess of 10 percent even after McDonald's introduction of the product. Although below the 20 percent gains achieved before the McDonald's entry, the Pizza Hut experience was by no means catastrophic.

Chapter 7

Wall Street and the Fast-Food Industry

Earnings Before Interest, Taxes, and Depreciation (EBITD) and Takeovers

The search for a single quantitative tool to value companies has evolved rapidly in recent years. Once the key valuation measure was thought to be the ratio of a company's stock price to its book value. The classic text for security analysts by Benjamin Graham stressed that measure. The emergence of rapidly growing technology stocks in the late 1950s and 1960s made the price-to-book-value measure suspect, however, since the explosively growing stocks of the day, IBM, Xerox, and Polaroid, sold at multiples of their underlying book values, yet their rate of profitability on their equity was sufficiently high that their stock prices rose manyfold even from a base that, by standards of the price-to-book school, seemed outrageously high.

The concept of valuing companies by their price-earnings (p/e) ratios came into vogue, with the thought that a company with more rapid growth prospects might be worth a higher level of valuation, or higher p/e ratio, on current earnings than a firm with less rapid growth. A rule of thumb in the 1960s was that companies could sell at p/e ratios equal to their projected growth rates. Some investors ranked companies by dividing their p/e's by their growth rates: the lower the quotient, the more attractive the stock.

An added wrinkle was to divide the p/e not by the growth rate alone, but by its "total return," that is, the sum of the growth rate and the current dividend yield. After all, if two companies have identical growth prospects and prices, surely the one that provides a higher yield is the more attractive.

New Valuation Techniques

The dominance of the corporate buyer in the 1980s has led to the use of different tools, with an emphasis on the ability of a corporation to generate surplus cash that can be used to retire the debt issued to acquire the firm.

EBITD as a Valuation Tool

The most widely used concept is that of EBITD, or earnings before interest, taxes, and depreciation. The prospective buyer views EBITD as the cash available to service debt that may be issued to acquire the company. This becomes the denominator in a calculation in which the numerator is the total cost of acquiring the company, including the total market value of the company's stock, plus all debt, less surplus cash. The objective is to determine the total cost of acquiring a company, including the assumption of its net debt, relative to the cash-generating capability of the company before allocating its cash to repayment of debt, maintenance of its physical plant, or payment of taxes. Table 7.1 provides an illustration of the above calculation, using PepsiCo as an example.

The end result of the calculation is expressed as a multiple of EBITD. In the example of PepsiCo, one sees that the company sold in the fall of 1989 at a price on 1988 EBITD of about 8.9 times. This multiple was in line with most high-quality, predictable-growth companies in the consumer products category.

Prices Paid for Acquisitions

Table 7.2 shows the multiple to EBITD paid for the major acquisitions in the restaurant industry since the beginning of 1985. Note that the typical price to EBITD averaged about

Table 7.1

PepsiCo's Value as a Multiple of EBITD
($ millions except where noted)

Depreciation & amortization	629.3
Pretax income	1,137.6
Interest charges, net	222.4
EBITD	1,989.3
Shares outstanding (million)	262.9
Stock price ($)	59.50
Market value of stock	15,643
Plus: Debt (March 31)	3,617
Less: Cash	1,638
Total cost of acquisition	17,622

seven times. Note, too, that the price to EBITD is generally a more stable series for all of the acquisitions than other ratios, such as price to book value or price to sales. This is reasonable, since a company with a high return on equity or book value will normally command a far higher price compared to book value than will a less-profitable one. Similarly, price-to-sales ratios can be distorted in the event that one company's profit margins can be far different from another's. Even p/e ratios are inadequate because one company may have more debt to be paid off than another, one may have far more cash on its balance sheet than another, or one may have unusually high depreciation charges that mask strong underlying cash flow. Hence, the cash-adjusted total-cost-to-EBITD ratio provides the single most stable tool for the acquiring entity.

Table 7.2

Data for Selected Restaurant Acquisitions, 1985–89

Acquired Company	Equity Value ($ million)	Equity/ Book Value Ratio	Equity/ Net Income Ratio	Total Value ($ million)	Total Value/ EBITD Ratio
TW Services	1662.6	3.3	30.3	2709.7	7.5
Church's	395.7	1.6	86.0	413.0	10.0
TGI Friday's	258.1	2.1	20.0	213.1	7.1
Foodmaker	244.2	2.1	31.7	769.9	7.8
Steak & Ale	431.0	2.5	59.0	522.4	6.1
Chi-Chi's	229.1	2.5	18.6	223.4	
Shoney's South	131.5	1.6	42.4	152.9	4.6
Int'l. Kings Table	58.6	2.6	30.8	67.8	6.5
Restaurant Assoc.	82.0	2.1	13.9	125.5	5.1
Calny's	53.0	1.3	33.1	94.3	6.3
Rusty Pelican	25.4	3.4	51.0	42.4	8.5
Denny's (by TW Services, 1987)	218.0	5.5		782.5	6.3
Pizza Inn	51.8	2.0		82.0	5.1
Ponderosa	285.0	1.8	23.5	285.5	5.4
Kentucky Fried Chicken	840.0	1.0	35.9		
Carrol's	88.0	2.4	23.2	123.8	7.5
Saga	502.0	2.7	26.4	592.6	7.2
El Torito	235.7	2.5	23.6	271.5	6.2
Chart House	83.0		16.9		
Restaurant Systems	42.3	2.7	22.3	41.9	7.2
Jack-in-the-Box	450.0	2.3	17.0	450.0	5.6
Hungry Tiger	20.2	1.2			
Diversifoods	382.9	2.0	27.4	491.2	8.6
Denny's (by management, 1984)	725.2	2.3	16.9	901.3	6.4
Unweighted average		2.3	30.9		6.8

Source: Montgomery Securities.

The IPO Craze of 1983

The summer of 1983 saw the emergence of a lively market for initial public stock offerings (IPOs) in specialty retailing, electronics, and the restaurant industry. Not since the late 1960s was there a spate of offerings in food service to rival what occurred in 1983 on the heels of one of the greatest stock market surges of the century. What distinguished the offerings, and subsequent failures of 1983, was the fact that few of the chains that came public had ever even achieved initial profitability. Some were sold to the public on the basis of a demographic promise—for example, Fuddrucker's was to introduce the "adult hamburger."

Concepts Better than Operations

Some were touted on the basis of a pricing strategy, for example, Po Folks was to offer the lowest-priced family dining imaginable. Vicorp was to buy up money-losing medium-priced restaurants at distressed prices, refurbish them, and restore to profitability. Some have actually prospered: Chili's was a member of the class of 1983, and has proven to be successful, but had to undergo a drop in earnings per share in 1984.

Fate of Unprofitable Chains

Of the great successes in the restaurant industry in the stock market over the last twenty years, only one, Chi-Chi's, was unprofitable at the time of its initial public offering. Virtually all other IPOs of unprofitable companies have proven to be fruitless speculations.

Table 7.3

Decade's Best-Performing Restaurant Stocks

Chain	Price Jan. '80 ($)	Price March 7, '88 ($)	% Change	Price Sept. 12, '89 ($)	% Change
Ryan's Family Steak Houses*	0.25	7.88	3052.0	8.50	3300.0
International Dairy Queen	0.88	26.75	2939.8	43.50	4843.2
Pancho's Mexican Buffet	0.63	11.75	1765.1	9.50	1407.9
Frisch's Restaurants	2.25	33.63	1394.7	20.75	822.2
TCBY Enterprises †	0.75	9.25	1133.3	21.88	2816.7
International King's Table ‡	1.75	20.00	1042.9	NM#	NM#
Shoney's§	3.00	24.50	716.7	12.13	304.2
Dunkin' Donuts¶	3.50	24.50	600.0	45.38	1196.4
Luby's Cafeterias	4.25	24.25	470.6	24.88	485.3
McDonald's	4.25	23.13	444.1	29.63	597.1

* Went public July 1982.
† Went public September 1984.
‡ Acquired.
§ Recapitalized, paid $16.00 dividend in 1988.
¶ Target of $45.00 a share takeover bid in September 1989.
#NM—not meaningful.
Source: Investor's Daily, March 7, 1988, p. 7.

Greatest Stocks Over Past Ten Years

Table 7.3 presents the most spectacular restaurant stock market successes of the 1980s. Ironically, the greatest winner was an ancient veteran of the fast-food wars. Note that Dairy Queen far outstripped any other stock in the industry in terms of the performance for the decade. Another great winner, TCBY, rode the crest of a boom in yogurt and ice cream sales outlined in Table 7.4.

Table 7.4

Franchised Ice Cream and Yogurt Stores

Year	Number of Stores	% Change	Sales per Store ($)	% Change	Total Sales ($000)	% Change
1977	5,525		67,595		373,464	
1978	5,960	7.9	94,366	39.6	562,424	50.6
1979	5,355	−10.2	111,766	18.4	598,509	6.4
1980	5,516	3.0	125,679	12.4	693,246	15.8
1981	5,427	−1.6	146,217	16.3	793,518	14.5
1982	5,547	2.2	154,402	5.6	856,466	7.9
1983	6,322	14.0	152,687	−1.1	965,285	12.7
1984	6,736	6.5	140,245	−8.1	944,693	−2.1
1985	7,772	15.4	158,275	12.9	1,230,115	30.2
1986	8,473	9.0	170,685	7.8	1,446,210	17.6
1987	9,272	9.4	173,710	1.8	1,610,646	11.4
1988	10,586	14 ?	177,611	2.2	1,880,191	16.7
Compound Annual Growth Rate (%)						
1977–88		6.1		9.2		15.8
1983–88		10.9		3.1		14.3

Source: National Restaurant Association, "Franchise Restaurants, a Statistical Appendix to Foodservice Trends," Washington, D.C., March 1988.

Chapter 8

Foreign Markets

International Markets

The prospect of U.S. fast-food operators entering foreign markets is a seductive one. Few local operators can match the experience, real estate expertise, and purchasing power of the American fast-food giants. Moreover, the markets are in their infancy in terms of saturation. Few foreign markets have rejected American fast food, and in many cases the sales per store exceed the experience in the United States. Ironically, this was not the case in McDonald's initial foray into Europe, an attempt to open in Dutch suburbs in 1971. Nor has Kentucky Fried Chicken's progress overseas always been smooth. Indignant Germans, for example, demanded to know what role Colonel Sanders had played in the war!

McDonald's progress in foreign markets has been slow and deliberate, stressing the development of infrastructure in both sourcing and real estate development. It has, above all, stressed partnerships with local citizens and the need to find dedicated local operators. According to James R. Cantalupo, president of McDonald's International, "We think globally and we act locally."

It is for this reason that McDonald's stands alone among the hamburger chains in its emerging dominance of the European and Asian fast-food markets. There is a market for fast food beyond the hamburger segment, however, and the operations of PepsiCo are among the leaders in capitalizing upon this opportunity.

Graham Gil Butler, who has been president of PepsiCo Food Service International since 1980, estimates the total size of the international fast-food market at $38.0 billion, with a 15 percent annual projected growth rate. In contrast, PepsiCo's research puts the U.S. market at $60 billion with an 8 percent projected growth rate.

Pizza Hut's dominance of the pizza segment in many countries is already well-established in the sense that it holds the leading position. Its market share, however, generally does not yet approach its U.S. dominance. In 1989, PepsiCo's research indicated that Pizza Hut

Table 8.1

Pizza Hut Market Share

	1988 Share (%)	Rank	1984 Goal (%)
Australia	40	1	49
United Kingdom	20	1	31
Canada	10	1	20
Germany	3	1	5
Mexico	12	2	26
Japan	7	2	17

Source: PepsiCo.

captured a 23 percent share of the U.S. pizza market. Table 8.1 indicates Pizza Hut's rank and share of market in its most important foreign markets, along with the company's target market share for 1994.

Note that by 1994 the chain will approach or exceed its current U.S. market share in four major markets. The conspicuous laggard for the chain is Japan, an anomaly in that Shakey's has the leading position in the market in contrast to a weak position in the United States where it is less than 5 percent of the size of Pizza Hut.

Pizza Hut's International Goals

With an estimated 1219 units in operation in foreign markets at December 31, 1989, Pizza Hut's management expects the chain to open 290 stores per year through 1994, bringing the system's foreign total to 2600 restaurants. The objective is to achieve average unit volume by 1994 of $1 million per store, compared with $735,000 at present.

In terms of profitability, a 17.0 percent operating margin at the store level and a 9.0 percent pretax margin are the company's targets, representing a 3.5 percentage point improvement in each measure over the five-year time period 1989–1994. The result, if achieved, would translate into 50 percent annual profit growth.

Key Differences Overseas

Worldwide markets are obviously not homogeneous, and the successful fast-food chains have been the ones that can adapt to the peculiarities of each marketplace. The two most critical differences lie in restrictions on marketing practices and in the resulting need for a different real estate strategy. Most foreign markets do not allow the unlimited entry to television advertising available to the chains in the United States. Hence, the need for billboard locations is critical.

Suburban Locations Failed

Initial attempts to duplicate the time-honored American pattern of opening stores in the suburbs, gaining sufficient presence to buy television time, then entering major cities as a last step have been reversed in many foreign countries. Instead, the strategy is to open stores in highly visible locations (on the Ginza in Tokyo, for example, or on the Champs d' Elyseé in Paris), then play on the exposure by gradually spreading outward into the suburbs. One of the side effects of this technique is extremely high real estate costs in most foreign markets. It is comparable to opening all of a chain's first hundred stores on New York's Madison Avenue or Los Angeles's Rodeo Drive.

Differences abound in labor practices, too. Especially frustrating can be local laws or customs frustrating the chain's efforts to use part-time workers. Because of an intrusive labor policy by the Australian government that results in very high effective wage rates, McDonald's crews in Australia must achieve the highest levels of productivity anywhere in the world.

Real Estate Costs Higher Overseas

Even low labor costs may not compensate for the high costs of real estate. In Hong Kong, very low labor costs are partially offset by staggeringly high real estate costs. McDonald's in 1989 bought one site for nearly $20 million, describing it as the best site in Asia. The site is in Kowloon, directly across from the Star Ferry. This, of course, is a prime example of what McDonald's refers to as a "billboard location."

The need for highly visible locations provides a significant barrier to entry to all but a very few players. In 1988 McDonald's affiliates made $153 million in capital expenditures, primarily in Japan and Taiwan. Inasmuch as only fifty-two restaurants were opened in those two markets, the implication is that each new unit cost almost $3 million, or more than double the cost in the United States.

The willingness of McDonald's to spend vast amounts in marketing dollars in developing markets makes the chain a formidable competitor against local operators, too. In its early attempts to achieve a toehold in Mexico, McDonald's used billboard and radio advertising, but found that neither of these media were well suited to communicate the McDonald's message. As a result, the chain elected to advertise on national television at a time when it had only eight stores in the entire country! The commercials, which promoted a package for children called the Happy Meal, proved so powerful that the chain soon began recording 85 Happy Meal sales for every 100 transactions.

Site Costs Decline

Once the billboard locations are in place, however, the costs of real estate may decline. In time, profitability in foreign markets will probably exceed that in the United States. Construction costs can fall dramatically for McDonald's as it gains presence and experience in foreign markets. Its first eight buildings in Mexico, for example, cost $1.4 million apiece for the structure alone (compared with $622,000 in the United States), but that cost has now dropped to $600,000, in line with the domestic experience. In its earliest ventures in Latin America, McDonald's typically signed three- to five-year leases, but now buys 70 percent of its sites. With high inflation levels in most Latin American countries, McDonald's occupancy costs will drop dramatically.

American Offerings Duplicated

Normally, the most successful strategy has been not to alter the menu offerings to suit local tastes, but rather to offer local residents exposure to the American fast-food experience. Some flexibility is necessary, though. In countries with very low incomes, McDonald's has been willing to expand its menu in order to make the product more affordable. In the Philippines, with $600 per capita annual income, McDonald's originally thought that it could open perhaps ten stores when it first entered the market in 1981, according to George T. Yang, president of McDonald's of the Philippines.

In a concession to local tastes and income, however, the chain placed a new, low-cost item on the menu, McSpaghetti. The item is hugely popular, selling 600 portions per store daily in the twenty-five units in the country. Moreover, the product lends itself to delivery, which McDonald's provides free of charge. With this flexible approach to a low-income market, McDonald's has found that its store-opening potential far exceeds earlier projections, and it now plans to open 200 stores in the market.

McDonald's Results in Hong Kong

Some indication of McDonald's potential in Asian markets can be derived from its achievements to date in Hong Kong, with a population of 5.6 million people. McDonald's managing director of Hong Kong, Daniel Y. C. Ng, believes that McDonald's can support "100 or maybe even 200" stores, noting that the 42 stores in operation in the market now enjoy the highest transaction counts within the McDonald's system. "Our biggest challenge is to open additional restaurants fast enough to satisfy that demand."

According to Noel Kaplan, senior vice president of McDonald's and zone manager for the Pacific region, "We sell an American experience. We cannot sell local food at the same cost [as local restaurants]. Only when consumers can't afford it [the regular McDonald's menu] do we offer local dishes." Examples include McEgg in Malaysia and McSpaghetti in the Philippines, both low-cost, locally popular items.

Product Uniformity

McDonald's strives for uniformity of product worldwide. In Japan, for example, until recently the only local product found on the menu was corn soup, which captures 0.2 percent of sales. In 1989, however, the company began experimenting with a teriyaki burger. Reportedly, however, the introduction of this product was designed more to frighten local competitors than to appeal to consumers.

The chain's pricing, too, shows a surprising degree of homogeneity, given the different stages of maturation and development worldwide. Table 8.2 indicates prices in U.S. dollar equivalents in nine major cities as of July 31, 1989. New York is used as the American example because, while its prices are higher than the U.S. average, it most closely resembles the major metropolitan areas in which McDonald's typically concentrates its efforts overseas.

McDonald's offers bone-in chicken in a number of Asian markets, including Malaysia and the Philippines. (This product is the basis for a new fried chicken product in test in

Table 8.2

**Price of Big Mac,
July 31, 1989**

City	Price ($)
Amsterdam	2.50
Frankfurt	2.31
Hong Kong	0.97
London	1.81
New York	2.35
Paris	2.36
Rome	2.69
Singapore	1.28
Tokyo	2.70

Source: McDonald's Corporation.

Houston in late 1989.) Yet McDonald's management remains skeptical of the long-term appeal and importance of local dishes. As Noel Kaplan, McDonald's zone manager for the Pacific, put it, "In Hong Kong we average $2 million a store: with no noodles!"

Franchising Terms

McDonald's franchising structure is generally similar in foreign markets to that in the United States except for the fact that it charges a significantly higher rental and licensing fee. The reason for this is the far higher costs of real estate in many European markets and McDonald's need to compensate for the resulting lower capital turnover. In most European markets, the franchisee pays a 5.0 percent royalty (versus 3.5 percent in the United States) and 12.0 to 14.0 percent of sales for rent (compared with 8.5 percent in the United States). Many foreign licensing agreements also call for percentage escalation over time, as is increasingly being done in the United States.

In certain cases McDonald's finds that in order to ensure quality it must become involved in food production to a limited extent. In Moscow, for example, the company has begun to explore the possibilities of a joint venture with a Soviet meat packer to assure uniform quality of supply.

Local Competitors

In Brazil, a 10-year-old chain called Bob's operates seventy stores, compared with McDonald's fifty units. McDonald's, however, records higher total sales.

In Mexico, a coffee shop chain patterned after Denny's operates nearly seventy stores, yet achieves less total sales volume than McDonald's does with eight units!

In Puerto Rico, Burger King has three times as many stores as does McDonald's, yet McDonald's achieves higher overall sales.

In the Philippines, the most serious competition for McDonald's is a local chain called Jolly B, which copies McDonald's format while offering local dishes. McDonald's has slowly begun to respond, with a menu offering unique to the Philippine market called McSpaghetti.

Foreign Profit Margins

As might be expected, foreign markets vary considerably in terms of their profit contribution. Labor practices, real estate costs, and the ability to absorb overhead with a large number of stores are all important determinants of profitability. Table 8.3 shows McDonald's foreign store locations by country from 1983 to 1988. Note that by 1988, foreign openings accounted for more than 43 percent of the chain's systemwide new stores.

Observe, too, that the largest markets, Japan and Canada, are already slowing their rate of store expansion. In Europe, however, the rate of growth remains rapid, with expansion in both the United Kingdom and Germany actually accelerating in 1988. Finally, note the explosive growth in the French market.

Table 8.3

McDonald's Foreign Locations

Location	1983	1984	1985	1986	1987	1988
Japan	395	455	532	573	604	653
% Change		15.2	16.9	7.7	5.4	8.1
Canada	442	465	492	515	539	568
% Change		5.2	5.8	4.7	4.7	5.4
W. Germany	190	208	227	245	262	295
% Change		9.5	9.1	7.9	6.9	12.6
United Kingdom	133	164	196	228	255	289
% Change		23.3	19.5	16.3	11.8	13.3
Australia	147	152	164	183	204	225
% Change		3.4	7.9	11.6	11.5	10.3
France	15	18	25	38	61	84
% Change		20.0	38.9	52.0	60.5	37.7
All other foreign	205	247	293	356	419	492
% Change		20.5	18.6	21.5	17.7	17.4
Foreign total	1527	1709	1929	2138	2344	2,606
% Change		11.9	12.9	10.8	9.6	11.2
Foreign as % total	19.6	20.6	21.7	22.7	23.7	24.8
Foreign openings as % total:		34.6	36.9	41.1	41.1	43.5
U.S.	6251	6595	6972	7272	7567	7,907
% Change		5.5	5.7	4.3	4.1	4.5
Grand total	7778	8304	8901	9410	9911	10,513
% Change		6.8	7.2	5.7	5.3	6.1

Product Acceptance Nearly Universal

In terms of acceptance of the product, the results are generally good and getting better with the passage of time. McDonald's initially experienced difficulties in the French market as a result of a poor relationship with the local franchisee. In France, which has been a market for more than ten years, McDonald's stores were still achieving 20 percent growth in sales per store in 1989.

Highest-Volume Stores

Most of the highest-volume stores in the McDonald's system are overseas. The company's first unit in Rome is generally considered to be among the highest-volume stores in the world, along with units in London and Tokyo. McDonald's worst market in Asia is in Malaysia, where its twenty-two stores achieve breakeven results on a cash-flow basis. In South Korea, the two McDonald's stores do not quite cover their general and administrative expense allocation, but are profitable at the unit level.

Initial Losses in Latin America

McDonald's has losing operations in two Latin American countries. The chain's four stores in Venezuela lose money, but management expects them to become profitable in 1990. Argentina also loses money, with no immediate turnaround in sight. The stores are profitable on a cash-flow basis, however. While precise data are not available, both Brazil, with fifty stores, and Mexico, with eight, do "very well," according to James R. Cantalupo, president of McDonald's International.

In Europe, McDonald's nine stores in Belgium lose money, while the four units in Italy, though profitable at the store level, do not cover their corporate overhead charges.

McDonald's Profits by Market

McDonald's profitability in its largest foreign markets, in terms of return on assets, is indicated in Table 8.4. Note that both Canada and Japan produce returns above the system

Table 8.4

McDonald's Return on Assets

Country	Return (%)
Canada	23.0
Japan	20.0
Australia	16.0
Germany	15.0
United Kingdom	13.5
France	10.0
System	17.4

average. Overall, McDonald's operating margins in foreign markets were 4 percentage points below those in the United States. Within five years, according to James Cantalupo, they should be the same.

Five Markets Key

McDonald's currently derives 80 percent of its foreign profits from five markets: Japan, Canada, West Germany, the United Kingdom, and Australia. France, with eighty-four stores at year-end 1988 and plans to open at least thirty stores per year in the future, will soon join that group. In 1987 the Pacific accounted for 39 percent of sales generated outside the United States. (Noel Kaplan, 1988 annual meeting)

Improvement in profitability for McDonald's has been dramatic in certain markets. In France, for example, McDonald's operated eighteen stores in 1984 and lost money: its return on assets was a negative 10 percent. By 1987, however, the chain was solidly in the black with a 6 percent return on assets, and by 1988 with eighty-four stores enjoyed a 10 percent return on assets.

Two Most Successful Markets

Switzerland and Canada are the two markets with the highest return on investment for McDonald's. Switzerland, with only 15 stores, enjoyed a 28 percent return on assets in 1988. Canada, which is the third largest market for the company (after the United States and Japan) recorded a 23 percent return on assets in its 568 stores in 1988.

Other Players Overseas

Table 8.5 shows the number of foreign stores for eight important American fast-food companies, along with the percent of their stores located in foreign markets.

Table 8.5

Foreign Operations of U.S. Fast-Food Operators, 1988

Chain	Foreign	Total	Foreign as % of Total
Kentucky Fried Chicken	2862	7,761	36.9
McDonald's	2606	10,513	24.8
Pizza Hut	955	6,662	14.3
Burger King	558	2,930	19.0
Dunkin' Donuts	321	1,764	18.2
Wendy's	144	3,762	3.8
Denny's	76	1,337	5.7
Taco Bell	52	2,930	1.8
Total	7574	37,659	20.1

Table 8.6

Foreign and Domestic Volumes

Chain	U.S. Volume per Store ($)	International Volume per Store ($)
Pizza Hut	520,000	735,000
Kentucky Fried Chicken	659,000	821,000
Wendy's	759,000	911,000
McDonald's	1,425,000	1,657,000
Burger King	1,006,000	1,075,000

Table 8.6, based on data from PepsiCo's market research, shows the foreign volume contrasted with domestic results for the five most important players in the international fast-food arena. Reflecting the high levels of profitability abroad, the established American fast-food chains are accelerating their foreign store-opening plans.

In Germany, McDonald's will open 30 stores in 1989 on a base of 295, and will continue at an annual pace of 35 to 40 stores in subsequent years. Capital costs are considerably higher in Germany than in the United States, with land parcels averaging $1.0 million and building costs an additional $1.0 million. Free-standing units achieve volumes 50 percent higher than "inn stores," that is, units located in downtown or mall locations, justifying the heavy capital outlay. Occupancy costs are very high, averaging 8.0 percent of sales in Germany, though this is lower than the 11.0 percent that prevailed just a few years ago in the market.

McDonald's is not content merely to develop its existing markets. In 1990 the company will enter Greece, Portugal, Czechoslovakia, Bulgaria, and Chile for the first time. In the following year, initial forays will be made into Indonesia, Pakistan, and Jamaica. The first McDonald's units in China, Ecuador, and Uruguay will follow soon thereafter. In West Germany McDonald's 300 stores are divided among company-owned units (40 percent of the total) and a group of 100 licensees with an average of 1.75 stores per licensee.

McDonald's is accelerating its rate of store openings in foreign markets. From 206 new units in 1987, the chain's openings rose to 262 in 1988, will reach 300 in 1989, and will range between 330 and 350 in subsequent years. In terms of the potential for market saturation, the future potential appears almost boundless. McDonald's has opened one store for every 30,000 people in the United States. In greater Los Angeles, according to the company's research, it has one store for every 50,000 residents. In the foreign markets in which it operates, however, the company has but one store for every 405,000 inhabitants.

Table 8.7 shows McDonald's increasing focus on foreign locations as a percent of its company-operated locations. Note that in 1988 more than 60 percent of the company-operated McDonald's stores opened were in foreign markets. This is surely the clearest sign of where this company's management believes the best return on investment can be achieved.

Table 8.7

McDonald's Company Store Openings

Year	Foreign Stores	Domestic Stores	Total System Stores	Foreign Openings	Domestic Openings	Total System Openings	Foreign Stores as % Total	Foreign Openings as % Total
1983	519	1430	1949				26.6	
1984	572	1481	2053	53	51	104	27.9	51.0
1985	631	1534	2165	59	53	112	29.1	52.7
1986	678	1623	2301	47	89	136	29.5	34.6
1987	718	1681	2399	40	58	98	29.9	40.8
1988	842	1758	2600	124	77	201	32.4	61.7

Although overstoring and saturation, together with problems of labor shortage, couponing, and site costs may plague the domestic market, the outlook for foreign expansion appears open-ended. Unlike the U.S. market, moreover, the investment that McDonald's and the PepsiCo subsidiaries have made in setting up an infrastructure of suppliers, site-selection teams, and proven local operators virtually precludes new competitors from encroaching on their turf.

Bibliography

Books Having Information on the Fast-Food Industry

Bernstein, Charles. *Great Restaurant Innovators*, Chain Store Publishing Corp., New York, 1981. Biographies of twelve prominent entrepreneurs and managers in the restaurant industry.

Boas, Max and Chain, Steve. *Big Mac: The Unauthorized Story of McDonald's*, E. P. Dutton and Co., Inc., New York, 1976. A highly critical attempted expose of the fast-food industry that chronicles some of the excessive practices of the early franchisors.

Emerson, Robert L. *Fast Food: The Endless Shakeout*, 2nd ed., Chain Store Publishing Corp., New York, 1982. Financial analysis of the chain restaurant industry, including interviews with five senior executives and franchisees.

Fishwick, Marshall, Ed. *The World of Ronald McDonald*. Collection of articles on the sociological impact of fast food. Particularly valuable for exhaustive bibliography.

Kroc, Ray. *Grinding it Out: The Making of McDonald's*, Henry Regnery Company, Chicago, 1977. Ghost-written autobiography by the founder of McDonald's. Emphasizes obsession with operations in the early days of the chain.

Love, John F. *McDonald's: Behind the Arches*, Bantam Books, New York, 1986. Exhaustive history of McDonald's Corporation, with emphasis on the personalities involved. This is absolutely the best study of fast food ever attempted, including both operational and financial analysis in great depth.

National Restaurant Association, *Consumer Expectations with Regard to Dining at Fast Food Restaurants*, National Restaurant Association, Washington, D.C., 1983. A survey of 1,000 adults concerning their reasons for choosing among fast-food restaurants.

National Restaurant Association. *Consumer Reactions to and Use of Restaurant Promotions*, National Restaurant Association, Washington, D.C., 1982. Data on 13,466 adults and children above age 8 analyzing their use of coupons and other promotional techniques used by chain restaurants.

National Restaurant Association. *Foodservice Numbers: A Statistical Digest for the Foodservice Industry*, National Restaurant Association, Washington, D.C., 1986. An exhaustive compendium of statistics on the restaurant industry, with annual historical data dating back to 1970. Also includes highlights of periodic surveys by the trade association, including studies of frequency of patronage, demographics of different user categories, etc. Updated yearly.

National Restaurant Association. *Meal Consumption Behavior,* National Restaurant Association, Washington, D.C., 1985.

Analysis of a sample of 14,255 people designed to survey their eating habits, including frequency of eating out, motivation for restaurant selection and demographic profiles of restaurant patrons.

Newspaper Advertising Bureau, Inc. *The Fast Food Industry: Your Newspaper's Opportunity.* Newspaper Advertising Bureau, Inc., New York, NY, 1986.

A compilation of demographic data on fast-food consumption.

United States Department of Commerce. *Franchising in the Economy, 1986–1988.* U.S. Government Printing Office, Washington, D.C., 1988.

An annual study of all types of franchising activity, including restaurants, auto parts, automotive dealers, dry cleaning establishments and others. Includes number of establishments by state, payroll information and sales projections. Also contains information on number of franchised outlets in selected foreign markets.

Wyckoff, D. Daryl, and Sasser, W. Earl. *The Chain Restaurant Industry,* D.C. Heath and Company, Lexington, Massachusetts, 1978.

A series of case discussions compiled by two professors at the Harvard Business School. Somewhat dated now, but presents considerable operating details on a small number of chains.

Periodicals Having Information on the Fast-Food Industry and Related Subjects

Consumer Reports, June and July, 1988. Consumers Union, Mount Vernon, NY.

Studies of nutritional quality of menu offerings at chain restaurants and fast-food units.

Nation's Restaurant News, Lebhar-Friedman, Inc., New York, NY.

A weekly news magazine that emphasizes developments affecting large restaurant chains. Annual survey of 100 largest chains, published each August, is particularly valuable source of data on privately owned chains.

Sales and Marketing Management: 1988 Survey of Buying Power, Bill Communications, New York, NY.

Magazine published 16 times per year has two issues that analyze income and spending habits in each of 3,138 counties. Invaluable source for detailed income and spending analysis.

U.S. Department of Transportation, Federal Highway Administration, *Traffic Volume Trends,* Washington, D.C.

Monthly survey of highway travel, a useful coincident indicator of restaurant sales trends.

Index